Iris Keltz's insider's experience of Palestine/Israel is exceptional. I often found myself in tears, probably mostly out of frustration, but also of being deeply moved by her descriptions of her relationships with everybody. Her intimate ties to both her Jewish and Palestinian families are exquisitely told, often very touching, and also heartbreaking. I learned more in this compassionate memoir about the history of Israel/Palestine than I have learned over many years from newspapers, books, television, news reports, and film documentaries. The author's insights into the facts and personality of that conflict are extremely detailed, carefully researched, and also made vivid by her personal experience on the ground, with friends and family on both Jewish and Arab sides that she loves. The memoir describes an unfolding tragedy, yet it is uplifting and also gives us hope.

— **John Nichols**
Author: *My Heart Belongs To Nature: A Memoir in Photographs and Prose; The Milagro Beanfield War; Missing; The Annual Big Arsenic Fishing Contest!: A Novel; If Mountains Die; The Last Beautiful Days of Autumn*

This is a unique and moving memoir. Iris Keltz is a Jewish-American woman whose long-term involvement in Palestine contradicts much of what American Jews were schooled to "know" about Israel, Palestinians, and Zionism. Decades before it became common to question the fear of faceless enemies referred to as "the Arabs," Iris lived in Palestinian towns and homes. Instead of enemies, she saw family; instead of hate, she felt love and acceptance. Iris made subsequent trips there spanning four decades, the last one in 2007. Readers will ponder the personal, the political, the local and the global, in the context of a tortured landscape and a tormented humanity.

— **Les W. Field**
Professor and Chair
Department of Anthropology, University of New Mexico

Anyone who wants to know what's really happened in Israel/Palestine over the last fifty years—in people's hearts—should read Iris Keltz's exquisitely written memoir. Blessed with clarity of vision and language, as well as bottomless compassion, she introduces us to both her Palestinian and Jewish families; in doing so she lets us wonder at the possibilities for a peace beyond war, religion, and ideology. Remarkably, the 20-year-old wandering free spirit and the 70-year-old grandmother are one and the same.

— **Mark Rudd**
Author: *Underground: My Life in SDS and the Weathermen*
Political activist, counterculture icon, mathematics instructor

P9-DVY-688

Mesmerizing! As a Jew with a profound love for Islam and a lifelong dedication to human rights, I am overjoyed to encounter this masterfully written memoir. With the ease of a bard and the rigor of a historian, Iris Keltz tells a deeply personal love story tragically set in a world on the brink of a war, the ripples of which have spanned the decades and left the Holy Land bleeding. I learned a great deal about the dynamics of Israel and Palestine from this book, and will refer to it often for intellectual clarity and political inspiration.

— **Mirabai Starr**
Translator of *Dark Night of the Soul: John of the Cross*
Author: *Caravan of No Despair: A Memoir of Loss and Transformation*

Unexpected Bride In The Promised Land creates a personal landscape that goes beyond statistics and rhetoric. With an eye for detail, Iris writes about rolling grape leaves, embroidery as a revolutionary action, eating *knaffeh* at Zalatimo's Sweet Shop, recording graffiti at the Separation Wall, and more. Even as someone who has traveled to the Middle East many times, reading this book opened my eyes to the human dimensions of the Israeli-Palestinian conflict.

— **Rev. Arnie Voigt**
Co-administrator for *Sabeel*-Colorado
Representative, Lutheran Ministries in Bethlehem, Palestine
arnievoigt@msn.com

A compelling, unique, and intensely personal examination of the Palestinian/Israeli conflict written by a Jewish-American woman, married to a Muslim Palestinian during the Israeli invasion of East Jerusalem in 1967. Iris Keltz offers an insightful eyewitness account of the brutality of the Occupation. Part autobiography, part travelogue, part political commentary, *Unexpected Bride In The Promised Land* deconstructs many Zionist arguments, concluding that "fear and racism are the enemy, not Palestinians." Keltz's sensitive treatment of this controversial topic belongs on the shelf of anyone concerned with realizing peace and justice in Palestine/Israel.

— **Stanley M. Hordes, Ph.D.**
New Mexico State Historian, 1981-1984
Author: *To the End of the Earth: A History of the Crypto-Jews of New Mexico* (New York: Columbia University Press, 2005)

UNEXPECTED BRIDE
In The Promised Land

&

Journeys in Palestine and Israel

IRIS KELTZ

NIGHTHAWK PRESS
TAOS, NEW MEXICO

Copyright ©2017 by Iris Keltz

Printed in the United States of America

Publisher: Nighthawk Press

PO Box 1222, Taos, New Mexico 87571

Print ISBN: 978-0-9862706-9-7

Library of Congress Control Number: 2017902100

Cover photos: This informal group portrait was taken in an Abu Dis olive grove on May 22, 1967, the day of Faisal's and Iris's marriage. Iris is standing between her new husband and her father-in-law, Ibrahim Khatib. The man wearing a *kaffiyeh*, Mohamed Dabu, was a family friend. The court appointed him to stand as Iris's paternal guardian and translator. His wife stands next to him. Photographer unknown.

Grapevine embroidery is from a Bedouin dress owned by Iris Keltz; photo by Josie Lenwell.
All other photos by Iris Keltz.

Cover design: Barbara Davis, Digerati Design, Taos, New Mexico

To my first teacher, my mother.

And to the Khatib family,

who welcomed a stranger into their home.

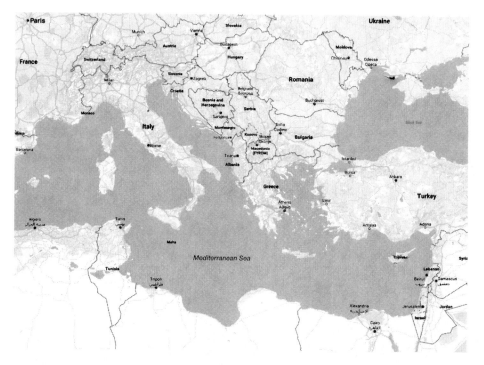

Keltz hitchhiked from Paris to the French Riviera and then followed the Mediterranean basin through Italy, Greece, Turkey, Syria, Lebanon, and East Jerusalem, Jordan. Map of Mediterranean: www.google.com/maps

"The whole world is a narrow bridge,

just a narrow bridge;

The thing is not to be afraid."

— *Rabbi Nachman of Bratslav, Jewish mystic, 1800s*

FOREWORD

I read Iris Keltz's manuscript one final time just before May 15, the day that Palestinians commemorate their *Naqba*, meaning their "Catastrophe." By the end of the first Arab-Israeli War in 1948, also known as the Israeli War for Independence, over 700,000 Palestinians became refugees, and over 400 towns and villages were depopulated. Historians, activists, and writers are finally telling the Palestinian narrative, as well they should.

Personal stories help us understand the enormity of that "Catastrophe." *Unexpected Bride in the Promised Land: Journeys in Palestine and Israel* gives context to the tragedy through the unlikely experiences of a young Jewish-American woman who decides to explore the world. By sheer chance, Iris finds herself in east Jerusalem, Jordan on June 5, 1967—the day that Israel started the Six Day War. She had no idea that she was in the heart of Palestine.

I grew up in Jerusalem. It is my home, so I feel a great affection for the places, flavors, fragrances and, most importantly, the people described in this book. They are all a part of me. I found it fascinating that this naïve young American woman embarked alone on a journey from America to Europe, across the Middle East, and deep into the Levant. Unaware that she should be afraid, she describes her experience crossing borders: "With a noncommittal shrug, guards at the Turkish-Syrian border returned the Hebrew dictionary they'd found in my backpack and motioned me across the border. When asked, I'd told them the truth—I'm on my way to Israel."

Unlike other young Jewish Americans who went to volunteer on an Israeli *kibbutz*, Iris took an overland route through Greece, Turkey, Syria, Lebanon and Jordan, arriving in what is now known as the West

Bank. *Kibbutzim* were Utopian agricultural communes that embodied the essence of socialism and justice, a place where everyone was equal and material wealth was distributed fairly. However, these ideals conveniently excluded countless Palestinians whose land and homes had been destroyed or stolen and given to European Jewish refugees.

In East Jerusalem, Iris discovered the ancient haunting beauty, the food, the culture, and the warm hospitality of the Arab world. And she learned a new word—*Palestinian*. After being thrust into the reality of the dispossessed, Iris would never be susceptible to racist narratives. By the time she arrived in Israel proper, she knew the cost Palestinians had paid for the establishment of the Jewish state.

Back in the U.S., and on subsequent trips to Palestine/Israel, Iris became involved with the same people and groups that have made up much of my own experience working with the Israeli "peace camp." *Neve Shalom/Wahat al Salaam*, The Families Bereavement Circle, Women in Black, *Zochrot, B'tselem*, Breaking the Silence, and other groups make up the sane, rational part of Israeli society that yearns to end the violent occupation. They understand that peace can only be achieved when justice for the oppressed and the dispossessed is realized. Like many of us, Iris saw hope in the Oslo "peace" process and was struck with despair by the murder of Yitzhak Rabin.

There is one quote from the book that I feel compelled to share. About 40 years after her initial experience in Palestine, Iris was in Buffalo, New York, visiting her former Palestinian husband. He said something to her that I've heard from countless Palestinians over the years: "It's not right for one people to be chosen by God for the real estate deal of the millennium. This is the time for all God's creatures to be chosen. The Israelis will never be able to kill every Palestinian, and as long as there is one left alive, the truth will come out. Someday the world will ask forgiveness for turning a blind eye to the suffering of the Palestinians, whose main sin was trying to survive."

This statement expresses their tragedy in a way most of us can never truly appreciate. Iris's response: "Clearly, those words had been locked inside him for a long time." Indeed, these words are locked inside the hearts of millions of Palestinians whose only sin has been trying to survive.

On a personal note, I owe Iris my deepest gratitude for encouraging me to write my personal story. I am thrilled she has finally completed her book, allowing others the opportunity to read this honest account written by a woman who is still as romantic, idealistic, caring and hopeful as the young woman in the story.

— Miko Peled
San Diego, May 14, 2016
Author: *The General's Son: Journey of an Israeli in Palestine* and *Tear Down the Wall: A Blog* – www.mikopeled.com

TABLE OF CONTENTS

PROLOGUE

Ramallah, Jordan, 1967

Ear-shattering explosions ring in my head long after the bombing stops. Fortunately our building never suffers a direct hit. The shelling feels like it has been going on forever, although it's only been days. Nine of us are hiding in the basement apartment of Khalti Suad, my husband's spinster aunty. Finally, on the morning of June 7, the glorious sound of human voices can be heard in the streets. We cautiously remove the cardboard covering the windows, placed there to protect us from the possibility of shattering glass. Sunlight streams into our twilight sanctuary as we peer into a world filled with soldiers, tanks, and jeeps. Israeli soldiers, known for their ferocity, are flooding the streets and entering homes.

"The Jews are here!" someone yells fearfully in Arabic. With a shock, I realize I may be the first Jew many of these people have ever met. For 19 years, Israel has been on the other side of a forbidden border.

"I don't understand what they're shouting," whispers Khalti Suad.

Faisal holds my hand as all eyes turn toward me. I trust and love this man who has been my husband for two weeks, whom I have known for barely a month. More than his dark eyes, lovely mustache, and velvet skin, it was his poet's soul and restless spirit that drew me to him. When we met, I told him I was Jewish and on my way to Israel. He smiled, curious to hear about the kibbutz where I planned to help harvest oranges.

A frightened father holding an infant in his arms beseeches me to run into the street, wave my American passport like a white flag of surrender, reveal my Jewish identity to the soldiers, and tell them the people in this apartment are friends. I fight the urge to remind everyone I am not part of the conquering army.

Fellow survivors, who not long ago were strangers, don't look terribly different from me; they have dark hair and skin tones ranging from fair to honey to molasses. Only my thick New York accent could identify me, but I imagine being shot long before having the chance to speak. The soldiers would discover too late that I was kin. My death would be mourned by my family, but the army would simply declare that innocent people die in war. I decide against running into the street. Terror is contagious.

The sound of boots and strident voices gets louder.

"Don't worry, habibti." Faisal speaks words of endearment just before helmeted soldiers burst into our sanctuary. Their impenetrable sunglasses reflect our frightened faces. Guns poised, fingers on the triggers, these fighters are young, and they are in control. No one is about to drive these Israelis into the sea, a fear ingrained in me since childhood. They search the apartment, confirm we are unarmed, and leave, but not before confiscating watches and gold jewelry, which everyone simply hands over. There is no resistance. The soldiers don't seem to notice the gold wedding band I keep nervously twisting—and they never recognize me as Jewish.

The guttural sounds of Hebrew are familiar to me, but I, too, cannot understand what is being said. I suddenly regret not memorizing the vocabulary lists in Hebrew school. From the haze of childhood, words come to mind: Ani lo medaberet Ivrit—"I don't speak Hebrew." Shalom—a universal greeting of peace. Bereshet—"In the beginning," the first word in the Bible. Shem—"name." To name someone is to recognize his or her humanity. Baruch HaShem—a traditional Hasidic greeting that means "Bless the Name," a reference to God.

I want to cry out, "I'm Jewish and these are my friends. My friends are your friends." But I remain silent, frozen by fear—and thoughts of my mother. Before admitting to these soldiers that I married a Palestinian, I must tell her.

PART ONE

CAST MY FATE TO THE WIND

A caprice of fate found me married into a Palestinian family within weeks of my arrival in East Jerusalem, Jordan. The odds of finding sanctuary with "the enemy of our people" during a war that changed the face of the Middle East were just about zero. I was born between two great historical moments for Jews: the liberation of the Nazi concentration camps in 1945, and the creation of Israel in 1948. My family stressed the Jewish narrative of suffering in a diaspora that lasted thousands of years, culminating in the Holocaust. On my *bat mitzvah*, I chanted from the book of Exodus about Hebrew slaves leaving Egypt with miracles and signs of wonder—ten plagues and the parting of a sea. Every time I read Anne Frank's diary, I prayed the horrors of the Holocaust would pass over the secret annex where she hid with her family just like the Angel of Death had passed over the homes of the Hebrew slaves. *Exodus*, a 1960 film based on Leon Uris's best-selling novel, was shown on the silver screen, and women fell in love with Paul Newman, who played a courageous renegade helping Holocaust refugees escape to Palestine. When Karen, a young survivor, was killed on a *kibbutz*, I sobbed as if she were my own sister. Perhaps the most influential story for my generation of American Jews, this narrative fed the yearning and justification for a state of our own.

In the summer of 1966, I was 20 years old, and thoughts of the Promised Land were far from my mind. I was casting my fate to the wind and paid little attention to the lunar orbiter taking photographs of earth from space, an event that forever changed the human perspective. College graduation three weeks earlier seemed like a distant past. I applied to the Peace Corps, but the bureaucratic pace of government was no match for youthful impetuousness. I resisted the temptation to repay student loans and used my graduation money to buy a one-way ticket on an ocean liner sailing to Le Havre, France.

My mother sat stoically on the couch watching me pack. Silver strands had begun to appear in her wavy auburn hair. I didn't have the heart to tell her I wanted to stay in Paris well beyond the summer, to live the life of a writer and wander the world in search of something I could not name, at least as long as my $900 in traveler's checks lasted. If my father were alive, he might have forbidden his only daughter from embarking on such a risky venture. His death from cancer when I was three had created a void in the family. I left home carrying a backpack, a duffle bag full of books, clothes for all seasons, and a sleeping bag.

I boarded the ship, terrified by my boldness. The New York City skyline and the Statue of Liberty receded in the distance along with everything familiar. Tugboats, guiding ocean liners and oil tankers in and out of the harbor, blew their horns of warning, a forlorn sound that echoed in my heart. Smaller vessels zigged and zagged amidst the maritime traffic. I stood on deck until I could no longer see my best friend, Kathy, waving wildly from the shore. Growing up, we'd had glorious adventures— attending the Newport Folk Festival when Bob Dylan went electric, watching foreign and experimental films on the Upper West Side, and listening to unknown folk singers and poets in Greenwich Village coffee houses. I gladly became part of her extended Italian family every Christmas, confident that there would be a gift for me under their tree.

Cannoli, manicotti, and lasagna slid down my throat as easily as bagels, lox, and potato latkes. Kathy and I crashed bon voyage parties at the Port of New York— drank champagne, danced, and made merry—as if we were among the lucky ones about to leave on a Caribbean cruise. A blast from the ship's horn, coupled with shouts of "All ashore who's going ashore!" would make us scurry down the gangplank.

Today the *bon voyage* was for me. Leaving was harder than I'd imagined. Kathy admired my courage but was not ready to leave the safety of her family. A passing ferry reminded me of riding the Staten Island Ferry with Grandpa when I was a kid. He would swear me to secrecy before buying us forbidden non-kosher hot dogs, which we greedily ate with gobs of sauerkraut and mustard. When the ferry docked, we hid in a toilet to avoid paying an extra nickel for the return trip.

New York Harbor was the first view my grandparents had of America when they arrived on Ellis Island in 1899 as part of a wave that brought 2.5 million Jewish immigrants from Central and Eastern Europe, most of them settling in large East Coast cities. Grandma told me about growing up in the Austro-Hungarian Empire. "Franz Josef was a great ruler," she said, meaning the emperor was good to his Jews. "My father managed a manor with a brewery, huge gardens, chickens, cows, and horses." Grandma blamed the philandering count-landlord for drinking up the profits that caused the estate to go bankrupt, ending her idyllic childhood.

Forced to leave family, friends, and country, her father traveled to America, where he found work as manager of a Lower East Side rooming house catering to new immigrants. Frugal living allowed him to save enough money to pay transport for his two daughters, 12 and 13 at the time. His wife and younger son had to wait. The sisters traveled steerage on an overcrowded ship, arriving on Ellis Island speaking only Yiddish. They were welcomed by a grey-green copper statue of a woman holding aloft the torch of Liberty while standing on a pedestal engraved with words they could not read:

> *Give me your tired, your poor,*
> *Your huddled masses yearning to breathe free,*
> *The wretched refuse of your teeming shore.*
> *Send these, the homeless, tempest-tost to me,*
> *I lift my lamp beside the golden door!"*
>
>   — Emma Lazarus

They were also welcomed by a father they had not seen for years.

My grandparents voyaged across the ocean to find work, shelter, and sanctuary. Travel in my family had always been about survival, not a privileged journey of self-discovery—until today.

I grew up in the last farmhouse in Queens, New York, which sounds more romantic than it was. Our ramshackle tarpaper-and-wooden shack was the neighborhood eyesore. Before our family moved in, two uncles, plumbers by profession, kindly installed hot running water and replaced a coal burner with oil. All the other houses on the block were red brick. Their walls touched as if in solidarity, and their yards met in a common concrete alley while ours stood alone on one wild acre. On hot summer evenings, our backyard came alive with kids digging for earthworms, catching fireflies, or telling scary stories while perched on branches in a tall hedge.

Something else set our family apart. We were prohibited from eating shellfish, bottom-feeders, and bacon, and from mixing dairy with meat. We were kosher. My brothers and I attended a public school that was white, middle-class, and predominantly Catholic. On Wednesday afternoons the school emptied out when most kids went to learn about the spirit world in catechism class, leaving a handful of students to wander through empty classrooms. Accused of killing God by neighbor kids who attended parochial school, we weren't prepared to defend ourselves. But that didn't discourage us from knocking on doors to ask for donations to plant trees in the Jewish homeland. We wanted to help make the desert bloom, a desert we could only imagine.

I was always drawn to those who spoke of faraway places. My wanderlust was likely embedded in my DNA. Even crossing the black line in the Holland Tunnel separating New York from New Jersey was thrilling. Occasionally the larger world would appear in the classroom like a new color in the firmament. In second grade, brown-skinned Rosita from Ecuador showed up speaking only Spanish; in fourth grade, a girl whose family had just escaped a revolution in Hungary taught me to say "I don't understand" in Hungarian.

In fifth grade, a teacher asked us to share the ethnic and cultural background of our grandparents for an assembly called "America, the Melting Pot"—a seemingly innocuous assignment. My paternal grandparents, whom I had never met, came from Minsk, the capital of Belarus, a landlocked country in Eastern Europe. "The borders were always changing. Sometimes it was part of Lithuania or Russia or Poland," Mom said. I never thought to ask my maternal grandparents— who lived to a ripe old age—the name of their ancestral village until long after both had died. Austria, Hungary, Poland, Lithuania, Russia—a mongrel, that's what I was. Pure nothing, except Jewish. But that was a religion, not a country.

"Can't I just hold an Israeli flag and dance the *Hora*?" I asked my teacher.

I enviously watched Linda stomp across the stage in black patent leather high-heeled shoes, a red polka-dot dress swirling beneath raised arms while her nimble fingers clicked castanets. Rouged cheeks and red lips set in a permanent smile let me know she was proud of her Spanish heritage. I performed a clumsy polka with another Jewish kid, paraded around with a Polish flag, shared *pierogis* as our national food, and felt a sense of confusion bordering on betrayal. Grandma had often told me how cruel the Poles had been to the Jews during World War II; fortunately our branch of the family was living in the States when the war broke out.

I worked to keep my balance on the slippery deck, suddenly realizing the "ground" beneath me was no longer solid. Grey gulls circled on a sea breeze before diving into endless whitecaps. In spite of feeling as if I'd binged on cheap red wine, I exulted in the moment. I had vague plans about what to do when the boat docked: go to Paris, find a cheap hotel, learn French, become a writer. The Lost Generation of Americans who'd flocked to Paris in the 1920s was dead and gone, but a new "lost generation" was gathering.

Salons and decks, filled with giddy college students, many leaving home for the first time, made the ship feel like a floating campus. The bounty of being served three meals a day was taken for granted. A rumor circulated that Paul Newman's son was on board, rendering every blue-eyed guy his possible progeny.

To keep from retching, I circled the deck, breathed deeply, and stared at the horizon. I met Hank on my second day out at sea. Leaning against the rail, his thoughtful demeanor was a refreshing break from the never-ending revelry. A chiseled nose and square jaw were softened by chestnut hair falling into brown eyes. From a height of more than six feet, Hank looked down on most of the world, which added to the serious tone of his words. "We must have power over decisions that affect our lives. The government has no right to draft 18-year-olds to fight and die in a war when we can't even vote." He challenged my assumptions about the

States and informed me of the evils of capitalism and imperialism.

Hank's ideology had been established long before I knew what imperialism meant. At the University of Chicago, he was president of Students for a Democratic Society (SDS), a radical left-wing student organization that believed civil disobedience was necessary to promote true participatory democracy. In stark contrast, my days at the State University College in New Paltz, New York, were filled with beer-guzzling fraternity and sorority parties, necking in the apple orchard, and slogging through uninspiring classes. History was taught as a series of factoids about wars and ensuing treaties that were ultimately broken.

My other on-board acquaintance was Alice, an art student heading to Florence to study the Renaissance and learn to speak Italian. A rather plain-looking woman, she had the audacity to imagine hooking up with a sexy Italian man. I admired her clarity of purpose and her confidence.

The crossing took twelve days. Sailors in Southampton greeted us shouting, "Welcome to England, mateys!" I entertained fleeting thoughts of disembarking, but Hank invited me to hitch with him to Paris: "I'm standing in solidarity with other internationals on Bastille Day at the anti-Vietnam War rally. Come with me!" I said *yes*.

In Le Havre, France, I ruthlessly pared down. Whatever books and clothes didn't fit in my backpack got put in the duffle bag, which I left on the dock. Hank and I caught a ride to Paris with a friendly trucker who asked, "*Vous êtes Américains?*" After we responded with an energetic, "*Oui, oui,*" the conversation fizzled. Neither Hank nor I spoke French. The curious driver wanted to tell us about himself, but all either of us could say was, "*Je ne comprends pas.*" The frustrating silence fanned my desire to learn French. I envisioned us through the driver's eyes—a lanky man with sleek brown hair forever falling into his eyes holding the hand of a short woman with dark, curly hair wearing a peasant blouse and jeans. My looks offered no hint that I was about to become an ex-pat

American writer, nor did Hank resemble a university graduate and leader of a nationally known political group.

"*Au revoir*," we recited in unison when the trucker dropped us off at Gare Saint-Lazare in the center of a city where we didn't know a soul. With help from Hank's guidebook, we navigated the Paris Métro and found a youth hostel run by Dō Hu Tai, the first Vietnamese person I had ever met. He was five feet four inches tall, the same height as me. After securing beds for the night, Hank and I relaxed in overstuffed chairs in an informal gathering room. Dō Hu Tai joined us. As an economics student at the Sorbonne, his English was fluent. Hank asked Dō if he was going the anti-war rally on Bastille Day. Without giving him a chance to answer, I parroted the domino theory, America's justification for the war. "If Vietnam fell to the Communists, every country in Southeast Asia would fall, one by one, threatening our way of life. America is saving your country from being controlled by an elite group of people. It's the opposite of democracy."

Dō responded, ignoring any reference to the anti-war rally or the domino theory, "I love my country just like you love yours. When my education is finished, I will return to Saigon and care for my elderly parents."

"My family is worried about my brother being drafted," I added tentatively.

"Your family should be worried. Vietnam is hell now. I hope your brother does not go there." Dō's calm voice held no trace of anger. Before Hank and I moved into a cheap *pension* in the Latin Quarter, Dō gave us his phone number and said to call if we ever needed help.

Our sunless room on the third floor reeked of stale smoke and old wine. Cardboard-thin walls covered with layers of flowered wallpaper barely muted the conversations in the next room. Occasionally a chambermaid came to change the linens and scrub the *bidet*. The nearest water closet was down a dark, winding staircase. We were tempted to pee in the *bidet*, which looked like a toilet without a seat, but we restrained ourselves as this left the unpleasant odor of urine.

Hank and I slept in the same bed, but I was conflicted about my precious virginity. Women's liberation was just beginning, and the sexual revolution was a breath away; it was the dawn of birth control pills. Part of me held onto the belief that women who slept around were "easy." I thought of Isadora Duncan, who arrived in Paris at the turn of the 20th century ready to dance the dance of life with every fiber of her being. Determined to lose her virginity, she seduced potential lovers. Her *joie de vivre* infected me; I, too, wanted to become a woman of the world. At first Hank seemed the perfect man on whom to bestow the gift of my virginity. We crisscrossed Paris, visited museums, held hands in the darkness of *the cinémathèque,* jumped on the Métro when tired, and drank endless cups of espresso in cafés, but his constant politicizing had become wearisome.

"Communism is not the greatest threat to our freedom. We've been lied to by our leaders and history books and betrayed by our government."

I had read *The Ugly American* before college graduation and vowed never to spend gobs of money on overpriced hotels, restaurants, and clothes, nor to take endless photos with an expensive camera—an easy promise to keep given my budget.

Hank and I picnicked on baguettes and Camembert cheese and drank *vin rosé* in the shade of overhanging trees on Île de la Cité, an island on the Seine near Notre Dame Cathedral. To all the world we looked like lovers in the city of love, and I *was* falling in love—with Paris.

On Bastille Day, July 14, Hank took me to my first anti-war protest. Having been the previous occupiers of Southeast Asia, the French had experience with the colonization of Indochina. Thousands of students, leftists, and internationals had gathered in La Place de la Concorde to express their rage over America's bloody war in Vietnam. Boot-stomping gendarmes wielded chains and clubs hidden beneath black capes while weaving an ever-tighter web around the protesters, whose chants reverberated through my being: *"Johnson Assassin! Johnson Assassin!"* They were accusing our president of being a murderer! Hank's hand was my lifeline. I dared not let go. With his free arm, he held a camera, focused, clicked, and captured history.

During the frenzied bloodletting of the French Revolution, King Louis XVI, Marie Antoinette, and Robespierre had their heads chopped off by the guillotine in this square. I imagined Madame Defarge, guardian of the French revolution in *A Tale of Two Cities*, knitting quietly on the edge of the mob, recording the names of traitors. A 3,300-year-old obelisk from the Temple of Luxor—a gift from the Pasha of Egypt in the 1800s—stood in the center of La Place de la Concorde, named for a dream of peace and harmony.

In the quiet of our room, after the protest, chants still echoing in my head, I rejected Hank's embraces for the last time. My intellect was stimulated by his perpetual politicizing, but there was no gravity holding us together. At the end of summer he returned to graduate school, and we made no pretense about staying in touch. If we ever chanced to meet again, I would tell him our adventures did not ring vainly for me, as he insinuated in the handwritten melancholic love poem he gave me before we parted. Hank was my first political mentor, but I saved my precious virginity for another.

KAREN TROTSKY

I kept the room at the *pension* on Rue Mazarin. Mornings found me in Café Le Buci, a watering hole for artists, writers, beatniks, and vagabonds from around the world. Waiters ruled this domain, but as long as you ordered something and left a tip, they let you be. Small round Formica-topped tables spilled onto a sidewalk that jutted daringly onto a sharp-edged corner surrounded by helter-skelter traffic. One day, an arrogant young black American filmmaker appeared and offered me the possibility of doing a nude shot for his upcoming flick, which I modestly declined. In this promiscuous world without rules, an invisible chaperone sat to my left. An ever-present journal held the musings of my mind in print so small it took a magnifying glass to read. Apart from random entries, letters home were my main writing accomplishments:

Dear Mom,
It's difficult to justify what I'm doing in Paris. My life makes no sense to you. It doesn't to me, either. I know it's hard but you must leave me to my mistakes.

Love, Iris

The thought of my mother's daily drudgery—commuting on overcrowded subway trains, cooking, shopping, laundry, house cleaning, constant worry about my brothers and me—sucked the wind from my sails and spun me into the doldrums. Although separated from Mom by an ocean and several time zones, my sense of expansive freedom was touched by a fatalistic resignation that someday, I, too would become part of that mundane reality. But for the moment I clung to the possibility of committing acts of free will.

Official working papers were not needed to peddle the international edition of the *New York Times* on the streets of Paris. Every vendor was given a canvas sack filled with newspapers and a hip-length navy blue jacket with "New York Times" printed on the back in bold white letters. The utilitarian garment kept me warm, dry, and highly visible. My first assigned beat was in the shadow of the symbol of Paris, where I sold only four newspapers the entire week. Tourists were far more interested in Taiwan-made trinkets of the Eiffel Tower than the latest edition of the newspaper. Hoping my next beat would be more lucrative, I cruised the late-night bars on Boulevard de Clichy in Montmartre. Lonely American G.I.s were said to have bought entire sacks of papers in exchange for conversation, but my presence in Harry's New York Bar only triggered a minor brawl when French prostitutes saw me as a threat to their trade. They kicked me out, which compelled the G.I.s to defend my honor. During the ensuing ruckus, I skulked onto the boulevard without having sold a single paper.

My third beat, in front of the swanky Café de la Paix on the Right Bank across from the American Express building, was where I was able to sell enough papers to pay for bread, cheese, wine, and pâté. Friendly rivalry between vendors and an abundance of tourists made time pass quickly. Passionate fights between an Irish-Greek couple who sold competing newspapers was endlessly entertaining. Bucktoothed blonde-haired Fritz from Germany dreamed of becoming his country's next great film director. Jon, a slender South African Jew with a mop of scraggly brown hair, always wore a black-and-white checkered scarf draped around his neck as an homage to Bob Dylan. When he saved enough francs, he insisted that he was traveling to Israel so he could live on a *kibbutz*.

When tourists asked to take my photo because I reminded them of the woman vendor in Jean-Luc Godard's *Breathless*, I began to charge ten francs, about two dollars. Before leaving the vicinity of the American Express, I would pick up my mail and take full advantage of the immaculate toilets filled with rolls of soft paper. Compared to the Turkish-style *pissoirs* in the café, with torn newspapers stuck to a nail and foot perches on either side of a dark hole ready for a rush of clean water upon pulling a nearby chain, the American Express was luxurious.

The people I chanced to meet seemed as lost as I was. Every afternoon a woman with flawless ivory skin sat in languid repose staring out the plate glass window of the café with a sack of newspapers leaning against her legs. She rarely spoke, and when she did, her mellifluous accent pointed to English aristocracy. What could she possibly have in common with the mangy musicians who stopped by her table? We spoke for the first time in the local post office. I discovered we were staying in the same *pension*, and our rooms faced the same sunless courtyard. A shameless *voyeur*, I watched the lights burning in her room all night and wondered if this enigmatic woman was lost in a weird world of drugs.

Sarah from Valparaiso, Indiana, was friendly, chatty, and open. A river of freckles crossed her pug nose, spilling onto rosy cheeks framed with curly brown hair always on the verge of escaping the barrette. She was not on a mission, was not an activist, anarchist, beatnik, communist, or socialist, and had no pretensions of becoming a writer. I don't think we ever discussed Vietnam, although most Americans got around to that subject. Spending time with her felt like sitting in a ripe cornfield. She, too, had just graduated from college and was wandering Europe with her bulky blonde American boyfriend who swaggered around the café like he'd just walked off the field after scoring a winning touchdown. I saw her alone in the café one day, which was unusual. She looked dazed, disheveled, and ashen. I quietly sat beside her. Before long, she hung her head and began to sob. Her boyfriend had just left Paris for parts unknown—and she had undergone an illegal abortion. *Abortion*—an ugly sounding word. Did it sound sweeter in French? That afternoon, Sarah moved into the *pension* with me.

I listened to her ramble about growing up in rural Indiana and falling in love with the star football player in high school. Pain ravaged her sweet face. I felt disgusted when she told me the doctor who performed the procedure had forced her to play with his penis. Her contracting uterus was causing severe bleeding. After several days, I realized she was beyond my care, so I took her by taxi to the American hospital. She offered no resistance when the nurse removed her clothes, covered her nakedness with a white gown, checked her pulse and heart rate, injected, inspected, and hooked her up to an IV. Dark circles under tired eyes made her looked haunted. I left Sarah sitting in a wheelchair in the sterile hospital.

In the shade of a tree on Île de la Cité, I pondered recent events while watching barges snake their way along the Seine. I envied the camaraderie of drunks sharing a bottle of wine and remembered having picnics here with Hank. Rows of stalls along the quay offered a welcome distraction. I bought an old postcard with a photograph of a decaying *chateau* blanketed by ominous clouds, a veritable Edgar Allen Poe setting. While trying to decipher the handwritten Gothic script on the back of the card, I was approached by a diminutive man with huge saucer-shaped eyes. He spoke as if needing to impart the secrets of the universe before it was too late. The mysterious yin/yang, a Chinese philosophy he described, divided the world into male and female principles. "You must eat so your body is in balance with these forces." He invited me to join him for dinner in a nearby macrobiotic restaurant. The grain-and-vegetable-based diet he detailed was far from the baguettes, cheese, pâté, and croissants of my normal fare. "Chew each mouthful one hundred times," he insisted. My jaw was tired long before the food was swallowed. As we parted ways, the little man with saucer eyes took my hand and read my palm. "I hope you're not getting married soon." Marriage? Not even a remote fantasy. Years later, I still wondered why this strange little man thought I might be married in a matter of months.

When I went to get Sarah from the hospital, the bloom had returned to her cheeks. She thanked me for taking care of her and cheerfully told me that a girlfriend had offered to share a two-bedroom apartment; the friend had also gotten her a coveted job hostessing in a popular Montparnasse jazz bar. From then on, Sarah hid under a layer of thick make-up, black eye-liner, dark lipstick, and tight-fitting skirts over knee-high boots. Her boyfriend never reappeared, and no one in Paris missed the corn-fed, homegrown, freckle-faced innocent from Valparaiso, Indiana—except me.

My loneliness was broken by a group of young French communists from the café who extended their hands in friendship. The walls in their tiny apartment were plastered with Revolutionary posters. I sat reading *Asterix le Gaulois,* a popular French comic book, and listened to names and words being thrown in the air like pizza dough—Lenin, Trotsky, Marx, Engels, right wing, left wing, fascist, anarchist, reactionary, and so on. They spoke passionately, loudly, and shrugged their shoulders in disgust, proclaiming, *"merde alors"* and *"malheureusement."* For me the jargon meant nothing, but the camaraderie meant everything. It was here that I conceived of an identity purge. Detachment from everything I had known—familial and cultural expectations, my mother tongue, and my name—exhilarated and terrified me.

Dear Mom,
Please address future letters to Karen Trotsky in care of the American Express, Paris.

Your loving daughter, Karen

I chose the name Karen because in high school I had admired a popular, sophisticated girl by that name and wished we were friends. Trotsky reminded me of my Russian-sounding surname, Devinsky. It would be decades before I discovered Leon Trotsky advocated worldwide revolution of, for, and by the workers—a sympathetic cause.

Mom wrote back, *"Like hell I'll call you Karen Trotsky."*

Time was running out. When summer turned to fall and I showed no signs of leaving Paris, Mom's letters and postcards, addressed as usual to Iris Devinsky, were filled with growing panic and a reminder of the road I should be taking—graduate school, marriage, babies, and a home in the 'burbs. I had no counter-vision to bounce across the ocean. It was a fool's mission to believe I could escape the agenda implanted since childhood with the ease of smoking a Gauloise and walking the sidewalks in uncomfortable black lace-up boots. Ironically, what I sought to escape was everything I was seeking.

It was a happy day when Lester shuffled into the café in ankle-high shoes too large for his feet with a stretched-out black boat-neck sweater hanging off one shoulder. His broad grin revealed a spacious gap between his front teeth. He shook hands with anyone in the café who smiled back and proudly shared his dream of becoming a sculptor, perhaps the next Rodin—but first he needed a foundry and a place to live with his wife and three children who were coming in a few weeks.

Having lived in Paris for three months, I tried to protect him from the ubiquitous seductresses and sirens who languished here.

Lester was still living in a room without a kitchen or bathroom when his family arrived in Paris. Drawn to the anomaly of California domesticity transplanted to Bohemian Paris, I offered to babysit. Entertaining a four-year-old girl and a six-year-old boy while nursing a baby in the confines of a hotel room was no small feat. I listened to Lester's wife, Joclyn, calmly explain to the children why they had left their home at the foot of Mt. Baldy to live in a hotel room. Either she was madly in love with her husband or was seething with secret resentment, or both.

Months later, an affordable *atelier* had yet to be found. After visiting every museum in the city, meeting other sculptors, frequenting smoky cafés and bars, riding the Métro, and walking along the Seine, Lester got the message: go to Greece, where the living is cheap, skies are blue, and beaches soft and welcoming. He packed up his family and left Paris before he smelled of cheap wine, stale tobacco, and greasy *pommes frites*. Joclyn and Lester promised to write when they got settled.

I dreamed of traveling but was not ready to follow my thumb, not even when tempted by a motley crew of internationals heading to Kathmandu for the world's first beatnik convention. What did one do at a beatnik convention? Smoke pot? Make love? Write poetry? Discover a new reality? I imagined my spirit soaring under starry skies, far from asphalt and electric lights.

A guy with tawny, rope-like hair stood beside a boldly painted van. Each uniquely designed letter of *Destination Kathmandu* pointed to an impressive artistic collaborative. "There's room for one more!" he beckoned seductively. Dressed in a loose-fitting rainbow tunic, he looked like the lion from *The Wizard of Oz* dressed as a court jester.

Raindrops like tears bounced off the concrete while I sat in a nearby café and wrote a letter.

Dear Kathy,

I remember the day I left New York filled with hope for a glorious future. It seems like the more I yearn to find a thread of meaning, the more elusive it becomes. Pasted smiles on waiters and store clerks reveal nothing. Are they resigned to their fate, or have they joyfully accepted the mundane? Circular pathways and dead-end streets describe my life. Predictability might not be so terrible. Marriage to a Jewish doctor almost seems inevitable. My fear is that one morning, I'll wake up a middle-aged matron ridiculing silly notions about living an unconventional life.

Love, Karen (Trotsky)

I walked the streets of Paris with a sack of newspapers slung over one shoulder. The implacable grey, wintry skies seemed to have forgotten the color blue. Afternoons often found me settled on a broken-down couch inside Shakespeare and Company, a well-known English library and bookstore on 37 rue de la Bûcherie, near Notre Dame Cathedral. The original independent bookstore founded in 1919 by American expatriate Sylvia Beach had been a sanctuary for avant-garde artists and writers since the Lost Generation of Americans began showing up in Paris after World War I. Beach was arrested during the German occupation of France but not before saving her precious books from being burned.

A hand-painted sign hung over the storefront. Seduced by books spilling onto the sidewalk, I walked into Shakespeare and Company as part of the next "lost generation" disillusioned with our country embroiled in a war that threatened the lives of our brothers, sons, and boyfriends. Like ghosts from another era, black-and-white photographs of Gertrude Stein, Ezra Pound, James Joyce, Hemingway, Scott Fitzgerald, and Picasso lined the walls. George Whitman, the current proprietor, a gaunt, tubercular-looking man, was every bit as welcoming as I imagined Sylvia Beach had been. Every week he hosted a tea party, free and open to the public. Among the dusty volumes packed on wooden shelves I discovered Henry Miller. His appetite for life rumbled across the pages of *Tropic of Capricorn*. He sounded positively drunk on unbridled freedom while I was desperately lonely with mine, but when it came to women, he sounded like a self-centered bastard traipsing around Paris with Anaïs Nin while his wife languished in Brooklyn.

One night, I had a lucid dream:

I'm alone in a desert surrounded by ceaseless wind and shifting sand. Shades of brown dominate a barren landscape. An invisible camera seems to be recording my every move, getting unnerving close-ups of my face. The camera pans back to reveal I am hiding in a sand dune. Someone familiar is next to me, but I have no idea who it is. Black specks on the horizon are growing larger. I feel trapped. Three men approach at an excruciatingly slow pace. One has a thick black beard. I pick up a gun lying on the ground.

I woke up sweating. This felt like a warning.

The decision to leave the flea-ridden *pension* on Rue Mazarine was mainly economic, but I also needed a change. The Vietnamese man from the youth hostel had said to call if I ever needed help, but that was over six months ago.

"Good to hear from you," he said warmly over the phone. "How is your friend, the tall man?" Dō Hu Tai remembered me. I was grateful. "Well, Hank has returned to the States. I'm selling newspapers, studying French at the Alliance Français, and looking for a place to live," I said, trying not to sound desperate. Dō offered to let me stay in his brother and sister-in-law's two-room flat for the week they were out of town. He advised me to check the bulletin board at the Alliance, where an entire wall of notices was devoted to informing its international student body.

I easily found a job as an *au pair* with a French family who offered a free room in exchange for twelve hours per week of childcare. The luxury apartment building on Boulevard Montparnasse had a back entrance for groundskeepers, maids, and nannies. Up a dark narrow winding stairway, my tiny *chambre des femmes* on the fifth floor was depressing. A naked light bulb dangled over a narrow iron bed wedged between a wall and a gas heater. There was no water, hot or cold, and the nearest water closet was on the floor below. I bought a chamber pot and a hot plate, but the room never felt like home. Still, it was exciting to live only blocks from La Coupole, La Rotonde, and Le Dôme—cafés where Miller, Anaïs Nin, and Hemingway had hung out, as had Picasso, Chagall, and Stravinsky. I sat in Miller's favorite café and copied meaningful passages from *Tropic of Cancer*. He wrote about remembering his life in NYC.

"I'm not American anymore, nor a New Yorker and even less a European or a Parisian. I haven't any allegiance, any responsibilities, any hatreds, any worries, any prejudices, any passion. I'm neither for nor against. I'm neutral."

I, too, had no allegiances. My only responsibility was to respond to my mother's letters.

Dear Iris,
It's time to come home. Apply to graduate school. Get a job. Buy a car. We want you back.
                                        Love and hugs, Mom.

As a widow, Mom's struggle was to raise, support, and nurture three children. She could never understand that I was on "*a heroic descent to the bowels of the earth*" so I could emerge "*cleansed of the past, ready to cast myself upon an alien shore."* I never mailed that letter.

Nanny duties included taking my two charges to the Luxembourg Garden. Confirming my employer's worst fears about undisciplined Americans, I allowed the children to go on the swings and get dirty in the sandbox. I hoped the boys wouldn't share the particulars of our outings with their mama, who worried about cold air seeping into their lungs, but with innocent exuberance, they told her everything. I was given a warning.

Dō invited me to celebrate Vietnamese New Year with his family. I felt like an Amazon walking beside his petite sister-in-law as part of a throng of Asians pouring into La Place Monge, which was surrounded by red banners waving over the doorways of nearby restaurants. Drums and flutes synchronized with the throaty sounds of Vietnamese prayer streaming from a nearby Buddhist Temple.

Dō was the only person in Paris who ever showed concern for my well-being. One night, when he hadn't heard from me for weeks, he climbed the dark spiral staircase to my fifth floor room. He knocked but got no answer. He knocked again, this time louder, and again got no answer. The pounding finally woke me. As I groggily opened the door, the smell of escaping gas followed me as I rushed into the hall. The pilot light on the heater had gone out. If Dō had not come over, I might have slept forever. He turned off the heater, opened the window, and walked me downstairs for fresh air and black coffee. "I kept thinking about you today. Your life is too lonely and chaotic." He shook his head disapprovingly. "You need family." But the prodigal daughter was not ready to return.

On an obscure shelf in Shakespeare and Company, I randomly found a book that offered a nugget of wisdom: *"What presents problems for thought is no block for action."* I suddenly understood that the union of thought and action was what I craved. I was reading *Bitter Lemons*, Lawrence

Durrell's book about the Greek island of Corfu, when a letter arrived from Joclyn and Lester inviting me to visit them in Corinth, Greece. A map was included. That week, I received a postcard with a photo of a cloudless blue sky shimmering over a body of water surrounded by sandstone cliffs and stark desert. It was from Jon, the South African Jew I had sold newspapers with by the American Express.

Dear Karen,

I'm living on a kibbutz *near the Dead Sea. My body and soul have grown stronger. You would love it here. We need help in the fields and gardens. Follow the map.*

Shalom, Jon

A letter and a postcard changed my life. This time there were no agonizing reflections. The tangle of streets that led to the Seine had become home, but it was time to head toward the lemony warmth and clear light of the Mediterranean. I quit my job selling newspapers but kept the New York Times windbreaker. The children offered sorrowful hugs when I gave notice, but the parents looked visibly relieved and invited me to my first and only dinner in their luxury apartment. A sumptuous three-course meal opened with an *aperitif*, followed by never-empty glasses of Beaujolais, and ended with fruit, cheese, and a sweet pear liqueur. Although all of us were drinking, I seemed to be the only one in an altered state. My ability to speak French had improved to the point where I could vocalize my obsession about the bloated pear floating in a narrow-necked green bottle—which they gave me as a *bon-voyage* gift. That dinner was my grand farewell in Paris. I went to say goodbye to Sarah from Valparaiso. She smiled without warmth as she finished applying her makeup, got dressed and left for work. There was no indication that we'd ever been more than fleeting acquaintances. Over dinner in a Vietnamese restaurant, Dō Hu Tai warned me I was heading toward treacherous waters. I thanked him for saving my life.

Alongside the Seine, I discovered a stall filled with maps, new and old, of every country and continent that ever existed or might have existed, including a map of the world when it was flat. I saw that if I traveled overland, Greece was on the way towards the *kibbutz* near Jerusalem. It never occurred to me to take a plane, boat, or train. Time stretched out like an infinite resource to be used as needed. There was no expected date of arrival. The journey was everything.

FROM THE LEFT BANK TO THE WEST BANK

I stuffed clothes, a sleeping bag, and a Hebrew-English dictionary into my backpack, mailed a postcard with a tentative route to my mother, and hitch-hiked toward the Promised Land.

Male travel partners were easy to find in youth hostels, which was where I met a California surfer heading to Italy. Survival concerns soon eclipsed the existential angst that had gripped me in Paris. Where would we sleep? Would the drivers who chose to pick us up deliver us safely to the next destination? Passports and traveler's checks had to be guarded. We lived on bread, cheese, fruit, wine, water, and adrenaline. I learned to read a man's character from his dashboard; pictures of semi-nude perky-breasted women usually meant the driver expressed his sexual desires with a girlfriend and would not become belligerent when his advances were refused. However, displays of Jesus nailed to a cross, haloed saints, or the Madonna cradling her baby put me on guard. Self-described pious drivers seemed to think if you weren't their mother, sister, or betrothed, you were most likely a whore. Darkness once found the California surfer guy and me between towns, forcing us to sleep under a bridge.

After a long week with many rides, a trucker dropped us off at the beginning edge of a town bordering the Mediterranean. To catch another long-distance ride, we had to walk through the entire town. My head bowed against the noonday sun, I plodded behind my perennially pissed-off road partner, barely noticing my surroundings until we stopped for a water break. Looking up, I saw a magnificent castle crowning a hillside adorned with wildflowers and gardens surrounding white houses that cascaded toward the sea. At the other edge of town, uniformed guards standing in front of a concrete barricade asked to see our passports.

"*Pourquoi?*"

"You are entering France, *mademoiselle.*"

"But we never left France!"

"Oh, but you are leaving the sovereign nation of Monaco." We had unwittingly walked through a kingdom on the French Riviera about half the size of Central Park. I thought of Grace Kelly falling in love with her prince and hoped she was living happily ever after.

Postcards from Mom begging me to come home greeted me at the American Express in Florence, where the youth hostel had once been Mussolini's brothel, or so we were told. Twenty metal bunk beds crammed into a huge room with high ceilings and tall windows overlooked vineyards, fountains, and statues of mythic heroes, nymphs, and goddesses. On the Ponte Vecchio, I met a local guide who believed himself to be Italy's answer to Humphrey Bogart. "This is where Dante met Beatrice," he said smugly before quizzing me on the flaw in Da Vinci's sculpture of David. "His penis is not circumcised because the model was not Jewish." As he hoped, my eyes were instantly drawn to the statue's groin. No doubt, he had shared this fact with a thousand tourist girls. I left him on the bridge and wandered into the straw market, where I ran into Alice, the woman I'd met on the ship, the one who had dreams of studying the Renaissance and falling in love with a sexy Italian. While I'd been living in Paris, she had been in Florence. She offered to show me the city she'd come to love and invited me to stay in her apartment. Like Odysseus, I was easily seduced and might have accepted her offer had I not met an English guy at the hostel that evening who was looking for a road partner to hitch to Greece.

Malcolm and I followed the highway to Naples, traversed the neck of Italy to Brindisi on the east coast, and caught the ferry crossing the Adriatic Sea to Corfu, an island off the Greek mainland. We walked into town along a narrow two-lane road, where smiling people offered us freshly picked figs. On a cobblestone road, I stopped in a café with panoramic views of the bay and the old Venetian citadel. A young man sitting at a nearby table asked in English what I was writing about.

"What I'm seeing. Who I'm meeting. What I'm thinking."

"Why?" he asked.

For someone not plagued with the instinct to record experience, there was no easy answer. This island, fishing, and the ocean filled his world. A week or so later, Malcolm and I watched the lush paradise fade from view as the ferry floated toward the rocky, barren Greek mainland. We hitched to Ioannina, then Patras, where we crossed the Gulf of Corinth, and found ourselves in Corinth, a city on a narrow stretch of land connecting the Peloponnesus to the mainland.

It was a joyful reunion. Joclyn and Lester welcomed us into their haven of domestic bliss, but the true nature of their bliss was soon revealed. Joclyn was having a clandestine affair with an acquaintance from California who had unexpectedly appeared at their door a few weeks ago. Chaos ruled for the children, whose main challenge was to keep themselves entertained without a television, but if they missed their California lifestyle, they didn't show it. Joclyn was learning to speak Greek and practiced every day with the vendors at the nearby food market. For me, the exotic diphthongs and lisping sounds fell on ears whose previous encounter with Greek had been college sororities and fraternities.

Idyllic days included snorkeling in the Ionian Sea. We visited a gypsy encampment, where a fortune-teller gave me new appreciation for my given name by telling me Iris was the Greek goddess of the rainbow. In a local *taverna*, our spirits were lifted by bitter Retsina wine, whose taste improved with each sip. A chorus line of sloe-eyed Zorbas, inspired by ear-shattering electric *bouzouki* music, moved like an interconnected wave, their shoulders barely touched as their arms reached heavenward. Thumbs clicked in unison. Onlookers showed appreciation by smashing plates and glasses at the dancers' feet. Compliments cost six *drachmas* per plate, three per glass. Waiters mysteriously kept track of broken crockery and presented bills to departing guests.

On the night before everything changed, a neighbor, Papa Feliz, invited us for a barbecue in his backyard, where he grilled *souvlaki* over an open pit fire. American rock-and-roll blasted from somewhere inside the house while his five daughters danced "the shake." (Usually Greek women were busy with domestic chores.) The next morning, a strident voice on the transistor radio announced a curfew.

"Anyone found in the streets after dark will be shot."

On the evening of April 21, 1967, we bolted the doors and took turns peeking through the window to see if anyone dared to walk in the deserted streets. Howling dogs and gunshots could be heard in the distance, but the streets remained eerily empty. We stayed inside for three days, eating nuts, drinking wine, and listening to a continuous broadcast of martial music, wondering what the hell was going on. American Armed Forces Radio did not announce the military takeover of the Greek government until cars and people began moving through the streets and life appeared to return to normal. Papa Feliz was crying when he came over to tell us there had been a *coup d'état* by a group of right-wing colonels who had formed a *junta*. It took an act of will to leave the cocoon of my accidental family. The road suddenly felt dangerous.

I hitchhiked alone on the main highway to Athens about 50 miles away. Heavily armed soldiers stood in front of random roadblocks, but traffic moved freely. In the Athens hostel, somber young travelers gathered around the radio had seen tanks occupy the city streets. They had listened to the pronouncement forbidding gatherings in groups larger than four people. Rock-and-roll music was officially considered part of a dangerous left-wing conspiracy. Ten thousand people had just been arrested, and the constitution had been abolished. The upcoming elections, which Prime Minister Papandreou was expected to win, had been canceled. A constitutional government had just been overthrown. I now understood why Papa Feliz was crying, and never doubted that his daughters would keep dancing.

A mature-looking man at the hostel introduced himself as an Austrian road engineer. He told the group he was driving a Jeep to Malaysia and would welcome company.

"If you're going near Jerusalem, I'd love a ride," I piped in without hesitating.

"It's a little out of my way, but I'd be willing to take you there. Name's Hugo." His strong six-foot frame was topped with long blond hair held in place by a wide-brimmed safari hat. I never asked to see his passport, driver's license, car registration, or any other official document, and I never looked at a map to see how much of a detour he was willing to take. I must have been protected by the angel of fools who looked upon my innocence and laughed. We followed the Aegean coastline north through Thessaloniki toward the Turkish border. Hugo wiped the sweat from his brow with an ever-present red bandana while paying verbal homage to every passing temple. He never asked why a 20-year-old woman was traveling alone through the Middle East—and he never seduced me. I never asked if he had a girlfriend or about the details of his surveying a virgin jungle in Malaysia. Our conversations were rarely personal. Not until he turned down an offer from a silver-toothed shepherd, somewhere between Athens and Istanbul, to buy me for a few goats and sheep did I discover he was a man of principle.

All roads led to Istanbul, the crossroads of the world. We ate fresh fish cooked on boats docked by the Galata Bridge and were showered with light from hundreds of stained glass windows in the Blue Mosque, named for the hand-painted tiles adorning the ceiling. The fabled market dazzled every sense. Istanbul deserved months of exploration, but the belly of Turkey was 400 miles wide, and Hugo insisted we be on our way.

The crescent moon and star of Islam topping village minarets became a familiar sight, as did the graceful Arabic script pirouetting on road signs, storefronts, restaurants, and hotels. We drove past kerchief-clad women pounding their laundry on rocks next to streams. Children screamed at us, but it was hard to tell if they were cursing or welcoming. We were often the only vehicle on lonely stretches of road. Ennui reduced the world to two people, a Jeep, endless black tarmac, nights in cheap inns, and an unquenchable thirst mixed with the taste of dust and gasoline. Days dragged on. I berated Karen Trotsky as if she were outside of myself. She was the crazy one who had opted for this venture, so she should be the one to beg for a one-way ticket home.

With a noncommittal shrug, guards at the Turkish-Syrian border returned the Hebrew dictionary they'd found in my backpack and motioned me across the border. When asked, I told them the truth. "I'm on my way to Israel." Because of hostile relations between Israel and Syria, Hugo thought this a reckless admission and didn't stop driving until we reached Damascus. I was unfazed when he told me we were on the same road as Saul was when he had a revelation about Jesus being the only son of God. Hugo's knowledge of history and mythology was impressive. I enjoyed our brief respite in Damascus, where we washed our feet in an outdoor fountain near a mosque and walked through the fabled silk market filled with endless piles of colorful, diverse, amazing textiles. I envisioned veiled women in unimaginably gorgeous gowns sequestered in the caliph's harem. Unfortunately, there was no time to shop.

If Turkey and Syria felt impossibly exotic, Lebanon was comfortingly familiar. Carved out of the Ottoman Empire after its defeat in World War I, the country had been a French protectorate until 1943, when foreign troops were finally withdrawn. Beirut had it all—crowded cafés along well-lit boulevards inspired by Parisian streets, mountains, sandy beaches, and a thriving international intellectual community. Before I could abandon my plans and enroll in the American University in Beirut, Hugo told me it was time to get back on the road.

I woke one night to the sight of Hugo trembling so hard it looked as if his limbs were about to shake loose. His red neckerchief was drenched. The intimacy between two strangers—brought on by traveling for days on the road—can feel like an enormous responsibility. When he chose not to sell me to the shepherd, he became my protector. There was trust between us. What should I do to help him? Seeing the horrified look on my face, Hugo whispered hoarsely, "Malaria attack. Got it in the jungle." In the morning, he appeared remarkably recovered, showered and was ready to drive.

Dusk found us looking for a place to sleep in a rose-scented Lebanese village. With permission from a white-robed man standing in front of a vacant building he claimed to own, we spread our sleeping bags on the rooftop. Unbeknownst to us, the whole village was aware of our presence. In the morning, another villager invited us home for breakfast. His family spoke French, which made for easy conversation. After eating and drinking to our heart's content, a woman led me into a blue-tiled room where the only furniture was a wooden bench. Clay pitchers filled with hot water rested on the concrete floor. I sat naked on a bench, allowing the woman's strong hands to scrub my scalp and pour hot water over my head and shoulders. I felt like Scheherazade being anointed for the king. An unexpected marriage proposal came when the oldest son discovered Hugo and I were merely travel partners. I politely declined his offer. We left the flower-scented air of Lebanon and drove toward Jordan. Our pace had quickened. Hugo was ready to get rid of his charge.

Visible heat waves shimmered over the two-lane highway that cut like a sword through the desert between Amman and Jerusalem. A sign in Arabic and English read *Dead Sea 10 kilometers*. The naked hills seemed unchangeable and eternal, as if time had stopped and only a thin veil separated me from seeing Lot's lament after God turned his wife into a pillar of salt. My body felt leaden in the oppressive afternoon heat. Thirsty and tired, we stopped at a Bedouin roadside encampment. They spoke no English but offered us glasses of hot, sweet, black minty tea with the graciousness of a tradition thousands of years old. We were strangers in need of sustenance.

As we ascended from the Jordan River Valley, Jerusalem appeared in the distance like a mirage. The mythic city seemed to be floating over elongated ridges. Ancient saw-toothed walls, church steeples, minarets, and a golden dome that dominated the cityscape slowly came into focus.

Hugo dropped me off at the Jerusalem youth hostel on the edge of the border between Israel and Jordan, and I never saw him again. After weeks of traveling together through Greece, Turkey, Syria, Lebanon, and Jordan, we parted as strangers.

DONKEYS, ALLEYWAYS, AND PROPHETS

I was ridiculously nonchalant about setting foot in the Old City of Jerusalem—and ignorant. A Canaanite city-state founded 4,000 years ago as an oasis for caravans crossing the Arabian Desert had become sacred to the world. Nomadic tribes once tended flocks of sheep and goats in the harsh Judaean Desert to the east, while farmers cultivated the fertile lands sloping west toward the Mediterranean.

Jews have dreamed of returning to Jerusalem ever since the Babylonian exile.[1] But for me it was simply a resting place on my way to a *kibbutz* where I would be welcomed—I hoped. Jordanian authorities informed me it took at least three days to get a visa allowing me to pass through the Mandelbaum Gate checkpoint into West Jerusalem, Israel. Permission to cross between Jordan and Israel was mainly reserved for visiting dignitaries and UN officials, except during Christmas, when worshipers from West Jerusalem were allowed to pray in Old City

---

[1] The Chaldean conquest of the Kingdom of Judah in 597 BCE marked the beginning of the Jewish exile in Babylon. The exile only included prominent citizens. People of the land were allowed to remain in Judah. Almost nothing is known about their fate. Babylonian Jews were permitted to return to Judah 70 years later when the Persians under Cyrus the Great conquered the area. From *The Jewish Temples: The Babylonian Exile (597-538 BDE)*, Jewish Virtual Library, a division of the American-Israeli Cooperative Enterprise. www.jewishvirtuallibrary.org/jsource/History/Exile.html.

churches, and twice a month when an armored Israeli convoy brought supplies to Mount Scopus, an isolated Israeli enclave inside Jordan. Once my passport had an Israeli stamp, I would never be allowed into an Arab country, but I didn't care. I would be in the Promised Land.

A sign posted near the hostel warned in English and Arabic: CAUTION! BORDER AHEAD! DANGER! MINES! I looked past the threatening-looking barbed wire and imagined the cries of mothers who'd lost sons and daughters in war. From the window of the hostel, I could see the flicker of lights in Israel.

The Damascus Gate, a massive portal in the northern wall of the Old City, was a short walk from the hostel. An imperious stone archway ushered me into a world where men dressed in ankle-length white robes and headscarves to protect themselves from the harsh desert sun. I walked aimlessly for hours, giddy with discovery. Donkeys stoically carried their burdens along narrow winding streets and alleys. Women surrounded by mounds of fresh fruits and vegetables gossiped and shouted to passersby while babies nursed at their breasts. Merchandise spilled out of stalls that were little more than windowless units with corrugated metal doors. Household goods, clothing, jewelry, and tourist trinkets were displayed near trays of fresh *baklava*, sesame rolls, fruit, nuts, herbs, and spices my nose could not identify. Succulent odors wafted from restaurants, but the scent of Turkish coffee with crushed cardamom prevailed.

A golden dome crowned with the crescent moon of Islam rose like a second sun over the Ottoman-built walls of Jerusalem. Like a moth drawn to light, I followed a road that appeared to be heading toward the dome, but I ended up on a broad cobblestone street in the Christian Quarter. Tourists in search of religious trinkets walked between monks in faded brown habits and priests in black robes. Shop windows displayed filigreed silver and gold jewelry, carved olive wood crosses, brass bowls and vases, leather goods, intricate wooden boxes inlaid with mother-of-pearl, and hand-blown glass. On a whim I entered a leather-goods shop and was approached by a dapper young clerk in a grey suit. With a polite bow, he asked in the Queen's English if I would like a cup of tea, and could he please help me find something?

"Just browsing," I said, determined not to be pressured into buying.

"How long will you be staying in Jerusalem?" The only clue that English was not his native tongue was his rolling "*r.*"

"A few days. I'm waiting for my visa to cross into Israel," I said tentatively, watching for any change in his expression. Not a twitch. "That is not enough time. There is much to see here." His understated comment was delivered with the suaveness of a diplomat. Customers came and went as I perused the merchandise, and I finally bought a large leather shoulder bag, engraved with camel caravans, that smelled of sheep.

"My name is Ahmed. It's closing time, and I'm going to visit my cousins. I invite you to join me. I think you would enjoy them. They live a short walk from here." His courteous manner was reassuring. Why not? In a few days I would be in Israel, forbidden to ever return here. We left the shop together and walked at a leisurely pace while Ahmed told me about the historical buildings.

"The Church of the Holy Sepulchre was built by Emperor Constantine's mother. She believed this to be the site of the crucifixion. Others disagree." We temporarily got swallowed by a group of pilgrims retracing the footsteps of Jesus as he carried the cross on the Via Dolorosa, the Way of Sorrow; and then we found ourselves behind a group of women impressively balancing ungainly sacks of produce on their heads. Late afternoon light slanted through the streets as they emptied of people. The clacking sound of corrugated doors swinging shut echoed through the market like a warning. A spasm of fear shot through me. I hoped my trust in this stranger was well-placed. If I disappeared, my mother would have no idea where to search. This man knew I was Jewish and on my way to Israel. He also knew I was traveling alone. Childhood warnings flashed through my mind: *Arabs hate us. They want to drive Israel into the sea.*

Ahmed finally led me into a walled courtyard that felt far from the bustling market. A barefooted middle-aged woman wearing an ankle-length flower print dress stood on an outdoor patio at the top of a stone stairway cut into the side of a two-story stone building.

"*Ahlan wa sahlan,*" were Amty's first words. Her high-pitched voice sounded almost like singing. She spoke only Arabic and felt very maternal.

"Amty welcomes you into her home and invites you for tea." Ahmed translated. I watched her pump a primitive but efficient one-burner kerosene camping stove until a blue flame hissed around the narrow rim. Loose black tea, fresh mint, and many teaspoons of sugar were spooned into a metal teapot filled with boiling water. We sat in the open-air stone patio on straw mats. Ahmed enthusiastically bragged about his cousins but revealed little about himself.

"My cousin Samira has recently come home after studying journalism at the university in Miami, Florida. Her older brother has just returned from traveling in Africa."

"And you?" I asked.

"Just a merchant." His reticence was fine with me. I didn't feel like talking about Paris, nor did I want to press the point that I was on my way to Israel. A call to prayer suddenly echoed off the ancient stone walls and poured into the courtyard. Amty prayed barefoot on a small Persian rug, her head covered and eyes closed. Her movements were fluid as she touched her knees and forehead to the ground, sat up, then stood straight-backed before returning to her knees, all the while repeating the litany: "*Allahu akbar.*" God is great. "*La ilaha illa Allah.*" There is no God but God. "*Al salat khayr min al naum.*" Prayer is better than sleep. The depth of her devotion was obvious.

I thought of my mother lighting Sabbath candles every Friday night, head covered with a cloth, eyes closed, hands circling the flames as she sang the blessing in her sweetly atonal voice. "*Baruch atah, Adonai elohaynu, melech ha olam, asher kidshanu bemitzvotav, vetzivanu l'hadlik ner shel Shabbat.*" Blessed are you, our God, Ruler of the Universe, who commanded us to light the Sabbath candles.

When Amty asked me to stay for dinner, which she had already begun to prepare, I accepted. My fear had vanished, and nobody was waiting for me at the youth hostel. Rice and vegetables were washed in a stone sink built into the wall. Gravity-fed water streamed from a spigot cut into the bottom of a two-gallon olive oil tin hanging on the wall, a clever way of creating running water. A well in the courtyard was the water source for all the families living in the compound. Amty easily climbed the uneven surface of the stone steps while balancing a bucket of water on her head.

Ahmed's cousins were about my age. Marwan was the first to appear. His job at the bank dictated he wear a suit and white shirt. Thick dark-rimmed glasses hid his eyes. "Who is this lovely young lady visiting us tonight?" He spoke as if he thought I might be part of a foreign delegation. Ahmed explained we had just met in his shop.

Moments later, a young woman with black hair pulled in a tight ponytail and kohl-lined eyes walked in and kissed Amty on both cheeks, greeting her in Arabic. Samira accepted my presence as if guests from America were a common occurrence.

Ibrahim Khatib, Samira and Marwan's father, arrived next. Except for a white *keffiyeh* covering his head, he dressed in Western garb—loose-fitting trousers and a short-sleeved buttoned shirt. A shock of silver hair and white stubble on his chin did not diminish his robust presence. His English was fluent. "I was a police officer when the British ruled Palestine. I had a uniform and rode everywhere on my horse." Ibrahim's milky eyes seemed to focus inward to a time when he was doing important work. "My friends were Muslim, Christian, Jewish—and British." I told them that my father had also been a mounted policeman in New York City. We had something in common. When the eldest son, Faisal, arrived, the entire family lit up. The only one in the family not fluent in English, he nodded politely and greeted me in Arabic.

Amty cooked a feast on the one-burner kerosene camping stove. Slices of lamb sizzled under a blanket of rice, fried eggplant, garlic, onions, and pine nuts. Moments before serving, the pot was flipped over, and the lamb found its rightful position on top, which explained why the dish was called *maqlouba*, or "upside down." We sat on folded floor mats around a communal platter and scooped rice, lamb, and vegetables with torn pieces of bread. They delightedly told me I was the first American they'd met who didn't mind eating with fingers. I laughingly replied, "And you're the first people I've ever met who consider the way I like to eat to be good manners." Amty spoke no English but could read hearts and knew everyone was having a splendid time. Samira served sweet Turkish coffee with crushed cardamom. Three sips from a tiny porcelain cup left a sediment of muddy grounds.

"Turn your cup upside down so Amty can read your fortune," Samira requested. The rivulets of coffee grounds trickled along the inside of my cup.

Amty smiled and spoke to me as Samira translated: "You will travel to many lands and meet a tall, handsome stranger."

After dinner, Faisal played the *oud*, his nimble fingers sliding up and down the fretless Middle Eastern guitar, its atonal notes sounding like a journey with no end. His appreciative audience, including me, clapped, clanged pots, and sang or hummed along.

Later that evening, a friend of Samira's stopped by, her curiosity piqued by rumors of a visiting American woman. In a deep and gravelly voice, Herminia introduced herself in halting English. "I live with my family in the Armenian Quarter." After several insistent requests, Herminia tied a scarf around her diminutive hips and began to belly dance, her hips pointing everywhere, especially toward Marwan—but my attention was drawn to Faisal. Ahmed had neglected to mention that women, especially foreign women, were attracted to this charismatic man with dark wild eyes, a thick black mustache, and honey-colored skin. The family went into paroxysms of laughter when Faisal told stories between songs, which Samira and Marwan had difficulty translating. Humor doesn't easily leap across cultural divides.

Music and joy oozed from this man, who held his *oud* as tenderly as he embraced his culture. That he was unpredictable was no family secret. Samira told me that instead of returning to Ankara, Turkey for his third year of university as expected, Faisal and his best friend Farid used the funds for a trip to central Africa. Farid came home after a few months, but Faisal remained for over a year and had only been home a little more than a month. Although his family was upset about the misspent money, they welcomed him like a prodigal son. I wondered what my homecoming would be like.

Sometime during the evening, I unintentionally insulted the family by taking my new leather bag with me into the water closet. They thought I was safeguarding my passport and money because I didn't trust them, but hidden deep within the recesses of my new purse was a roll of precious toilet paper. Eventually we had a good laugh over this. I felt so at home with the family, the food, and the music that I didn't hesitate when they invited me to spend the night. After all, I might never pass this way again.

Samira said she had to catch a bus to her mother's house and left. This confused me, since I assumed Amty was her mother, but I was too tired to worry about the details of their family relations. I slept comfortably on a feather-filled mattress in the back room. By the time I woke, Amty was serving tea to Marwan, Ibrahim, and Faisal on the open-air patio.

"*Sabah al khayr, Erees.*" Good morning. I loved how they pronounced my name: two long e's sandwiched between a rolling *r*, sealed with a soft *s*. The morning sun warmed our backs as we sat on the stone floor, using warm bread to scoop up a creamy dip topped with olives, pickled turnips, and pine nuts floating on a thin layer of olive oil. The flavors rioted favorably on my tongue. I tore another piece of bread and scooped more of the dip. Ibrahim demystified the exotic. "Hummus is made from mashed chick peas, tahini, garlic, salt, and lemon. *Khalas*. That's all." I thanked them for the recipe. The hot tea quieted my palate as I listened to everyone's suggestions about what I should see, given my three-day limitation. Faisal offered to be my guide.

"Let's go to the Wailing Wall," he announced.

"I'm not religious," I cautioned.

"Of course you want to see the Wailing Wall. You're Jewish. All Jews love this wall."

"So do the big, bad, scary Palestinians," Marwan joked.

That was the first time I had ever heard the word *Palestinian*. Who were the Palestinians, and why should I be afraid of them? I followed Faisal through the winding streets and alleyways of his childhood into the clamor of the *souq*. In a city saturated with religious and cultural memories, it was hard to isolate the significance of one wall.

The Wailing Wall stood unmarked and unnoticed in the middle of a poor, overcrowded neighborhood. Hebrew school teachers had taught that this wall was the last remnant of King Solomon's Temple, destroyed by the Babylonians in 587 BCE. But archeology has yet to find evidence of this magnificent temple, which may or may not be buried beneath the earthen rubble of the Temple Mount. The wall was actually built by Herod the Great to shore up the Temple Mount when he restored the second temple, which was destroyed in 70 CE by the Romans. When Palestine was a British mandate, Jews were allowed to pray in the twelve-foot alley beside the Wailing Wall, but were prohibited from blowing the *shofar* (ram's horn) on the High Holy Days. Egalitarian in their repression, the British also prohibited Muslims from practicing *Zikr*, a ceremony in which supplicants repeatedly glorified the name of God.

"Next year in Jerusalem." Every year my family spoke these words during the Passover Seder when retelling the story of the Hebrew slaves' walk from bondage to freedom. The world knew how Jews felt about Jerusalem, which was why Faisal insisted our first excursion be to the Wailing Wall.

Israelis may have been forbidden to pray here because of a hostile border, but no one cared that a Palestinian man was encouraging an American Jewish woman—who had entered East Jerusalem through Jordan—to place her forehead on these time-worn limestone blocks quarried in the Jerusalem hills.

The Temple Mount, known to Muslims as the Noble Sanctuary or *Haram al-Sharif*, was above the Wailing Wall. Two mosques, built after the Muslim conquest of Jerusalem, have graced either end of the plateau for

over 1,300 years. The Dome of the Rock was the golden structure I had been drawn to on my first day in Jerusalem. Cobalt tiles imprinted with Quranic verses wrapped the outside walls of the mosque like a sacred blanket. Faisal secured permission for a non-Muslim to enter. We rinsed our feet in a nearby fountain, leaving our shoes outside, and walked into the mosque through intricately carved wooden doors. A turbaned man handed me a shawl to cover my head, shoulders, and arms. Scattered around the immense room, people sat on prayer rugs studying the Quran. The dome protected a massive, sharp-edged black granite stone like a giant womb. Many believe this rock to be the site where Abraham (called *Ibrahim* by Muslims) almost sacrificed his son Isaac (Muslims believe it was Ishmael), where farmers threshed grain during the reign of King David, and where the Prophet Mohammed began his earthly ascent to heaven. We walked the perimeter of this enormous space before descending a flight of stone steps into the darkness of a cave formed when the earth tried to follow Mohammed to Paradise. History, religion, and mythology had woven diverse narratives on this seemingly ordinary vein of black bedrock.

I suddenly felt claustrophobic and needed to be outside. The blinding afternoon sun sent us into the shady part of the *souq*, where a relentless current of humanity was intent on buying, selling, and making the best deal. Donkeys had the right-of-way, followed by pilgrims and camera-toting tourists walking between white-gowned men and women squatting beside mounds of produce. We emerged on the crowded Via Dolorosa near Zalatimo's Sweet Shop.

"*Salaam aleikum*," Faisal greeted the owner of this well-known bakery.

"*Aleikum al salaam*, Faisal," Abu Khalid, a short stocky man, answered from behind the counter. Having known the Khatib family for decades, he regarded me with curiosity, getting ready to record another personal history into his mental repository. He reminded me of Bernie, the owner of the corner candy store near our Queens farmhouse. Bernie sold cigarettes and newspapers to tired commuters and served ice cream sodas to kids who came to buy comic books.

Faisal ordered *knafeh* and carrot juice for two. The flat roof of Zalatimo's bakery overlooked the Via Dolorosa, one of the most trafficked streets in the *souq*. We sat on dilapidated chairs on opposite sides of a packing crate used as a table and toasted with carrot juice as if it were exquisite champagne. From the first bite of the buttery cheese-filled pastry drowning in syrup and garnished with pistachios, I was hooked.

The sum was greater than the ingredients. Faisal regaled me with stories about his African travels. "I was welcomed in villages wherever I went. A chief in Niger gave me a grass hut to live in—and a wife!" In exchange, he taught them Arabic and the Quran. Faisal's humor and adventure shone through his struggle to speak English.

We left the Old City through the Damascus Gate, where money-changers and falafel vendors were forever shouting at the passing crowd, hoping to drum up business. Faisal pointed to a legless man rolling around on what looked like a primitive skateboard. Without a moment of pity, he told me which war had sliced this man at the waist, adding that he was a well-known cheat. We walked along Nablus Road to a secluded, walled-in garden known as the Garden Tomb. Let archaeologists decide whether this garden or the Church of the Holy Sepulcher was the true site of Christ's crucifixion and resurrection. We didn't care. We were two young people living in a temporary state of grace. I told Faisal about my mother and two brothers, the farmhouse in Queens, and a backyard filled with kids perched in tall hedges catching fireflies on hot summer evenings. I told him about the death of my father when I was three. "His name was Max. I missed not having a father when I was growing up." I shared concerns about my brother being sent to Vietnam.

"War is scary," was all Faisal said.

"I called myself Karen Trotsky in Paris, but you can call me Iris." He laughed. "*Erees* is a beautiful name." The self-imposed loneliness of my Paris life was unfathomable to him. Like me, Faisal had the soul of a wanderer, but when he wandered, his poetry, tradition, and music came with him. He had no need to strip himself of cultural or familial expectations. That we were raised on opposite sides of the world only fanned our mutual curiosity. That neither of us had much money, a job, or a direction in life didn't matter. In a few months Faisal planned to return to the university in Ankara, Turkey, and I might be living on an Israeli *kibbutz*, but at this moment a world was being unveiled before my eyes, one that held an undeniable attraction.

The ancient, haunting beauty of Jerusalem was washing away a thousand miles of road dust and survival angst. We sat on a bench in the Garden Tomb surrounded by azaleas, bougainvillea, and hibiscus bushes, shaded by gnarled olive trees that may have witnessed world-altering events. Faisal leaned over, put his arm around my shoulder, and kissed me in the flower-scented air. Our lips touched, and our lives intertwined like sudden spring growth. I delayed my passage through the Mandelbaum Gate for a few more days.

ROLLED GRAPE LEAVES AND DOOMED CHICKENS

We had no intention of sharing the stirrings in our hearts. Back in the Old City with Amty, she smilingly told us that Faisal's mother had invited us for dinner. His mother lived near Ramallah in a modern home with electricity, flush toilets, and a hot shower—things I had come to appreciate.

We left the walled city through the Damascus Gate and walked along Sultan Suleiman Street to the bus depot. Few people owned cars, so the rickety buses that arrived and departed with surprising regularity were a lifeline. Wearing blue jeans and a T-shirt with a new leather purse slung across my shoulder marked me as a foreigner. The village women wore ankle-length dresses and carried their babies in slings close to their bosoms while balancing cumbersome sacks on their heads. Modern Arab women, like Samira and Herminia, who preferred western garb, always dressed modestly.

Considering the amount of vehicular road traffic that drove through the helter-skelter crowds of pedestrians, the bus was outside of Jerusalem in a surprisingly short time. Cruising on a two-lane blacktop, we passed through bucolic villages with lovely sounding names—Wadi al-Joz, Sheikh Jarrah, Shu'fat, Beit Hanina, Qalandiya, and, finally, Kafr Aqab, where we got off. Faisal told me that King Hussein was in the process of building a minor palace on this empty stretch of highway, but I never saw imperial gates or guards signifying royalty.

Faisal told me Hussein was a teenager when he watched his grandfather, King Abdullah, get killed as they were leaving the Al-Aqsa Mosque after Friday prayers. A second bullet, meant for Hussein, ricocheted off a medal he was wearing. He became the King of Jordan when he was 18. Faisal was not shy about expressing his rage toward Hussein's grandfather, who he considered a traitor and collaborator. "For the promise of a kingdom, Abdullah helped the British and agreed to give away the golden triangle of Palestine."

However, the British may have been the ultimate betrayers. Believing a British promise that their victory would bring "territorial independence from the eastern Mediterranean to the Persian border," Arabs fought against the Ottoman Turks in World War I. But in 1916, the European powers had already carved up the Ottoman Empire for themselves in a secret agreement known as Sykes-Picot.

Another conflicting British promise came with the release of the Balfour Declaration in 1917: *"His Majesty's Government view with favor the establishment in Palestine of a national home for the Jewish people."* The borders of this "national home" were left undefined, and it was unclear whether a Jewish state meant political sovereignty or a sanctuary. The declaration included concerns for the indigenous population: *"Nothing shall be done which may prejudice the civil and religious rights of existing non-Jewish communities in Palestine, or the rights and political status enjoyed by Jews in any other country."*

Faisal's family was part of the overwhelming majority of more than 700,000 Muslims and Christians referred to as "the non-Jewish community." European Jews, responding to anti-Semitism and poor economic conditions, were coming to Palestine in increasing numbers, and by 1936 they totaled about 30 percent of the population.[2] Palestinian farmers watched as absentee landlords sold village lands they had farmed for centuries. In my family, Sykes-Picot was nothing more than a forgotten footnote in the history books, but the Balfour Declaration was as important to us as the U.S. Constitution.

On this lovely spring day, I was not thinking about secret agreements, declarations, constitutions, conflicting promises, shifting alliances, or mass migrations. I was entranced by the passing landscape that seemed to vibrate under the desert sun. Faisal pulled the wire signaling the driver to stop across from the Semiramis Hotel. We stood for a moment in the wake of bitter-smelling exhaust before walking toward a white house built from bricks that appeared to have been quarried from the hillside where it stood. Faisal's mother met us at the door.

"*Ahlan wa sahlan.* I am Yusra. Be welcomed in my home." Black curly hair framed her milky-white moon-shaped face. Dark eyeliner emphasized narrow brows that arched over her robin's-egg-blue eyes. Samira was in the kitchen helping her mother prepare dinner. Afternoon light filtered through a large open window, where Marwan sat in an overstuffed living room chair reading an Arab newspaper. On a crowded bookshelf sandwiched between Arabic volumes, I noticed an English translation of Virginia Woolf's *A Room of One's Own.*

"I understand you are on your way to Israel," Yusra said, sipping her tea. For a moment I worried this was going to be an interrogation, but she quickly slipped into reminiscing about life in British Mandate Palestine during the thirties and forties.

"Faisal and Samira were born in Ein Karem, an Arab village in what

---

[2] From 1919-23, about 35,000 Russian and Eastern European Jews immigrated to Palestine. In 1924-28, worldwide depression and anti-Semitic outbreaks in Poland caused another 78,000 Jews to immigrate there. The rise of Hitler and the Nuremberg racial laws triggered the next wave of well-funded German immigrants. This was followed by another wave between 1933-36. From *A Concise History of the Arab-Israeli Conflict* (Englewood Cliffs, NJ: Prentice Hall, 2004), Ian J. Bickerton and Carla L Klausner. pages 37-42.

is now West Jerusalem. People believe that water from a natural spring in the center of town has the power to heal. You should visit there when you go to Israel."

Ein Karem, the birthplace of John the Baptist, was one of the few depopulated Arab villages to have survived the 1948 war with buildings intact. According to the United Nations Partition Plan of 1947, this village was designated to be under international control along with the Old City of Jerusalem. Upon the creation of Israel, Palestinian homes were given to European Jewish immigrants. Yusra's voice was filled with resignation but no animosity. She continued, "It was cheaper to rent a house in Ein Karem than Jerusalem. We had no running water or electricity. Faisal and Samira were delivered by the same midwife. Amty helped take care of them. When Faisal was five, the British Police transferred Ibrahim to Zahiriya, ten miles south of Hebron. So we moved. Marwan, our third child, was born there."

"My brother was delivered on the dining room table by a one-eyed midwife," Faisal interjected, obviously having heard this story before. Yusra continued, "Our Yemenite Jewish neighbors taught us about kosher. We once offered them a huge goose, but they couldn't accept it because it wasn't slaughtered correctly." Talking about *kashruth* and Jewish neighbors was comfortingly familiar.

"The Jewish family missed their home in Yemen but could not return. They spoke only Arabic and had arrived in Israel without an education or money."

Changing the subject, Yusra asked, "What did you do before traveling?"

"Studied French in Paris after graduating college," I said, offering the clipped version of my life. She became excited.

"My mother was a French woman who lived in Palestine during the British occupation." That explained her fair complexion. "She died when I was a baby." Yusra never stated the cause of her mother's premature death but was full of stories about her late father, Sheikh Mahmoud al-Askary, a well-known writer, scribe, scholar, and mystic.

"Kings and political leaders of the day consulted with him in person or through correspondence. His dream interpretations were highly valued, and his poetry was read throughout the Arab world." Yusra intimated her eldest son had inherited the sheikh's psychic and intellectual powers, as well as his charisma.

"*Tfadali*. Please help yourself," Yusra added in Arabic. Baba ghannouj, hummus, pickled turnips, olives, tabouli, and feta cheese were served with warm bread. We ate dinner from individual plates while sitting on chairs around the dining room table.

"I received my nurse's training at the Augusta Victoria Hospital on the Mount of Olives. Have you been there yet?" I had not. "Now I'm the head midwife of the Jerusalem maternity hospital. We have no doctors, only nurse-midwives," she said proudly.

"I wish a midwife had been there for my mother," I lamented. "During her labor, she was given so much ether, the doctors wouldn't allow her to hold me for 24 hours. My mother has no memory of giving birth." Yusra clicked her tongue as if to say what a shame. After dinner we drank cardamom-flavored Turkish coffee, ate almond cookies and listened to the transistor radio.

"That's a live broadcast from Cairo," Samira told me. "One of Umm Kulthum's songs can last up to an hour. Everyone loves her—cab drivers, government officials, students, young and old. Her voice is the voice of the Arab soul."

The singer's oceanic vibrato challenged the tiny speakers in the radio. At the end of the broadcast, Faisal was inspired to sing and play his *oud*. He had one in each home. The muses had gifted this man with music, poetry, and song. And with the seeming ease of plucking ripe fruit in an orchard, he also told the most entertaining stories.

"*Erees*, you are most welcome to take a hot shower and borrow any book in my library." Yusra had noticed me eyeing the Virginia Woolf book. Besides being a nurse midwife, Yusra had a degree in literature from the American University in Cairo. "I love Greek mythology. Zeus and Apollo are my friends," she joked. "I must get up early for work, so I'll say good night, *layla saida*." That Yusra, a divorced woman with three children, lived independently and was able to support her family forced me to revise my image of Middle Eastern women forged by Hollywood and *A Thousand And One Arabian Nights*.

Yusra left sheets and blankets on the living room couch where I would be sleeping. Samira had already gone to sleep. Marwan reluctantly retired to the bedroom he shared with his older brother, leaving Faisal and me alone in the living room. We spoke in whispers so as not to disturb the others. What happened next had a gravitational inevitability. Faisal rubbed my tired shoulders. I relaxed under his touch. He murmured in Arabic, but the only word I understood was *habibti*, a term of endearment. I was a beloved. My fingers traced the outlines of his face, lips, nose, forehead, mustache, hoping to imprint them in memory. Touching became a wind that fanned a growing fire. Arms, neck, belly, everywhere burning until there was no turning back. A thousand dandelion pods parachuted into unknown territory as I freely gave myself to this man who never knew I was a virgin. When Faisal entered me, my entire being welcomed his entire being—including his world. I had crossed the Atlantic; lived the Bohemian life in Paris; hitchhiked across Europe, Turkey, and the Middle East in search of something I could not name; and somewhere near Jerusalem, I found a home in the bosom of a Palestinian family. No pain or blood testified to the fact that I had become a woman.

Slamming drawers and doors from another part of the house broke the quiet. Faisal went to the room he shared with his brother. They argued in Arabic, but it was easy to guess what the yelling was about. Marwan overheard our lovemaking and became jealous. I quickly put on my clothes, turned out the lights, and wrapped blankets around myself like a cocoon. The arguing woke up Yusra, who called out to her feuding sons. I listened to her calm, high-pitched voice speaking Arabic and tried to imagine what she was telling them. Minutes later a luminous presence in a white nightgown walked into the living room and flicked on the lamp, creating an instant spotlight. I pretended to be asleep. What was I thinking? I was not Isadora Duncan learning to dance the dance of life. This was not bohemian Paris where being a virgin was a mark of failure. Yusra and her family were educated, worldly people steeped with respect for Palestinian culture, including its traditional values. The pit of my stomach contracted. I whispered, "Forgive my behavior. Please don't kick me out in the middle of the night."

Yusra's soothing voice broke the tension. "I apologize for my younger son's rudeness. He does not understand the ways of Western women. In our culture, sex before marriage is forbidden, *haraam*." She offered me and Faisal the privacy of her bedroom. I was speechless. My own mother would have thrown me the hell out, but I knew Yusra's rules for me were different from the rules for her daughter. Ashamed and embarrassed, I resolved to go to the youth hostel first thing in the morning and stay there until it was time to cross into Israel.

In the morning light, last night's incident seemed like an improbable story from a cheesy romance magazine. I could hardly wait to get my visa. I imagined joking with my friend Jon, "Guess what happened to me on my way to the *kibbutz*? I lost my virginity." To which he would have responded, "Karen, if I knew you were a virgin in Paris, I would gladly have relieved you of your burden." We'd laugh. I wished I'd let him know I was on my way. What if he was no longer living on the *kibbutz*? Would I still be welcomed just because I claimed to be Jewish? I had no official papers to prove my religion, no circumcision, and no rabbi or Jewish mother to confirm my Jewishness. I could read Hebrew, but Faisal's father could speak it.

Yusra had already left for work. Marwan broke the awkward silence filling the kitchen as we ate breakfast. "Can I please beg your pardon, *Erees*? I would feel personally responsible if you chose to leave, but I would understand." His contrite manner was far from the agitated man of last night. He invited everyone for a picnic by the Dead Sea. "You can always leave tomorrow." Samira seemed unaware of the previous night's drama.

"*Erees*, please stay for another day," Faisal said, pushing a stray hair from my eyes. In spite of strong misgivings, I accepted the invitation.

Marwan took the day off from work and Samira from job hunting. She called Herminia, the Armenian nurse, and invited her to join us. We packed up last night's leftover food, threw bathing suits into a sack, and met Herminia at the Jerusalem bus depot.

The two-lane asphalt road descended to the lowest point on earth—1,286 feet below sea level. Sandstone escarpments glowed in the noonday sun. Heat waves quivered over the metallic surface of the Dead Sea. The life-giving Jordan River emptied into this dying body of water. Pointing to a cluster of date palms on the horizon, Faisal proclaimed, "That's Jericho, the oldest city in the world. I would like to take you there someday."

Marwan added, "Their natural spring runs year-round, so the people can grow a lot of fruit and vegetables." In this unyielding desert, water was the gift of life, which might explain why thousands of years ago, Joshua and the Israelites chose to invade this city.

Instead of a Bedouin encampment with camels tied to palm trees as I'd imagined, we ended up on a sandy beach with shaded picnic tables, fresh water showers, and a concession stand. I ran barefoot on the hot sand toward a sea that appeared to offer respite from the blistering sun. Faisal's warning came too late. The fire in my eyes was put out by tears. Almost ten times saltier than the ocean, the slightly slimy mineral-rich water could sustain no plant or marine life. People bobbed about reading newspapers as if sitting on chairs. It was impossible to sink. We sat on the edge of the sea with a 45-mile coastline and slathered ourselves with mud. When it caked dry, we rinsed our salt-encrusted bodies under the fresh water shower. The desert air-dried us instantly, leaving our skin tingling and rejuvenated. We picnicked on hummus, cheese, olives, bread, and cold drinks from the concession stand before taking another swim. This time, I closed my eyes.

The old bus laboriously ascended the steep hill to Jerusalem as I watched heat waves belly dance on the horizon. Sunlight and shadow played on sandstone escarpments. Faisal talked about ancient cities, ruins, monasteries, coral reefs, his family village—all the places we would visit together.

The next day, I wrote to my mother, telling her I had decided to extend my stay in Jerusalem, hinting at a romantic liaison. Her alarmed letters, which I picked up at the American Consulate, begged me to leave immediately and questioned my ability to think rationally. "War might break out at any time, and you are living with Arabs. It's dangerous." Looking around, I saw Faisal, Samira, Marwan, Herminia, Yusra, Amty, and Ibrahim. There were times I found Marwan's contrite manner annoying, Samira's beauty rituals tedious, Ibrahim too macho, Amty too saintly, Yusra too understanding, and wished Faisal spoke better English—but I never saw dangerous enemies.

Squawking chickens ran aimlessly around in the open-air butcher stall. "Choose one," Faisal said. Amty was planning to bake *jaj* and *bamia* (chicken with okra) for dinner. I reluctantly pointed to a doomed chicken betrayed by her eye-catching colorful feathers. Grabbing the chicken by her legs, the butcher swung the bird around his head so fast it created a halo. Seconds later he mercifully slit its throat. The headless chicken continued to run in circles for another few minutes. We left the shop carrying a featherless bird wrapped in white paper.

Nearby stalls displayed mounds of fresh fruits and vegetables, salted nuts, burlap sacks filled with chickpeas and barley, colorful confections, and waist-high stacks of sunflower centers without their golden petals. Each seed-filled center looked like a nautilus-shaped mandala, nature's perfect package. We bought apricots, tomatoes, okra, and onions from village women shouting over the din, "*Yalla mish mish! Yalla bandoura!*" Get your apricots and tomatoes here! I was beginning to discern the sounds of Arabic and knew some words, phrases, and even sentences. *Ana biddi mai* was a request for water. Faisal motioned to a passing vendor carrying a carved metal cooler on his back. The man leaned over and held a glass under a slender spout, which released a prune-colored liquid made from the pods of the tamarind tree. The thirst-quenching juice was unlike anything I'd ever tasted.

Sitting on the rooftop of Zalatimo's Sweet Shop while eating warm *knafeh* and watching the never-ending stream of human traffic in the *souk*, we began to breathe life into an impossible dream. There never was a romantic marriage proposal. Faisal's mother had given us a bedroom in her home, but we knew this arrangement was temporary. In traditional Palestinian society, living together without being married was forbidden—*haraam*.

"*Erees*, come to Ankara with me when I go back to university."

"I don't speak a word of Turkish. What would I do there?"

We considered London—friendly pubs, fish and chips, four o'clock tea with cream and sugar, Beatles music on every corner—and everyone spoke English.

"Or Paris," I suggested. "*Je parle français.* We could rent a cheap place in the Latin Quarter, and you could study French." Not eager to sell newspapers again, I became a pragmatist. "But we'd have a problem getting jobs and visas in London and Paris."

Suddenly, the skyscrapers of New York City loomed large in my mind's eye. The world's greatest melting pot, a vibrant, eclectic, cacophonous, multicultural, multiracial city that happened to be where my family lived, where I could get a job and Faisal could get a green card—if he were married to an American. Our tenuous liaison would have withered on the vine if we had not been willing to make decisions based on innocence, optimism, and lust. Under the influence of divine *knafeh*, I promised myself to a man I had known for about two weeks, extinguishing Mom's dream of marrying her only daughter to a Jewish doctor. My capricious decision to marry a foreign man living on the other side of the world, who spoke broken English and came from a family considered the enemy

by my family, was more complex than either of us was willing to admit. But our tango with realism was finished for the day.

Yusra was at Amty's house when Faisal and I announced our intention to get married. Amty joined two fingers in a gesture of happy union. "*Mabrook, mabrook!*" she said, congratulating me with a hug. I felt guilty knowing how much she longed to become a grandmother, a dream I had no intention of fulfilling any time soon. As if reading my mind, Ibrahim added, "May you have many healthy babies!" Yusra seemed to have accepted this unlikely decision with equanimity. "You should do well together. You have much in common. Both of you are restless spirits who love travel and meeting people." Marwan seemed neutral, and Samira appeared mildly shocked. No one advised us to slow down, and no one seemed concerned that a Muslim Palestinian Jordanian was about to marry a Jewish American.

Most of the time, we stayed with Amty and Ibrahim; an arched hallway separated our room from the rest of the house. My belongings were scattered beside the mattress sitting on the stone floor. In the quiet of our room, I wrote a long chatty letter to Mom. I told her about living in the Old City with a wonderful Arab family, how I loved shopping in the Jerusalem market, that I was learning to cook, and about our excursion to the Dead Sea and visiting the Wailing Wall.

I told her everything—except that I was about to get married. In my arrogance and naiveté, I reasoned that Mom wasn't missing my "'til death do us part" wedding. That would happen in the future. I was merely using the institution of marriage to bypass bureaucratic red tape and immigration. Faisal and I were friends and lovers who wanted to live together—until we decided to part. Part of me clung to the elusive ideal of being a free spirit.

On the other hand, the words of Faisal's mother kept rumbling through my brain: "A girl from here would never sleep with a man unless she was his wife." At that moment, traditional values trumped the nihilistic, let's-be-lovers-today-and-who-cares-about-tomorrow philosophy, and to my surprise, it was a relief. Drifting through ever-changing landscapes, surrounded by strangers, hitchhiking, and sleeping under bridges or in hostels had lost its allure. Foreign cities had become hurdles to get through. My journey seemed without end. Faisal offered me companionship, family, a home, and love—everything I yearned for.

Now that I was about to become her daughter-in-law, Yusra wanted to take me shopping—immediately. Shopping with her was much like shopping with my mother. Both had strong opinions on what constituted appropriate fashion, and both knew where to find the best quality at the lowest price. From an early age I was trained to be a bargain hunter. Mom would have approved of the blue-and-white knee-length cotton-linen dress that Yusra chose for me to wear on my wedding day. I thought it looked matronly and wished Samira had come along for another opinion. There was no discussion of a white gown. We decided on an informal ceremony in a government office. Since everyone admired how I looked in the blue-and-white dress, and there was no full-length mirror, I came to think it was attractive. Certainly it was more comfortable than jeans.

Cooking was women's work, but it was not lonely. Amty offered to teach me how to stuff and roll grape leaves, but first she had to perform her morning rituals. I watched her chew on an old piece of frankincense gum as she ran a wide-toothed comb through her long silver hair. She reminded me of Grandma Minka who wrapped braids around her head while regarding her reflection in the bathroom mirror. At the sound of the *muezzin*'s call to prayer, Amty reached for her head scarf and prayer rug. "*Allahu akbar. La ilaha illa Allah.*" The haunting chant hovered everywhere.

We were washing rice when a neighbor stopped by. Samira had warned me about Umm Khalid. "She's very nosy. She wants Marwan to marry her oldest daughter, although he always tells her, 'No, thanks.'" Umm Khalid's curiosity prompted an offer to help us roll grape leaves. Amty placed a finger-sized portion of uncooked rice mixed with spicy ground lamb and pine nuts in the center of a leaf, folded it on top and bottom, and rolled it into a cylinder shape, creating a perfect package. It was similar to making stuffed cabbage with my mother, except Mom used toothpicks to keep the mixture intact. Neither Amty nor Umm Khalid spoke English, so we worked in silence until Herminia showed up, which allowed Umm Khalid to release a barrage of questions: "Are you going to marry Faisal? What does your family think about you living with an Arab family?"

"*Khalas,* enough." Herminia grew tired of translating, and a relaxed quiet took over as we tightly stacked the stuffed grape leaves inside a giant pot.

"When will they be ready to eat?" I asked. Amty rolled her eyes heavenward and raised her arms to indicate hours. Time for a coffee break. Rivulets of coffee grinds running along the inside of my tiny porcelain cup revealed the same fortune as before: "You will travel to foreign lands and fall in love with a dark handsome stranger." We all laughed.

"The Khatibs own many *dunams* of land in Samua," Herminia told me. One *dunam* equaled a quarter of an acre. "Marwan took me there once. It's very, very beautiful. These grape leaves come from their village." Herminia clearly considered marriage to Marwan the gateway to a glorious future, as did the nosy Umm Khalid.

The sun was low in the sky when Faisal came home after a visit with Farid. Surrounded by minarets, church steeples, towers, and domes, we relaxed on the communal rooftop terrace which was a gathering place where people gossiped and read the paper while children played marbles and old men threw dice during spirited games of backgammon. Pigeons cooed in large metal cages. Against this backdrop of haunting beauty rose a translucent full moon. Umm Khalid's daughter, a gangly 14-year-old with sad eyes, came over to say hello. She was sweet but much too young for Marwan. In my opinion, Herminia was the perfect choice. I asked Faisal about Samua. "I would love to take you to the village," he said.

But first we had to get married.

Yusra generously offered to buy us gold wedding bands. On a broad street in the Christian Quarter, we entered a shop with an amazing window display of gold jewelry. "*Mabrook*, Faisal and *Erees*! Congratulations on your marriage." Abu Musa, the proprietor, already knew the reason for our visit. We chose matching gold bands with the date 5/22/67 engraved in Arabic numerals.

Faisal and I followed Yusra and Ibrahim along Saladin Street. Casual observers would never have been able to identify this as a wedding procession: Faisal, in dark trousers and a short-sleeved white shirt, kept his eyes hidden behind tinted glasses; I wore the new blue-and-white linen dress; Ibrahim and Yusra wore modern clothing. The four of us entered an old stone building that blended, chameleon-like, with others on this bustling street—not my image of a courthouse, which was a white-pillared edifice lined with broad steps. Faisal's parents told the court clerk I was a Christian woman converting to Islam. A moment of panic. What was I doing? Were Jews forbidden to marry Muslims? Faisal's family knew I was Jewish, so why couldn't the court know? I kept my head bowed, half expecting the clerk to look me in the eye and declare, "I can tell you are Jewish." He never even looked up. In the eyes of the court I was an orphan, so a friend of Faisal's was appointed to stand as my paternal guardian and translator. They called him "Abu Max," after my father.

Suddenly, thoughts of my father invade my being: I'm three years old, walking the length of the living room with a dish rag on my head, blissfully unaware my father is dying. Dressed in pajamas, he sits in a chair at the far end of the long narrow living room. He is singing, "*Here comes the bride, all dressed in white."* We never tire of this game.

He died at 35, but gave me his wedding blessing when I was three.

All I have from him are story fragments and a few photos. My favorite: a smiling dark-haired man in a blue police uniform is holding the reins of a chestnut mare. According to Mom he was one of the few cops in Brooklyn who refused to take bribes. I thought of him as righteous. Another photo is a formal portrait of both parents: Mom, dressed in an elegant floor-length gown, stands beside her handsome husband in a dark formal suit. My father's arm rests on my shoulder as if he's trying to stop me from squirming. I have no idea what the occasion was. Mom always worried when Max swam out to ocean liners anchored off shore. I imagined him plopping his tired muscular body in the sand next to a brunette in a leopard-skin bathing suit, the one Mom wore when she won a beauty contest in Coney Island. Mom was already engaged when they met on a handball court and fell in love. She wrote a Dear John letter to her *fiancé* in the army and followed her heart. I was doing the same.

I held Faisal's hand, determined to restrain the tears that mocked the free spirit who claimed to take these proceedings with a grain of salt. The court-appointed guardian was about to give me away in exchange for a number of sheep and goats to a man I'd known for less than three weeks. I wanted to shout, "I'm Jewish. My name is Iris Devinsky. My father is dead and I've missed him my whole life." Would my father have prohibited his only daughter from traveling the world by herself at the tender age of 20? If I'd rebelled and left home, would Max have brought me home with tactics stronger than guilt-provoking letters?

From behind a chest-high counter, the presiding clerk declared in Arabic, "In the eyes of this court you are husband and wife." Faisal leaned over and whispered, *"Ana bahibbik.* I love you." Yusra and Ibrahim were our only witnesses.

Shakespeare argued that a rose by any name would smell as sweet.

While that may be true, there's no doubt that names tell a story. *Devinsky*, my maiden name, hinted at Russian ancestry. *Karen Trotsky* represented freedom from familial and cultural expectations. *Umm Ibrahim Khatib* was the wife of a Palestinian and mother of our yet-to-be conceived son.

Amty, Samira, and Marwan welcomed us home with a feast. Baked *kibbeh*, an exquisite mix of ground lamb, pine nuts, butter, onions and spices, was served with yogurt, rice, a cucumber-tomato salad, and warm pita bread. Ibrahim filled glasses with *arak*, an anise-flavored liquor, which was followed by joyous shouting, "*Mabrook, mabrook!* Congratulations! A long healthy life to you both. May you be blessed with many babies. In a few weeks, we will have a wedding celebration with all our family and our friends." I had no idea how many people were part of their extended family. The anise liquor burned my insides and calmed my nerves. Samira and Marwan welcomed me as their new sister-in-law. The nurturing and acceptance of this family with roots as deep as the ancient olive trees shielded me from certain realities. I had no idea that church steeples across Jerusalem were flying black flags to commemorate the death of a soul because they believed a Christian had converted to Islam. There were no local synagogues to grieve that a Jewish woman had made a paper conversion. Nor was I told Faisal's mother had bought a vial of blood from the local butcher so she could hang a bloodied sheet during the night to prove to the world that the bride had been a virgin.

Unbeknownst to all of us, on May 22, 1967, the day we married, President Gamal Abdel Nasser of Egypt closed the Straits of Tiran to Israeli ships and any ships carrying goods to Israel, an action that set off an international crisis. The narrow straits between the Sinai and Arabian peninsulas were only three miles wide at the mouth of the Gulf of Aqaba. They held Jordan's only seaport and Israel's only access to the Indian Ocean. Israel immediately declared that any interference with freedom of shipping was considered an act of aggression. Nasser expelled the United Nations forces that had been monitoring a cease fire by the Suez Canal, and replaced them with Egyptian troops.

Oblivious to world events, Faisal and I affirmed our intention to share our lives—until we chose not to. We spoke of a honeymoon in Petra. This ancient Nabatean city, carved into the side of a rose-colored mountain, was only a few hours away by bus. Faisal had been there once. He described riding a donkey through a narrow canyon and up a steep cliff to a monastery with views stretching for eternity. My travel partner was now my husband, but our tenuous liaison was being transformed into a historical moment.

THE VILLAGE

The sun had barely risen, but the depot on Saladin Street was already bustling with travelers. We were going to Samua, the family's village. Ibrahim handed Amty the satchel filled with food and clothing while he bought four glasses of tamarind juice from a passing vendor. The morning coolness was beginning to wear off when we boarded the bus.

Two kilometers outside of Bethlehem, the bus passed through a thick pine forest laced with wildflowers. Ibrahim, who sat behind Faisal and myself, leaned forward anxious to share the significance of this pristine landscape. "We call this forest Abu Ghneim. The owners live in Bethlehem, Sur Baher, Umm Tuba, and Beit Sahour, where the shepherds and the wise men saw a star announcing the birth of Jesus." After a brief stopover in Bethlehem to drop off and pick up passengers, the bus continued riding on the Jerusalem-Hebron highway, passing kilometer after kilometer of stone-terraced hillsides, olive groves, and minarets marking distant villages. Depending on weather and traffic, the trip took about 50 minutes.

Hebron, like Jerusalem, is sacred to Jews and Muslims, but in Hebron few tourists wandered the streets in search of holy shrines or religious trinkets. Village women balanced ungainly sacks of produce on their heads while they walked straight-backed through a bustling market. Buses and cars shared the road with donkeys and camels. Faisal and Ibrahim wore loose-fitting trousers and cotton shirts, Amty her usual floral-print ankle-length dress, her head covered with a white *hijab*. Holding onto shards of my former life, I stubbornly wore blue jeans, which were much too heavy for a warm spring day. Everyone protected themselves against the intense sun with some sort of headscarf. When asked about the city's history, Ibrahim shook his head.

"Years ago, there was a community of Jews living in Hebron. They were still here when the British ruled Palestine." I wondered what had happened to them. Ibrahim hinted at recent violent confrontations with Israel, but all he said was, "The people of Hebron are very suspicious of outsiders." I took a deep breath. I was *Umm Ibrahim*, mother of this family's future grandchild—Jewish, but not an outsider.

We walked past the mosque where Abraham, known to Muslims as *Ibrahim*, the Patriarch for both religions, lay buried beside his wife Sarah in the Cave of Machpelah, but not even Amty felt like going inside to pray. I smiled, imagining our great-great-grandfather many times over blessing our union. Faisal and I were from the same lineage, but I had forgotten about Hagar, Abraham's concubine and mother of Ishmael, his eldest son. When Abraham's wife, Sarah, birthed their first child Isaac in her old age, she jealously demanded that her husband send Ishmael, his first son, and Hagar, his mother, into the wilderness. Abraham must have felt enormous sorrow and guilt for this action, but instead of perishing, Hagar and Ishmael were saved by a miraculous spring bubbling up through the desert floor. Isaac became a Patriarch for the Jews, and Ishmael, his half-brother, a Patriarch for Muslims. Everyone revered Abraham.

In May 1967, Hebron was a hub of commerce for outlying villages, including Samua, whose main link to the outside world was one bus. For lunch, Ibrahim bought spicy kebab sandwiches from a roadside stand. I had almost finished eating the succulent sandwich, confident it was not pork (forbidden to Jews and Muslims), when Ibrahim teasingly told me it was camel meat. I wasn't sure how I felt about eating the ship of the desert.

A stocky man with a thick black mustache walked toward us, waving. It was Omar, the village bus driver. Faisal, Ibrahim, and Omar embraced before offering the traditional greeting. *"Salaam aleikum."*

"Aleikum al salaam, Omar. Let me introduce Faisal's new wife, our daughter-in-law, *Umm Ibrahim."* I liked how that sounded—wife and daughter-in-law.

"Mabrook, hamdulillah!" Congratulations and thanks be to God. Twice a day Omar traveled the 15 kilometers between Hebron and Samua. We dallied over lunch, certain the driver would wait for us like he did for everyone, which caused an erratic bus schedule. Omar welcomed people aboard the bus as if he were the captain of a ship, gently scolding latecomers, warning them that next time he wouldn't wait, but according to Faisal, he always did.

Stark desert, rolling hillsides, endless vistas, and occasional minarets pierced the cloudless sky in the South Hebron Hills. The two-lane highway became a narrow road trafficked by donkeys, children, and shepherds guarding their sheep and goats. Flat-roofed homes made of stone, brick, or mud were surrounded by low stone walls, orchards, and gardens. Roaming dogs and clucking chickens announced our arrival. Samua, a village of about 5,000 people, reminded me of Chagall's paintings of his Russian *shtetl*, a place of mud and poverty—and the home of my grandparents. Instead of a fiddler on the roof, Samua would have an *oud* player.

Omar dropped us off in front of the two-room cinder block house Amty and Ibrahim rented from a cousin. Because there was no running water or electricity in the village, and no furniture in the house except for mattresses, the function of a room was arbitrary. Faisal and I unfolded mattresses, set them on the concrete floor, and claimed the back room as our bedroom. The other room served as Amty and Ibrahim's bedroom, living room, dining room and kitchen. Before going to sleep, I went outside to stand beneath the river of stars spanning the blackness—my first sight of the Milky Way with naked eyes.

In New York City, the sparkle was dulled by a trillion electric lights. Modern people do not depend on celestial events; calendars mark seasonal changes, and sophisticated technology guides us on land, sea, and air. Staring at these jewels of past light, I felt the immensity and mystery of the universe. Comforting sounds in the sleepy village—the lowing of a cow, a baby's cry, barking dogs—brought me back to earth.

By the time Faisal and I woke, Ibrahim was visiting friends, and Amty, with help from a neighbor girl, had hauled water and was preparing bread dough. Waving at me to follow her, I went outside where the girl handed me a bar of soap and poured warm water over my cupped hands. I brought the precious liquid to my face for a moment of running water.

We were sitting on straw mats drinking tea, eating olives, tomatoes and cucumbers with chunks of sheep's cheese and warm bread sent over by a neighbor, when Ibrahim came home excited and full of plans. "Omar has slain a sheep in honor of your marriage and invited us to a feast in his home." The bus driver was a highly respected man in this village.

"Tomorrow we'll ride donkeys to our land and check water levels in the well, but today we will show *Erees* around." Faisal and I were greeted by everyone we met. The entire village seemed to know that the son of Ibrahim Khatib was visiting with his new American bride.

Khal Mohammed lived with his two wives and numerous children. Their stone house was immaculate and comfortably cool inside. The younger wife proudly pointed to four children and then to herself, letting me know they belonged to her. A woman's worth increased with the number of babies she bore. I was digesting the idea of two women living harmoniously under one roof, sharing household duties, childcare, and a husband, when the older wife, Umm Nyfeh, took my hand and led me down the road to where a group of women sat on the ground weaving.

One of the women invited me to join them; it was like being asked to dance and not knowing the steps. No one spoke English. Communication became an ongoing game of charades. As morning wore on, I became lulled by the rhythmic weaving and the babble of voices. My mind wandered freely while my hands flung the wooden bobbin between rows of magenta, umber, and grey, as if I'd been doing this all my life. I watched the threads form an intricate geometric pattern and envied these women whose lives were like their rugs—each warp and woof intertwined into a life-sustaining fabric. They worked hard caring for children and livestock, gardening, cooking, weaving, hauling water, gathering fuel for the ovens—but their lives did not give the impression of hardship. They were as much a part of their village as the rocks and mud that made up the walls of their homes. My life in Paris as a street philosopher, aspiring writer, newspaper vendor, vagabond, and lost soul seemed fragmented and alienating by comparison. Umm Nyfeh broke my reverie by tugging on my arm and gestured me to follow her.

Sweating in the noonday sun, we walked on the black asphalt to her home where a young woman worked in the shade of ten-foot stone walls beside an igloo-shaped oven called a *taboun*. The young woman clapped, licked her fingertips, and clapped again, always keeping her eyes on the glowing coals created by a mixture of dried animal dung and dead branches. To avoid getting burnt by chunks of hot gravel embedded in the dough, she had to move fast, very fast, her arms becoming wings as she pulled round loaves out of the clay oven. The older wife smiled and pointed to herself and to the young woman. "*Hadha* Nyfeh." That's my daughter Nyfeh. At the sound of her mother's voice, the young woman looked up.

Except for my fair complexion, our resemblance was uncanny. We both had hazel eyes, a bridge of freckles covering a small nose, and dark curly hair. Umm Nyfeh introduced us in Arabic. The animal pens were near the oven. Nyfeh patiently tried to teach me how to milk the cow, but after several failed attempts, she laughingly took over. Accustomed to her smell and the sureness of her strong hands, the cow gratefully yielded the contents of its udder, and soon warm milk was pinging into a metal bucket. When Faisal came to see how I was doing, he was wearing

a loose-fitting ankle-length white tunic like all the men in the village. It took a moment to recognize this exotic-looking man as my husband.

Faisal photographed Nyfeh and me standing on either side of a cow in the stone animal pens. I'm wearing jeans, Nyfeh a traditional ankle-length embroidered dress. Both our heads are covered with scarves.

We ate lunch in Khal Mohammed's grape arbor next to the garden. His two wives served trays of hummus, olives, sheep's cheese, tomatoes, and the bread Nyfeh had just baked. They worked well together and appeared to be friends. Ibrahim cut up a fresh watermelon while Faisal and I picked grapes from a nearby vine. I spent the hottest part of the day inside the cool house, watching Nyfeh work on a Singer treadle sewing machine that was just like my grandmother's. She taught me to discern the difference between machine and hand-stitched embroidery, which was marked by tiny knots and random threads. Nyfeh had learned to embroider from her mother, a skill passed down through generations of women. The machine-embroidered dresses, still quite beautiful, were for sale. Opening a wooden chest sitting in a corner, Nyfeh carefully unfolded the dresses that would never be sold in the market. Faisal later explained that this was her trousseau.

Nyfeh showed me the wedding dress she had made for herself. The neckline was edged with a saffron zigzag appliqué outlined in red, yellow, and blue threads. Grapevines laden with fruit climbed their way from the hem to the bodice. On the back, two birds perched on a fountain surrounded by verdant growth appeared to be chirping songs of joy. With tiny cross-stitches on black satiny fabric, Nyfeh had painstakingly embroidered her vision of Paradise. The skill, concentration, commitment, and patience required to complete this dress was beyond anything I had ever attempted. Nyfeh insisted I wear one of her old dresses. The lightness of the cloth cooled my body as we walked arm-in-arm up the road to pick grapes, waving to everyone who passed by.

The sun had just crested the horizon when Faisal, Ibrahim, and I set out on donkeys. After realizing my donkey was never going to break into an uncontrollable gallop, I relaxed into its plodding rhythm while Ibrahim told me about his family.

"We come from Al-Arish, a small town on the Mediterranean south of Gaza. My family moved to the Hebron area when Palestine was ruled by the Ottomans. I had two brothers. All of us could read and write. We became teachers of the Quran. If people had no money to pay us, we traded for land. Between the three of us, we have 5,000 *dunams* on the edge of Samua." In spite of owning more than 1,000 acres, Ibrahim had never built a house there.

"We paid the villagers to help us plant over 300 olive trees." Ibrahim stressed the importance of these trees. All the food was cooked in olive oil, and no meal was complete without olives. Money earned from the sale of the oil and olives bought life's necessities. During the fall harvest, the most important occasion of the year, entire families camped out in their groves.

With outstretched arms, looking like the embodiment of his namesake, Ibrahim indicated the expanse of the family's land—land that would someday belong to Faisal. "From here you can see across the border into Israel," Ibrahim declared. There was nothing to mark an international boundary—no fences, survey flags, or striking land formations.

We tethered the donkeys to an olive tree while Ibrahim searched for a hidden well. Lifting the lid on a concrete slab, he announced, "The water level is high. This is good, very good, my son." The clear water reflected our delighted faces. Ibrahim plunged a bucket into the well, splintering our images into a thousand splashes. We thirstily drank the cold, clear water. It was a windless day, so Ibrahim lit a brush fire to clear away weeds. The earth was still warm when we dug up the wild onions that had gotten roasted in the ground during the fire, and ate them with bread, cheese, and olives. It was the most delicious sandwich I'd ever tasted.

Riding back to the village in silence, I witnessed a moment of harmony I will never forget. The sun, magnified through undulating heat waves, was sinking in the West just as the translucent full moon was rising in the East against darkening shades of indigo. Natural cycles frame even the most chaotic life—whether or not we take time to notice.

Amty was cooking lamb organs, a gift from Omar, over an open pit fire. Tradition demanded that meat from a slain animal be shared with family and friends. Nyfeh, who was helping Amty, offered me a taste of roasted liver and heart. I accepted her offer. In the privacy of my room, I rinsed my body with a basin of heated water, put on the dress Nyfeh had loaned me, and was ready for the feast.

Faisal and I held hands while walking on the road to Omar's house. I wondered if our public display of affection was appropriate, but he seemed unconcerned. We were newlyweds, after all. Omar's bus was parked in his front yard like a precious ornament. The savory scent of roast lamb filled their prosperous-looking home.

"Ahlan wa sahlan!" Soon after the traditional greetings, Amty disappeared to help the women, leaving me in a room filled with men sitting on mattresses arranged in a circle around straw trays. White ceramic floor tiles reflected light from kerosene lamps that burned in every corner. Faisal or Ibrahim occasionally translated the animated conversations happening around me. Women served salads, hummus, lamb, rice with okra, and fresh bread, the feast sealed with baklava and cardamom-flavored Turkish coffee. The other women ate when the men were finished. I would have preferred to eat with them, but I was treated like an honored guest.

We walked home beneath a trail of stars that perpetuated the illusion of a vast, unchanging universe. Faisal chose this moment to tell me that Amty was Ibrahim's first wife. When she remained childless after years of marriage, Ibrahim took a second wife, Yusra, who gave birth to Faisal, Samira, and Marwan. The children loved Amty as dearly as their biological mother—and she loved them with a nurturing devotion. I had no problem with Ibrahim or Khal Mohammed having two spouses, but made it perfectly clear to Faisal that I would never accept another wife into our family. He reassured me I was his one and only *habibti.*

Nyfeh and I spent as much time together as possible, and when the language barrier frustrated us, Faisal helped. She wanted to know how we'd met and what my life had been like before I married. There were no simple answers. In a world where it was uncommon for a woman in her twenties to be single, Nyfeh was considered an old maid. Faisal told me she was in love with a cousin who was studying at the university in

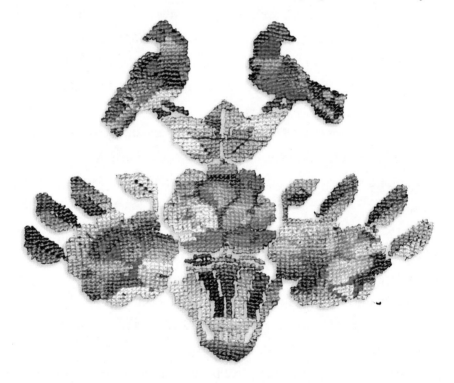

Damascus. She dreamed of marrying him when he graduated, but Faisal doubted that her cousin would marry an uneducated village girl, which disturbed me. I hoped her cousin had the brains to marry this woman, who was beautiful, smart, charming, and ready to be his devoted wife.

Nyfeh and I basked in the joy of a new friendship. She planned to attend our wedding celebration in Jerusalem. Unbeknownst to us, we were about to be separated by the abyss of war. As we said goodbye with a warm embrace, Nyfeh thrust a dress into my arms. "Tell *Erees* to wear this at the party," she told Faisal. It was the hand-embroidered dress she was saving for her own wedding day—the one with the songbirds perched on a flowering fountain. Her generosity overwhelmed me. I didn't know how to thank her with words or deeds.

My heart's desire was born in Samua. Someday I hoped to live in a village, have children, watch them grow, share life events with family, friends, and neighbors, plant a garden, raise chickens, and in time become a grandmother and elder. A traditional village is a personal landscape that survives by handing down knowledge from generation to generation. A nation-state defined by arbitrary borders straddling a continent, filled with diverse ethnicities and languages, felt too abstract. I imagined thousands of interdependent, sustainable villages strung across the globe—an idea as appealing as birds-of-paradise singing on flowering grapevines.

WARNINGS

*IRIS STOP WAR IMMINENT STOP GET OUT NOW STOP TAKE FIRST
BOAT OR PLANE TO CYPRUS STOP MOM*

A telegram was waiting for me at the American Express in Jerusalem. If I had bothered to look at a newspaper, I would have understood the cause for my mother's alarm. On May 14, 1967, Cairo announced their armed forces were on maximum alert. On May 18, Egypt demanded the recall of all UN troops stationed in the Gaza Strip and the United Arab Republic. Egyptian troops crossed the Suez Canal and took over UN positions in the Sinai. On May 22, the day Faisal and I got married, Egypt closed the Gulf of Aqaba to Israeli ships and ships carrying goods to Israel.

Blissfully uninformed about world events, Faisal and I continued to travel freely between his father's home in the Old City, and his mother's home in Kafr Aqab where we enjoyed the comforts of electricity and hot running water. One afternoon, the mysterious elixir bubbling on the stove in Yusra's house did not smell like an incredible home-cooked meal. I watched as Samira spread a taffy-like substance across her arms and legs—and then, with a quick yank, she pulled it off. The process of stretch, paste, and yank was repeated until all bodily hair was removed.

She then anointed her skin with olive oil, leaving it soft as a baby's bottom. Samira was in the middle of a beauty treatment.

"All married women do this," she informed me. "Arab men like their wife's skin to be smooth, without any hair." I hesitatingly agreed to try this razorless hair-removal technique. Samira placed the sticky substance on my arms and legs and then, to my surprise, she suggested we remove my pubic hair! A searing pain jolted through me when the pubic hairs were pulled out by the roots. Back to razors, I announced. Better to have hairy armpits and legs than ever submit to this procedure again. Faisal would have to love me as I was. On Samira's advice, after a long hot shower, I rubbed olive oil on my tender skin.

When the dinner dishes were washed, Yusra took a close look at the dress Nyfeh had given me. "This had to take more than a year to complete. Nyfeh must have been saving it for a special occasion."

"Her wedding," I answered.

"Embroidery is a Palestinian tradition handed down from mother to daughter. It's a way of remembering our history. Every region has a style and design. People weren't able to travel much, and villages were relatively isolated. Some designs are 3,000 years old." Nyfeh's gift was a historical treasure, something I would cherish the rest of my life.

"*Erees*, why don't you meet me at work when Faisal visits Farid," Yusra suggested.

The next day, Faisal dropped me off at the Jerusalem Midwifery Hospital in the Old City. I sat in Yusra's comfortable office while uniformed midwives stopped by for consultations. She clearly enjoyed a great deal of collegial respect.

"We have no doctors on staff. If there is a complicated delivery, the midwife calls me." As if on cue, one of them rushed into her office, speaking with great urgency. Yusra turned to me. "*Erees*, would you like to see a birth? A woman is about to deliver breech and needs help."

"Sure," I said nonchalantly, having no idea what a breech birth meant. Someone handed me a hospital gown and mask while Yusra sterilized herself. Screams echoed in the hallway before we entered the white-walled room where a woman lay in a hospital bed, her stupendous thighs supported by metal stirrups. She looked like Mother Earth about to birth the world. Seeing the look of horror on my face, Yusra took a moment to explain that after ten births, the woman's uterine walls had become flaccid. She deftly extended her arm deep into the woman's womb and came out with a tiny leg. Reaching in again, she came out with another leg—two miniature feet sandwiched between gargantuan thighs. As if panning for gold, both of Yusra's arms disappeared up to her elbows inside the woman. Back and forth, she slowly rocked the infant trapped in the birth canal. Rotating the legs and torso 180 degrees allowed the head to be released, and out popped a beautiful baby. I didn't know enough to be impressed with her expertise, but I did understand I had just witnessed a miracle. Yusra calmed me down with a cup of mint tea.

"Her nine other children were born here," she told me. I hoped Yusra would be around when my turn came. She must have had similar thoughts, for she quietly called me "Umm Ibrahim."

When Faisal arrived at the Midwifery Hospital to get me, he was whistling. All he could talk about was Farid, the friend who had been part of his African sojourn. As children they had both attended Collège des Frères in Jerusalem and later the university in Ankara.

"Farid cannot believe I got married while he was visiting family in Syria. He wants to meet you."

After dinner that night, we listened to the radio as we often did. I was shocked when the program was interrupted by a broadcaster announcing that all Americans were requested to register at the American Consulate. Faisal tried to calm my rising fears. "*Erees*, *habibti*, don't worry. Nasser talks big, but it's a war of words."

Samira concurred. "He believes all Arabs are brothers and we must stand together to be strong." Nasser was a champion of Palestinian rights and had rejected the UN vote that created the state of Israel. I remembered a childhood slogan learned somewhere between home and the synagogue, angry words meant to instill fear of Arabs who wanted to drive the Israelis into the sea, every last one of them. In the story of Exodus, the mighty Egyptian army drowned in the waters of the Red Sea after pursuing the Hebrew slaves who, with help from God, passed to freedom on the opposite shore. But Nasser was not Pharaoh. When Syria needed help to halt Israel's water diversion plans, Egypt did nothing. Nor did they help when Israel violated Syrian airspace by shooting down six planes in April 1967.[3] Egypt was a poor country and Israel did not need divine intervention.

Neither Samira, Faisal, Marwan, Yusra, nor I were privy to the glaring deficiencies of the Egyptian military and its allies, although I suspected as much while watching a group of Jordanian soldiers across from Yusra's house trying to attach a machine gun to something that looked like a tripod. Every time it collapsed, the gun fell to the ground, and the soldiers covered their ears in mock alarm, pretending an explosion had just occurred. A place in my heart that I barely understood—tribal loyalty perhaps—was reassured by their inefficiency. The Jordanian soldiers were playing war, not making war. They would never drive Israel into the sea.

I wrote to my mother, telling her war was not imminent. Nasser fought with words, and I had no intention of taking the next boat or plane to Cyprus. I willfully ignored my mother's warning. If a cataclysmic moment was hurtling toward us, I would find refuge with Faisal and his family. I was a beloved wife with two mothers-in-law, a father-in-law, a

---

[3] Ian J. Bickerton and Carla L. Klausner, *A Concise History of the Arab-Israeli Conflict* (Englewood Cliffs, NJ: Prentice Hall, 2004), page 148.

brother- and sister-in-law, not to mention aunts, uncles, cousins, and friends. But that was not in my letter.

Dear Mom,

The bakery up the street has the only phone in this neighborhood. Everyone brings their bread dough and uncooked chickens there. For a few pennies (called piasters*) you can buy space on a shelf in the huge oven. Call this number in case of emergency.*

Love, Iris

When Faisal and I dropped two chickens at the bakery, I warned the baker he might get a frantic call from my mother. As the neighborhood confidante and counselor, he shook his head understandingly. We mailed my letter at the post office and headed to the American Consulate, where a lady bureaucrat refused to answer any questions. Unlike my mother, she did not advise me to take the first plane or boat to Cyprus, although both of them seemed to believe something dangerous was about to happen. All she said was, "We're registering all Americans as a precautionary measure."

Café was a glorified name for Ibrahim's business, which was nothing more than a windowless room with barely enough space for two tiny tables, a few tottering chairs, and an old fridge filled with soda pop. When the door leading to the outside was closed, the café became as silent as a tomb. An unseen source of electricity illuminated a dangling light bulb. Ibrahim introduced us to his patrons. "This is my son Faisal and his wife Umm Ibrahim." A few white-robed old men with tanned leather skin sat around smoking a *narghile* and playing *shesh besh*, better known as backgammon. When someone wanted tea or coffee, Ibrahim called a street kid who, for a few *piasters*, would run to a nearby restaurant and return with tiny porcelain cups and glasses carried on a metal tray.

After introductions, I sat on the stone step outside the café and read the current issue of *Newsweek*. Exciting things were happening in the States. Photographs of long-haired barefooted hippies dressed in gypsy clothes with flowers entwined in their hair were dancing in Golden Gate Park. A year ago, when I left the States, the dominant artistic, intellectual, and cultural movers were folk singers and beat poets. Black was the color howling the message of doomsday. A spontaneous combustion had occurred, freeing the locked-up colors in the rainbow.

I thought of Hank's admonitions. An unpopular draft was forcing thousands of young Americans to choose between becoming draft dodgers or being sent to a horrific war in Southeast Asia. Soldiers were bringing home drugs along with lifelong traumas. Bob Dylan advised, *"You don't need a weatherman to know which way the wind blows."* Thousands of war protesters filled the streets of America, and I wanted to stand with them.

I averted my eyes when Amty greeted me with outstretched arms. She was always checking to see if I was pregnant.

"Keef halik inti?" How are you? she asked.

"Ana mabsoota." I'm fine. I lied. I was homesick.

Before going to sleep that night, I looked at the *Newsweek* again and wondered—who were the "flower children" and what was a "love-in"? Those photos were luring me home more surely than a thousand of my mother's anxious letters.

Ahmed worked long hours in the shop to help support his mother, father, seven sisters, and brother, so we rarely saw him after he introduced me to the Khatibs. Ahmed's 90-year-old father, who lived with his family in a refugee camp inside the Old City, had just welcomed a baby girl. "They live in two rooms with a dirt floor," Faisal explained as we walked through the narrow alleys of the overcrowded camp. People lived in a complex of half-demolished buildings without running water or electricity. I understood why Ahmed invited foreign women to Faisal's house. Abu Ahmed welcomed us into his tent, where his young wife sat nursing a rosy-cheeked plump infant. With a shawl to protect their modesty, Arab women were allowed to nurse on buses, in the market, and at home, even when visitors were present. Dangling gold filigree earrings emphasized the blackness of Umm Mohammed's hair. Had family circumstances forced this beautiful young woman to marry an old man, I wondered? She hauled water from a spigot somewhere in the camp and washed clothes and dishes in a basin. Showers and baths were an unheard-of luxury. The white-turbaned old man spoke to Faisal as if they were alone. I felt as invisible as his young wife who served us tea. Faisal later told me that the old man had been complaining about his sex life. Ever since the baby, his wife refused to sleep with him.

Although Faisal and Farid would never again enjoy the camaraderie they'd had as students and fellow adventurers, they met whenever possible. They discussed philosophy and literature and reminisced about past escapades, laughing until tears ran down their cheeks. Farid spoke no English, and humor was hard to translate. I rarely joined them. With Farid and myself vying for Faisal's attention, it was an awkward threesome. I understood they shared a past, whereas Faisal and I hoped to create a future. With unflinching honesty, Farid was the only person who expressed wariness that Faisal had married a foreign woman he barely knew. I looked at Farid's eyes, the color of burnt almonds, and secretly agreed with him.

In spite of his doubts, Farid invited us to his home for a congratulatory wedding feast. The two-story stone house built by Farid's great-grandfather sheltered his elderly parents, four brothers, and a sister. Perched on a steep hillside in Ras al-Amud, a Palestinian village near the Old City, the house had sweeping views of the fertile Kidron Valley fed by the Gihon Spring.

"Ahlan wa sahlan." The family's warm welcome helped offset my disappointment—or, should I say, sense of entitlement—that I expected people to speak English, even if I was visiting their country. We were shepherded into a shady courtyard. The family had known Faisal since he was a child and offered many *mabrook*s along with hugs and delicious food. Farid's mother and sister served course after course, starting with salads, olives, pickles, *hummus*, and pita bread. When the roast chicken and rice with vegetables arrived, I was already stuffed. Although everyone appreciated the few words I'd managed to learn, my inability to speak Arabic was a handicap. Questions about me were directed to Faisal, my husband and translator. I thanked Farid's father, who was a sheikh at Al-Aqsa Mosque, for getting me permission to enter the holy shrine. He smiled and continued gliding around the courtyard in a white turban and flowing robe, looking as if he already had one foot in Paradise.

An American film was playing in Ramallah. I didn't care what it was, as long as the characters spoke English. Pedestrians and vehicles filled the broad streets of this city with a blend of modern and traditional architecture. We had an hour before the film started, so we stopped to visit Faisal's spinster aunt, Khalti Suad, whom I had never met. Faisal, Samira, and Marwan were like her children. She was surprised and delighted to see us. Khalti Suad had the same sparkling blue eyes as her younger sister, Yusra, but dyed black hair and a prune face made her look much older. She, too, was a nurse and spoke perfect English. Faisal's aunt believed war was imminent, and she was scared. Faisal reassured her.

"Don't worry, Khalti. If there is a war, *Erees* and I will stay with you." Faisal may have had psychological insight into Nasser's reluctance to start a war, but he didn't understand that Israel's fear of being driven into the sea had caused them to create the most powerful, aggressive, and efficient military possible. Khalti Suad's anxiety and fear confirmed my own.

We finished our coffee and walked to the movie theatre near Al-Manara Square, a parklike area in the city center. In the cool darkness of the theatre, a bag of popcorn on my lap, I was ready to be transported to the American Wild West for two hours. Except for two people in the balcony, the theatre was empty. I was sorely disappointed when cowboy John Wayne began to speak Arabic. The film was dubbed. When the lights were turned on, we discovered the people in the balcony were Samira and Herminia. "I should have guessed the only other crazy people going to the movies tonight would be you guys," Samira laughed. "I think we're the only ones who don't believe there's going to be a war."

"Let's go home and hide under the bed," Faisal said, opening his eyes wide like an owl.

"Any excuse to get in bed with your bride," Herminia teased.

I mustered a smile. War was feeling like a real possibility.

"We'd better catch a bus while they're still running," Faisal said prophetically.

The four of us caught a bus in front of the movie theatre. Faisal and I got off at his mother's house in Kafr Aqab. Samira and Herminia continued on to Jerusalem.

WAR

By the time Faisal and I awoke on June 5, Israeli pilots had effectively destroyed the Egyptian Air Force in a surprise attack lasting less than two hours. Long-range bombers, fighter jets, transport planes, and helicopters, exposed in open-air hangars, were bombed like sitting ducks. One-third of Egypt's pilots were killed. Israel also destroyed two-thirds of the Syrian air force, leaving it unable to retaliate. Israeli pilots were ordered to *"destroy and scatter the enemy throughout the desert so that Israel may live, secure in its land, for generations."* [4] They succeeded beyond their dreams.

Radio Amman announced that Jordan had been attacked by Israel and the *"hour of revenge had come."* Israeli tanks were moving steadily through the Sinai on their way to the Suez Canal while Radio Cairo played patriotic music between calls to liberate Palestine. Official Egyptian communiqués falsely claimed they were shelling Israeli towns and their military had downed more than 150 Israeli bombers. International phone lines had been cut, and Israel did not contradict these lies.

All this happened before we had lunch. Later in the day, Faisal's mother called from Augusta Victoria Hospital on the Mount of Olives to

---

[4] Michael B. Oren, *Six Days of War: June 1967 and the Making of the Modern Middle East* (New York: The Random House Ballantine Publishing Group, 2003), 309.

tell us she had been recruited to be a nurse for the Jordanian army. "Go stay with Khalti Suad in Ramallah."

Just after sunset, distant explosions from the direction of Jerusalem pierced the night. They might have been Israeli mortar and artillery shells securing Mount Scopus, the isolated Israeli enclave on Jerusalem's highest hill. Since 1948, an agreement between Jordan and Israel allowed weekly convoys to bring supplies to this one-square-mile garrison, home to Hadassah Hospital and Hebrew University. Or the explosions may have been the Jordanian army safeguarding positions on the Mount of Olives overlooking the Old City to the east—the site where Jesus wept at a vision of Jerusalem lying in ruins.

To protect ourselves from the possibility of shattering glass, Faisal and I moved a mattress into the windowless dining room and closed every door leading to this inner sanctum, but an urgent curiosity drew me to pull back the heavy curtains covering the huge living room window. Three huge spotlights were casting an eerie orange glow over the landscape. Most likely flares and search beams, they looked like vacant eyeballs staring into the void. I returned their merciless stare, willing them to disappear. These surreal, incomprehensible events seemed to be happening in the safety of a darkened movie theatre. I was Scarlett O'Hara watching Atlanta go up in flames.

New rounds of artillery shells or bombs broke my reverie. Ignorant of the sounds of war, I had no way to distinguish them. Sleep, the only escape, was hard to come by. We listened to broadcasts from Egypt, Jordan, Syria, and Israel. Faisal translated as best he could. If we had understood Hebrew, we would have heard an Israeli broadcaster warn, "All of Israel is the front line." Believing another Holocaust was imminent, Jews from around the world were boarding planes bound for Tel Aviv, ready to defend their precious 19-year-old country. I, too, wanted Israel to survive but could not fathom how Faisal and his family posed an existential threat—to me or to Israel. The voices on the radio eventually melted into a monotonous stream of static, lulling us to sleep in the safety of each other's arms.

The next morning was quiet. I thought perhaps last night had been a nightmare, but when we turned on the radio, Nasser's bombastic shouting confirmed what we already knew. War had started. The only words I understood were *"Allahu Akbar!"*

I worried that if our house, resting on concrete pillars embedded in the hillside, incurred a direct hit, we could be crushed. On Faisal's mother's advice we went to stay with his aunt, walking from Kafr Aqab to Ramallah, about four miles up the road. Buses were no longer running, and few people owned cars. With backpacks filled with clothes, food, and water, we joined the throng of people heading in both directions on the two-lane highway. Heavy burdens were balanced on heads or backs. Arms were saved for babies, hands for children. The lucky people rode in cars or on donkeys.

Many were becoming refugees for the second time in their lives, exacerbating the unresolved refugee crisis created in 1948, when over 800,000 Palestinians were expelled from towns and villages. Many still held tattered documents proving ownership of land and keys to homes that had been destroyed or given to Jewish Holocaust survivors from Europe and Russia. That Israel had been created on the backs of over 500 destroyed Palestinian villages[5] was not taught in Hebrew school.

Faisal and I had little sense of the historic import of this moment— that this was another life-changing moment for his family, for the Palestinians, and for Israel. All we thought about was finding a sanctuary.

History books offer a range of possible provocations that ignited the flames of war: Nasser's bravado, Russian miscalculation, Syria and Israel's struggle over water in the Golan Heights, Jordan's misinformation,

[5] Bickerton and Klausner, *A Concise History of the Arab-Israeli Conflict,* 104.

or Israel's dream to extend its borders to the Jordan River. This much is clear: Israel struck the first blow in what they called a preemptive attack. Believing that Egypt had succeeded militarily, Jordan lobbed shells into West Jerusalem and seized UN headquarters in No Man's Land. Once the Pandora's Box of war was open, Israel did everything to conquer the Old City, something they had failed to do in 1948.

Khalti Suad wept with unabashed relief when we arrived at her door. "Thanks be to God you are here." The squat windows of her apartment were covered with cardboard, creating a false twilight. When our eyes adjusted to the dimness, we saw that other families had also sought sanctuary here, mainly people living on the upper floors in this building. A young couple took turns cradling their infant. A sweet scent wafted through the house. Women were baking bread and cooking rice while there still was electricity. We filled plastic jugs with water, and gathered every candle and match we could find. No one knew how long we'd be here, so we prepared for a siege.

Since we were supposed to be on our honeymoon, Khalti Suad insisted on giving Faisal and me the privacy of her tiny bedroom. Everyone else slept on mattresses in the living room. They teased us about spending so much time in the bedroom. Imagining us making passionate love in the midst of war was reassuring, but if they had put their ears to the door, they would have heard Faisal reciting poetry and telling stories. Along with food and water, his survival gear included a black hardcover journal hand-written with original poetry, most of which he knew by heart. Faisal's attempts to translate barely survived the linguistic divide. The words and images sounded excessively romantic to my ears, but the rhythmic cadence of his voice kept me from succumbing to abject fear. The inspiration he drew from these poems touched my heart and ignited my body. For brief moments we were able to create a cocoon of pleasure that overwhelmed the ear-shattering explosions followed by eerie silences. The uncertainty of not knowing when or where the next explosion would occur triggered his memories of another war.

"I was five years old. We were living in Ein Karem outside of Jerusalem. I watched my mother cry every time she read a paper or heard the radio announce more towns being taken over—Lydda, Ramle, Jaffa. One day we watched British airplanes flying overhead in low formation; they were saying goodbye to Palestine. The British left without securing the borders, and we were afraid of the Jews. They had strong weapons. We called them the *brin* and the *stin*, every bit as scary to me then as the atomic bomb is today. When the Jews pulled the trigger, their guns just kept shooting and shooting. Many of our friends and neighbors were killed."

"Faisal, you knew I was Jewish and on my way to Israel, but your family was so welcoming."

"*Habibti*, there was nothing about you that reminded us of war."

The bleating and braying of terrified sheep, goats, and donkeys was heartbreaking. Without their human caretakers, the animals were thirsty and starving. Our greatest fear was a direct hit to the building that sheltered us. Time was measured by shades of darkness and light. During a period of uneasy silence, Faisal again described our future honeymoon to Petra.

"We will ride donkeys into a canyon so narrow you can touch both sides, and pass into a valley with temples carved into the side of a rose-colored mountain. A steep winding trail leads to a monastery, where we will sit on the edge of a cliff and watch the sky turn purple. We won't be worried about my mother traveling with an army or my family hiding in Jerusalem." Neither of us said who we hoped would be the victor. We just wanted the war to be over.

I wondered where I'd be if I'd used the visa and gone through the Mandelbaum Gate—perhaps living on a *kibbutz* near the Dead Sea or hiding in an Israeli bomb shelter. Maybe I would have flown to Cyprus or returned to New York. At such moments people become religious, or insane. I held imaginary conversations with my mother.

"I told you to take the first boat or plane out of there," she'd say, to which I would humbly reply, "You were right, Mom, I should have left when I had the chance, but I discovered that Palestinians are not our enemy. We can live together," something I hoped to convince her of someday.

"*Habibi*," I whispered, "surely no one would bomb Jerusalem. That city is sacred to everyone," but my words hinted at underlying doubts. Radio Damascus falsely announced they had begun to bomb Israeli cities in the final battle for liberation from Zionism. In fact, two-thirds of their air force had been destroyed, and Israeli soldiers were poised on a hillside outside the Old City waiting for orders to break through the Lions' Gate. Abba Eban, Israel's foreign minister, had flown to Paris, London, and the United States to make a case for his country in the court of world opinion. During a speech at the United Nations on June 6, Abba Eban declared, *"Israeli streets are dark and empty with an apocalyptic sense of approaching peril."*

Few people knew that in the Negev desert, Israel had already built a facility capable of assembling a nuclear device.[6] Israel kept this incredible accomplishment a secret. The international community feigned ignorance or truly had no idea, and the myth of Israel's apocalyptic danger prevailed. King Hussein of Jordan appealed to the UN Security Council for an immediate cease fire, but a 24-hour delay gave Israel the opportunity to seize complete control of the West Bank. All this happened while Faisal and I dreamed of riding donkeys in Petra and remained hiding in Khalti Suad's basement apartment.

Ear-shattering explosions kept ringing in my ears long after the

---

[6] Ari Shavit, *My Promised Land: The Triumph and Tragedy of Israel* (New York: Spiegel & Grau, 2015), 178-182.

bombing and shelling stopped. Fortunately our building was never hit. It felt like the shelling had been going on forever, although it was only days.

On the morning of June 7, we heard the sound of human voices. I had no idea what the Israeli soldiers were shouting, but we all understood Ramallah was being occupied.

"*Hadha Yehudis hon!*" The Jews are here! Khalti Suad screamed in Arabic. I realized they shared Faisal's childhood terror. It hardly seemed necessary to remind everyone that I was not with the conquering army. We had just survived a war together.

"I don't understand what they're shouting," whispered Khalti Suad.

Sunlight streamed into our twilight sanctuary when we removed the cardboard from the windows. Tanks and military vehicles were flooding the streets. Israeli soldiers known for their ferocity were entering homes. One of my fellow survivors implored me to go outside and wave my American passport like a white flag of surrender.

Terror is contagious. I didn't look terribly different from my fellow survivors. Only a thick New York accent could identify me. I imagined being shot while shouting, "I'm American. Jewish. These people are my friends, my family. My friends are your friends." The soldiers would discover too late that I was kin. My death would be mourned, but the army would declare that innocent people die during war. I decide against running into the street.

I held Faisal's hand as helmeted soldiers, guns poised, barged into our sanctuary. The Israeli army had not been driven into the sea. Soldiers searched the apartment, confirmed we were unarmed, and confiscated watches and gold jewelry, but they didn't seem to notice the gold wedding band I tried to hide with the palm of my right hand. I held my breath until the soldiers were gone. My silence at that moment has come to haunt me.

On the morning of June 10, we heard Arabic being spoken in the street. The war was over! We had survived!

A shrill voice on Radio Amman announced that East Jerusalem, the West Bank, Gaza, the Golan Heights, and the Sinai Peninsula were under Israeli military control. And the Jordanian army had retreated.

Concern for Faisal's family in Jerusalem and an urgent need to send a telegram to my mother forced me to enter this strange new world immediately. The only transportation linking Ramallah and Jerusalem was the Israeli military. As the likeliest person in our group to find safe transport with the army, I once again donned the navy blue jacket with "New York Times" printed on the back in bold white letters. The jacket had served me well in the streets of Paris, and hopefully it would offer protection through the streets of a postwar zone.

One last hug, kiss, touch and words of reassurance from Faisal before I stood, vulnerable and alone, on a Ramallah street corner thumbing a ride to Jerusalem. Bullet-riddled, gouged-out walls looked like an insatiable monster had feasted on concrete and brick. Mercifully, our building had been spared. Air-conditioned tourist buses filled with soldiers viewing the newly conquered territories drove by, as did armored vehicles and trucks. It felt like a long time before an officer driving a Jeep stopped to offer me a ride. My New York Times jacket made him assume I was a journalist. In stunned silence, he listened to the short version of my saga. Taking his eyes off the road for a moment, he looked at me and asked, "Does your mother know where you are?"

I laughed for the first time since the war started and got in his Jeep. We drove past Yusra's house in Kafr Aqab. The house on stilts was standing, untouched. Faisal and I would have been safe there. Other places weren't so lucky. Bombed, gutted, burned-out buildings were everywhere. The war had been swift but deadly. Before dropping me at the Damascus Gate, the officer handed me a piece of paper with his name and phone number. "Call in a few weeks. I would like to talk with you again." It was unclear if the invitation included my Palestinian husband.

The throng of people entering and leaving through the Damascus Gate now included armed soldiers. I walked through the narrow streets and alleys inside the Old City feeling unfamiliar eyes staring at me. Clearly I was not an Israeli soldier or a local Palestinian, and tourists had not yet returned. Arab vendors and civilians likely assumed I was with the conquering army. "Walk like you're a journalist on a mission," I told myself to calm my rising fear. White flags of surrender draped over homes looked like there had been an unexpected summer blizzard. Blue and white Israeli flags flew from random rooftops. Conquerors and conquered were identified by flags.

Thankfully my feet remembered the way. I spotted the neighborhood bakery, ran up the broad steps, and bounded into the walled courtyard, relieved to find Amty, Ibrahim, Samira, and Marwan inside the house. We locked in a quiet embrace.

"Faisal is safe and so is Khalti Suad," I said immediately.

"We don't know where my mother is or when she'll be released from the army," Samira said apprehensively. "Or if the Israelis will ever allow mom to return." Her statement echoed fears from 1948. "Herminia and her family are safe," she added.

We all had war stories now. Samira began hers. "Early one morning, the sound of machine guns woke us up. All day we heard shooting and explosions, but had no idea what was happening. The streets were deserted. We watched two Jordanian soldiers enter the courtyard, take off their uniforms, change into street clothes, and run, so we knew the army was in trouble."

Marwan continued. "Just when I thought, 'I can't stand this bombing anymore,' we heard singing and the blast of a horn. Neighbors began to yell, 'The *Yehudis* are here!' But I thought, 'My new sister-in-law is *Yehudi*, and we love her.'" I bit my tongue. Marwan had no idea that from an early age, American Jews were taught that Arabs hated us and wanted to destroy the only Jewish sanctuary in the world. We feared and distrusted them.

"Farid's family is safe," Samira said. "He came to see us yesterday, right after civilians were allowed in the streets." Faisal's old friend Farid's walk from Ras al-Amud to Jerusalem took him past a burned-out city bus positioned to block entrance into the Old City through the Lions' Gate. The bus had likely been destroyed on the morning of June 7, when the Israeli army blasted open the twelve-meter-high Lions' Gate and drove tanks into the Old City. Farid hoped no one had been trapped inside the bus.

From the vantage of their hillside home, Farid's family had watched Israeli planes bomb the Mount of Olives, one of the mountains between Jerusalem and the Judaean Desert. They had also seen Jordanian soldiers change into civilian clothes, abandon their tanks, and run. Panicking neighbors sought to join the exodus to the east bank of the Jordan River, but just as their car was pulling out, there was a random bomb explosion. The driver swerved in time to avoid killing himself and his family. They all returned home. Farid's family never considered leaving—they'd learned that lesson 19 years ago.

None of us witnessed the unstoppable human tide of Israeli soldiers fan through the Christian, Muslim, and Armenian Quarters. Disoriented soldiers on the Sacred Plateau asked an old Arab man directions to the Wailing Wall. If Faisal had not been stranded in Ramallah, he would have taken the soldiers there, just like he had done for me. We had no way of knowing that a delegation of Palestinian notables had already offered to surrender in exchange for being treated humanely by their latest conquerors.

We never heard Israeli radio announce, "The Temple Mount is in our hands"; we never saw the army raise an Israeli flag over the Wailing Wall, although Amty, Ibrahim, Marwan, and Samira were close enough to hear their jubilant singing and a ram's horn echo across the rooftops. A *shofar* was only blown on the most sacred Jewish holidays.

By June 8, the Israeli military was in full control, and on June 9, they began to register people, house by house. Farid walked twelve kilometers to tell Faisal about the census. Passing the Palestine Archaeology Museum (now called the Rockefeller Museum), he saw young men carrying dead bodies to a nearby cemetery. He walked past Sheikh Jarrah, Shu'fat, Beit Hanina, and Tel el-Ful before reaching Yusra's house in Kafr Aqab, only to find it empty. Faisal and I were still in Ramallah. Farid returned to Jerusalem the same day. He later told us, "My shoes were full of holes and my feet ached for days."

Farid understood the significance of the census. When Israel annexed East Jerusalem shortly after the war, those registered were given a residency permit allowing them to work inside Israel and receive health insurance benefits—but Israeli identity cards were not passports and did not offer the rights of citizenship. Israel's Absentee Property Law that came into existence in 1948 provided a legal framework for claiming Palestinian homes and real estate left by fleeing refugees. The law was extended to include Palestinians in the newly conquered territories. Once under the control of the Israeli government, the property belonged to worldwide Jewry and could never be sold.

I didn't want to go to the American Consulate alone. Samira hesitated, for a moment, then lined her dark eyes with *kohl*, put on lipstick, and offered to come with me. Soldiers randomly stopped people to ask for IDs and to inquire where they were going. We linked arms. Our gait said, "Don't you dare stop us." Nobody did. We were modern-looking young women walking confidently through the streets of a postwar city.

A disinterested clerk at the consulate took no joy in my survival. "Notify my family immediately that I am unharmed," I said, hoping to sound authoritative. The clerk nodded perfunctorily, as if I were filing for a driver's license. After giving my vital information, I assumed my mother would be notified of my safety within hours. Unbeknownst to me, the State Department's communiqué took weeks to arrive.

We passed by the bus terminal, a ghostly specter of its former self. A few pedestrians milled around as if hoping to conjure the vehicles back to life, but the buses did not run that day, or the next, so I donned my New York Times jacket and hitchhiked to Ramallah. Palestinian civilians were driving cars now, but I have no recollection of who offered me a ride.

Years later, a former Israeli soldier whose platoon was among the first to enter East Jerusalem told me that soldiers immediately began stealing cars with Arabic license plates. When the Palestinians realized what was happening, tires everywhere were slashed to ribbons—their first act of nonviolent resistance.

"Al hamdulillah ala salama." Thanks be to Allah for your return. Faisal and Khalti Suad welcomed me as if I were a hero. They were relieved to hear everyone was safe, including Farid and Herminia's family, but upset to learn there had been no word from Yusra. When I reported that her house in Kafr Aqab had been untouched, Faisal and I decided to go there. Before leaving Ramallah, we bought a roast chicken, cheese, and bread. Civilian buses were still not running, so once again, we walked.

Without warning, an Israeli soldier on a motorcycle pulled over and pointed his Uzi at Faisal's chest. "Ma zeh?" What's that? he demanded. Faisal dropped the chicken to the ground, leaving the soldier free to explore the package with the butt of his gun. After mutilating the bird, the soldier got on his motorcycle and left us angry and shaken. "Kus ummak," Faisal cursed under his breath.

We didn't speak until we were across the road from his mother's house, where a deadly stench emanated from a truck parked in front of the Semiramis Hotel. We gave a wide berth to the vehicle, trying not to imagine what was inside. The electricity was on in Yusra's house, so we listened to the radio and ate bread, cheese, and olives, hoping the buses would start to run before our food ran out. Faisal and I were eager to return to the Old City. A few days later, Ahmed appeared at the door. After a night's sleep, we filled our backpacks with leftover food and water, and walked to Jerusalem, once again joining the throng of people on the two-lane highway.

Instead of being swept into the sea, Israel had completed the occupation of historic Palestine. They conquered 42,000 square miles, including the West Bank and East Jerusalem, the Golan Heights, the Sinai Peninsula, and Gaza. Israel's brazen victory left them with a dangerous hubris. Had I been living on a *kibbutz*, helping with the orange harvest, I might have been part of the euphoria, but I felt disheartened, and shared the humiliation, fear, and confusion of people about to be crushingly displaced. About 1.3 million Palestinians living in these territories suddenly came under Israeli military control, and became Israel's responsibility. I tried to imagine my family being kicked out of our home in Queens by an advancing army who claimed Queens as their ancestral homeland, forcing us to resettle in Brooklyn—only to be displaced and occupied 19 years later. I could not fathom such trauma.

General Rabin was given the honor of naming the war. Considered possibilities were The War of Daring, The War of Salvation, and The War of the Sons of Light. The general chose The Six-Day War, evoking the words in Genesis.[7] But Israel had created a new world in less than six days. With the destruction of the Egyptian Air Force, the war had been won in the first few hours. Arabs call it The 1967 War and might just as easily have called it their second *Nakba,* for that's what it turned out to be—another Catastrophe.

[7] Oren, *Six Days of War,* 309

BEYOND THE CITY WALLS

My memories of the days immediately following the war are like a well-used patchwork quilt; some are as vivid as if they happened yesterday while others have faded into near oblivion. What remains has allowed me to weave between the spaces. The Khatib family, who had offered sanctuary and treated me like a daughter, were on a roller coaster of uncertainty. To reassure himself, Ibrahim recounted stories of times past, when he was a police officer in British Palestine and rode all over the country speaking English, Hebrew and Arabic with his friends. The ultimate pragmatist, he hoped his Jewish daughter-in-law and his ability to speak the three languages of this region would help him find work. Everyone wanted to remain in their homes, re-open shops, businesses, and schools, and return to a normal life.

Occupation had not yet settled upon the land. The fluid situation immediately after the war allowed for a cautious flirtation. People were free to cross a formerly forbidden border to meet "the other." Yusra called from Amman to tell us she'd been released by the Jordanian army, but Israel had prohibited her, along with thousands of others, from returning to Jerusalem. Everyone missed her calming presence. Faisal and I never went back to her home in Kafr Aqab. We stayed in Jerusalem where we witnessed the initial merging of a city once divided. *Dinars* were still accepted currency in the market. Palestinians clung to their Jordanian passports. The Jordanian army had withdrawn so quickly, Faisal was convinced King Hussein had made a secret deal with Israel. To me it looked like the West Bank had been abandoned by Hussein, as if he had fatalistically accepted a divine decree. Losing the Old City of Jerusalem, a sacred site attracting millions of international tourists, and the fertile Jordan River Valley was a devastating loss to Jordan—and a humiliation.

Local Palestinians met their latest conquerors in shops, small bars, and cafés inside the Old City, which is how Professor Minkovitch entered the Khatib family's life. Ahmed had met the professor at his shop and invited him to meet his family over dinner— just like he'd done with me. A tall, wiry man, the professor hid his baldness under a narrow-brimmed working man's brown cap. I helped Amty serve the chicken, rice, and tomato-okra stew, holding my tongue until it was time to eat. Instead of retreating to the kitchen like most women did, I sat down with the men and joined the conversation.

"What do you think is going to happen now?" I asked in an obvious American accent.

"Who are you?" asked the stunned professor. I reiterated my unlikely saga—hitchhiking, courtship, marriage, and living through the war. These revelations inspired the professor to share his own journey. He taught psychology at Hebrew University and lived in Ein Karem, the Palestinian village where Faisal and Samira had been born.

"I left Russia in the late thirties to live in Palestine. Most of my adult life I have fought in wars for Israel, but now I am profoundly sad about the direction of my chosen country. We, Jews and Arabs, should be living like brothers." He encouraged all of us to explore beyond East Jerusalem. The professor became a frequent visitor and remained a close friend to the Khatib family, especially Marwan, for the rest of his life. Oh, that this wise Russian-Palestinian-Israeli Jew could be standing next to me when I told my mother about my marriage.

Faisal and I were among the first people to leave the Old City through the western gate. Built by Suleiman the Magnificent, the portal is called the Jaffa Gate by the Israelis because it leads to the famous port city; Palestinians refer to it as Bab al-Khalil, meaning the Hebron Gate. Under Ottoman rule this gate was the main egress between the old and new cities of East and West Jerusalem. When the Jews were unable to conquer the Old City in 1948, the commander of the Israeli military, Moshe Dayan, sat with his Jordanian counterpart, Abdullah el-Tell, in a deserted house in the Musrara neighborhood of Jerusalem and drew a two-mile line using a green wax pencil that became known as the Green Line. At the time, it was believed to be a temporary ceasefire line. The Jaffa Gate, on the edge of this line that became the internationally recognized border, had been closed until 1967.

Faisal was five years old the last time he walked through the Jaffa Gate into what was now called No Man's Land. Although this area was known to be littered with land mines, we felt no sense of danger. Perhaps Israeli soldiers had already swept the area. Without the intrusion of people or traffic for almost two decades, vegetation rioted between barbed wire, rocky hillsides, refuse, and abandoned homes. Oleander bushes with little need for water proliferated alongside white jasmine and thistles. Untended for so long, olive, fig, and almond trees matured into exotic shapes. Faisal was searching for his grandfather's house: Sheikh Mahmoud, the visionary, scribe, mystic, and scholar of his time, had not been forgotten. Other people wandered through this landscape also, seeking their past. Enterprising Palestinian farmers set up makeshift stands to sell fresh watermelon. Nineteen years of solitude for No Man's Land was over.

I was not convinced that Faisal's childhood memories would lead him to a lost past, but he recognized the house immediately. The flat-roofed building stood intact under the canopy of a leafy fig tree. Broken and missing windowpanes testified to the house's vacancy. Overgrown vines blanketed stone walls. Wild irises and hollyhocks sprouted randomly near stone steps leading to a door that proved to be unlocked. The desert sun burned hot outside, but inside the house was cool. Faisal reached for a handful of figs. Tasting the fruit seemed to evoke childhood memories.

"I loved visiting *Sidi* here. One day my grandfather gave my older sister a bag of candy, and me half a British pound. I got so jealous. My clever sister said, 'I'll give you my bag of candy if you give me the piece of paper *Sidi* gave you.'" Faisal laughed. "She cheated me. Later that afternoon guns started shooting. We ran up the steps and lay down on the floor in Khalti Asma's room. She was my mother's half-sister, who died of cancer at a young age. Bullets flew over our heads. They left deep holes in the stone walls." Faisal had no idea how long the attack lasted, but the terror from that day left an indelible imprint on a young boy growing up in British Mandate Palestine.

Faint flecks of violet and gold paint remained on the inside wall of the room that once belonged to Khalti Asma. Strewn all over the floor in the otherwise empty rooms were papers and notebooks, yellowed from time and streaked with animal excrement. We wiped filth off the pages as if handling the Rosetta stone. Under a pile of debris in the corner of the room lay a faded cloth sack tied with silk thread. Inside was a handwritten Quran.

"This book is over one hundred years old," Faisal said, tracing his fingers around the intricate design on the inside cover. The brittle pages threatened to become dust under his touch. He gently slipped the Quran back into the faded sack and continued to examine the musty papers while I sat in the shade of the fig tree, dreaming of what it might be like to live here.

"Ahlan wa sahlan," I imagined saying to guests leaning against soft pillows scattered around the room. "Be welcomed in our home. Our home is your home." We would serve sweet mint tea with baklava while telling them the story of how we found Sheikh Mahmoud's house.

Faisal's voice broke my reverie. *"Erees,"* he said excitedly, "There are handwritten letters from King Farouk of Egypt thanking my grandfather for his dream interpretations and a letter from Mohammed Ali Jinnah." Ali Jinnah, a lawyer by profession, voiced the notion of a secular democratic Muslim state carved out of British-ruled India, similar to the idea of partitioning a Jewish state in British-ruled Palestine. At first Ali Jinnah had advocated for Hindu-Muslim unity, but he came to believe that Muslims needed a state of their own. Pakistan was created after widespread violence and the death of hundreds of thousands of Muslims, Hindus, and Sikhs. I wondered what advice Sheikh Mahmoud had offered to Ali Jinnah, the father of modern Pakistan.

Believing he would soon return, Faisal's grandfather unwittingly abandoned his home. He was not alone. On the morning of April 9, 1948, the village of Deir Yassin was attacked by two Jewish militias, the Stern Gang and the Irgun. The villagers believed they would be safe from the militias because Deir Yassin was 18 miles outside the boundaries of the Jewish state, as delineated by the UN partition plan.[8] The massacre of 254 people, including women and children, led to widespread panic across Palestine. During the course of this war, over 700,000 Palestinian Arabs were expelled from their homes, and more than 500 villages were destroyed and over four million acres of land were confiscated. Days and weeks of people waiting to return home became generations of people living in refugee camps scattered across the Middle East. This moment in Palestinian history is called *Al-Nakba*—The Catastrophe.

In my family, the UN proclamation officially establishing the inde-

---

[8] Bickerton & Klausner, *A Concise History of the Arab-Israeli Conflict,* 103.

pendent Jewish State of Israel on May 14, 1948, was cause for celebration.

The afternoon passed quickly. Bursting to tell Faisal's family about Sheikh Mahmoud's stone house, we gathered the correspondence, unfinished manuscripts, and handwritten Quran. Carrying our miraculous harvest back through No Man's Land, we entered the Old City through the Jaffa Gate, feeling as triumphant as Kaiser Wilhelm II in 1898, when thousands lined the streets to welcome the visiting German monarch and his wife, Augusta Viktoria. We walked through the Jaffa Gate like General Allenby did in 1917, when he led British soldiers into Jerusalem, signifying the end of 400 years of Turkish Ottoman rule. General Allenby immediately proclaimed the Holy City to be under martial law but assured people that "every sacred building, monument, holy spot, shrine, traditional site, endowment, pious bequest, or customary place of prayer of whatsoever form of the three religions will be maintained and protected, and every person is free to pursue his lawful business without interruption." A similar declaration from the Israelis would have been very welcome.

But Faisal and I were not visitors, nor triumphal dignitaries. We returned the next day with Amty, Ibrahim, Samira, and Marwan, eager to show them the stone house and have a picnic in the shade of the fig tree. But we were too late. The house was gone without a trace, as was the leafy fruit-filled tree. Concrete and stone mixed with mangled uprooted trees, shrubs, and garbage. We walked in circles, not believing the devastation. An army of bulldozers had leveled the area—for a park, we were told. Instead of the anticipated figs, we ate dust mixed with tears that formed rivulets of grief running down our cheeks. No trace of the neighborhood remained except in the hearts of those who would never forget.

Shocked by the loss, our procession walked slowly back through No Man's Land, through the Jaffa Gate, returning to a home that no longer felt like a sanctuary. Hope, a rare commodity in this part of the world, had been crushed along with the stone house and the fruiting fig tree.

The physical border between East and West Jerusalem may have been gone, but the psychological barrier remained. No one asked for passports, but the moment we crossed the former international border between Jordan and Israel, we were aware of having entered another country. In West Jerusalem people did not dress as if the prophets were still alive, and most commerce happened in shops and offices, not in the outdoor marketplace. We followed Jaffa Street, past stone houses, restaurants, clothing shops, banks, and the post office. Cars, buses, and taxis jockeyed to beat the red light on Ben Yehuda Street. I carefully sounded out the Hebrew letters on a blue awning and declared, "Ka fay ba ru ka len—*Café Brooklyn!*" Since Arabic and Hebrew are both Semitic tongues, Faisal was often able to translate words from Hebrew into English after I phonetically read them. We played with language. *Lechem* is Hebrew for bread, and *lahmeh* Arabic for meat. Both words have the same three root letters. *Beit* means home in Arabic and Hebrew. We decided that Bethlehem must mean the "home of your sustenance." If you were a shepherd, that would be meat; for farmers, it was bread.

We bought two orange sodas and falafel sandwiches in Café Brooklyn and enjoyed our picnic in a nearby park. No one pointed fingers or eyed us suspiciously. After lunch we walked along King George Avenue past the famous King David Hotel, which had once served as the British military and civilian headquarters during Mandate times. This heavily fortified hotel was bombed in 1946 by the Irgun, a Zionist militia led by Menachem Begin that had survived the Nazi invasion of Warsaw, Poland before fleeing to Palestine. The British considered Begin a terrorist and offered 10,000 pounds for his capture. This violent act that resulted in the death of about 90 civilians, including Jews and Arabs, was the proverbial last straw that drove the British out of Palestine. Begin became the Israeli Prime Minister in 1977, and went on to share a Nobel Peace Prize with Egyptian President Anwar Sadat. Although he supported returning the Sinai Desert to Egypt, Begin remained opposed to the establishment of a Palestinian State in the West Bank and Gaza.

A concentration of soldiers guarding the hotel intimidated us from entering the historic lobby, so we headed toward the Mea She'arim, the Orthodox Jewish district. On the Sabbath, everything except synagogues was closed, from Friday afternoon until Saturday dusk. Fortunately this was a weekday, and the streets were full of people. Women and their older daughters wore long matronly dresses, hair covered by hats, wigs, or scarves. Young men's side curls hung beneath skullcaps. Bearded men in wide-brimmed hats and long black coats walked distractedly as if reciting prayers in their minds. Bakeries displayed a variety of breads and sweets—challah, babka, apple strudel, rugelah, all fresh from the oven and every bit as enticing as the treats in Zalatimo's.

This world was alien to Faisal, but the Mea She'arim reminded me of the Lower East Side, where my grandmother had a candy stand in the Essex Street Market. There, haggling was accepted and expected. The price tags on clothing, furniture, and household goods were mere suggestions. Tailors with pins in their mouths were ready to alter a newly bought suit, skirt, dress, or coat. Many Jews dressed in traditional Eastern European garb. Shop signs printed with Hebrew letters were common. Every corned beef or pastrami sandwich served in a kosher deli included unlimited pickles. But the Lower East Side felt friendly and accessible, whereas here, in the Mea She'arim, no one made eye contact or said hello as we walked through streets and in shops—not a single *"shalom."*

Our relief to see the familiar minarets and domed roofs of the Old City turned to sorrow as we stood in silent witness to an old mosque being blown up. In the seconds it took Faisal to focus the camera and snap a photo, the sacred building ceased to exist, becoming part of a buried history—like his grandfather's stone house. The destroyed mosque was likely in the old Moroccan Quarter, where Israeli bulldozers and demolition teams were mercilessly churning landmarks into the ground, readying the area for the world's largest open-air synagogue next to the Wailing Wall. Faisal appreciated the way Jews prayed there, forehead pressed to stone. It reminded him of Muslim pilgrims reciting the Quran and circling the Kaaba, a sacred cube-shaped stone covered in black and gold velvet. "Amty dreams of going on the *hajj* to Mecca, the direction Muslims face when they pray."

"Jews face Jerusalem," I added. Sharing each other's religion, culture, and traditions did not create conflict between us. Some prayed by a wall, some by a stone cube, but in the end, all prayer spiraled toward the same heaven. What gave us joy was the thought of traveling to the ends of the earth together. We were global pilgrims.

The hope that every person would be allowed to pursue his lawful business without interruption, as General Allenby once promised, was giving way to uncertainty. Rumors circulated. Jews were returning to the Old City, and people feared eviction. When we'd first met, Ibrahim told me their home was located in the former Jewish Quarter. Faisal, a born optimist, turned to me before going to sleep that night and said, "*Erees*, we will have the greatest wedding gift of all—an international passport." He envisioned Jerusalem as a sanctuary for all religions and never doubted the United Nations would quickly declare Jerusalem an international zone, like Vatican City. We imagined our passports filled with exotic stamps. Faisal's dream echoed the 1947 UN Partition Plan, which carved Palestine into Jewish and Arab sectors and declared Jerusalem an international city.

❧

Two smiling women were sitting with Amty in the open-air courtyard one morning. *"Sabah al khayr, Umm Ibrahim,"* they said in unison. Gold coin necklaces framed their sunburnt faces. A gold ring seemed to sprout from the nose of the larger woman. Amty and her Bedouin cousins from Beersheba were having a family reunion. For the first time in 19 years, the women were able to take a bus to West Jerusalem and walk to East Jerusalem, no longer on the other side of a forbidden border. Amty invited me to join them for a cup of tea, but Faisal and I had errands. We left the women twittering like a flock of birds at a watering hole.

I still had not heard from my mother. Before the war, her letters and postcards arrived as predictably as the sunrise. On our way to the American Express, we walked through the *souq*. Stars of David, menorahs, and mezuzahs were being sold alongside crosses, Virgin Marys, incense, and the Hand of Fatima. This ancient symbol, also called a *Hamsa*, was common to Jews, Muslims and Christians and found throughout the Middle East. Shaped like a hand with three extended fingers and two curved thumbs on either side, it protected against "the evil eye," which can be understood as jealousy or malice. The amulet can be worn as a pendant, used as house decorations, key chains, and more. Vendors gladly stocked anything they thought would sell. Commerce was delightfully democratic. Zalatimo's Sweet Shop had been discovered by soldiers and civilians alike. When Faisal and I held hands and wore Western-style clothes, the soldiers greeted us and made eye contact. We *shalomed* them right back.

Today there was a letter waiting for me:

Dear Iris,
My nails are chewed to the cuticles. Yesterday I finally got a call
from the State Department asking if I had a daughter living in

Jerusalem. Before they told me you were alive and unharmed, I just about passed out. I've been calling government offices for weeks and praying for you in shul. Thank God you are safe. I want to remind you that we have a cousin living in Tel Aviv. Meyer's mother and your grandma were sisters. He survived because the Nazis took advantage of his expertise as an engineer. His entire family was killed. He met his second wife in an Israeli Displaced Person's Camp. She died a few months ago. They had no children. His letters are in Yiddish, and I'm not sure he speaks English. Please visit him and call.

Love, Mom
P.S. Here's Meyer's address.

A trip to Tel Aviv was not the honeymoon we dreamed of, but Petra was on the other side of a border we dared not cross now. I thought of visiting the *kibbutz* by the Dead Sea where my South African friend might be living, but I wasn't sure Faisal would be welcomed. Ibrahim, who understood the sorrow of families being separated, encouraged me to visit my cousin. A language barrier is best overcome in person, so instead of a phone call, I decided to show up at his doorstep. I looked up useful sentences and phrases in the Hebrew/English dictionary still tucked in my backpack. Faisal spoke Arabic, Turkish, and broken English. I spoke English and broken French, understood a little Yiddish, and could read Hebrew. Meyer spoke Hebrew and Yiddish and, if we were lucky, some English. I hoped the desire to communicate would override the barriers.

The modern bus terminal in West Jerusalem was no less confusing than the one on the eastern side of the city. Hebrew signs were getting easier for me to read. After finding our way through a maze of caged ticket sellers, we bought two round-trip tickets to Tel Aviv. We wore modern clothes suitable for a hot summer's day and spoke English; no one searched or questioned us before we boarded the comfortable air-conditioned bus.

The bus descended on a road that wound through miles of pine forests. Minarets from the mosque in Abu Ghosh were visible from the highway. Many believe that Abu Ghosh was not destroyed like other Arab villages in the area because they cooperated with the Zionists in 1948. Further down the mountain, rusty carcasses of blown-up Jeeps were left as reminders of the lost battle for control of the Old City. The road finally opened into a broad coastal plain, with irrigated fields of wheat, barley, sesame, and citrus. It only took a few hours to traverse the narrow neck of Israel.

Before attempting to deal with the heat, noise, and congestion of Tel Aviv, we decided to relax on the beach. Before the war, a journey to this beach would have been forbidden to Faisal. Among what seemed like miles of high-rise buildings and hotels, Faisal asked Arab street vendors for directions. War felt far away as we walked barefoot in the sand, our feet cooled by the sea, our hearts calmed by the rhythmic surf. When we felt ready to navigate the streets, Faisal got directions from Arab construction workers.

Meyer's apartment was on a quiet residential street near Dizengoff Circle. An old man with glasses sitting on a shiny skull opened the door just enough to keep the chain latched. Three generations identified me as his cousin from America. "*Ani* Iris. *Bat* Janet. *Bat* Minnie. Niece of Aunt Edith." I had forgotten to look up the Hebrew word for niece. Before allowing us into his modest apartment, his watery blue eyes focused on my face as if searching for something familiar. A formal portrait of himself standing next to his deceased wife, a pale woman in black, hung on the wall. Their smiles looked staged. The mirror above a wooden hutch created the illusion of a room on the other side of the glass. Faisal and I sat on a couch drinking water. Meyer asked if I understood Yiddish, the secret language between Mom and Grandma.

"*Ich fashtein a bissel.*" A little, I answered. Pointing to Faisal and myself, I joined two fingers to indicate a union. "My husband, Faisal." Meyer did not react to this disclosure. Either he didn't understand or he understood all too well—a long-lost cousin from America had shown up with an Arab husband.

Meyer had arrived in Israel destitute and alone. Aunt Edith, Mom, and Grandma helped pay for this apartment and sent him money whenever they could, which was surprising. I would have thought all Holocaust survivors were taken care of by the state. But as late as 2014, around one-quarter of Holocaust survivors in Israel were living below the poverty line. One in five had to choose between food and medication.[9]

"*Nu*, how is Mama, Aunt Edith?" he asked in Yiddish.

"*Gut, gut*, they're good." I answered. After a stilted conversation, Meyer invited us to a nearby restaurant where we ate grilled chicken sandwiches with generous portions of tabouli salad. It was a short walk from the restaurant to the zoo. In an ongoing game of charades, we pointed at animals and commented on their looks or behavior. I cherish a photo of the three of us standing outside the cage of an old lioness sleeping lazily on her perch. Back at the apartment, Meyer gave me gifts for Mom and Aunt Edith. Time had bent him over and worn him smooth, but he endured. Having met a relative in Israel made me feel part of the fabric of this tiny country. I slept on the bus ride home and woke in time to see the familiar domes, minarets, and steeples of Jerusalem bathed in rose, lavenders, and deep purple.

Years later Mom told me that after the visit, Meyer wrote to Aunt Edith expressing his horror that I had brought an Arab into his home. It surprised me to learn my aunt responded by telling Meyer that Faisal was

---

[9] "Holocaust survivors in Israel living in poverty, report finds." *Jerusalem Post*, April 23, 2014, www.jpost.com

a respectful young man who came from a good family.

Everything changed with mom's next letter:

Dear Iris,
Aaron has finished basic training and is being sent to Vietnam. You
have to come home before he leaves.

Love, Mom

Suddenly my days in Jerusalem were numbered. I told Amty and Ibrahim I had to return to the States. Amty cried. She was afraid that once I left I would never return—that I would disappear from their lives as quickly as I had appeared. I could not admit that possibility to them or to myself.

"Of course I'll be back. *Ana bahibbek*. I love you." Ibrahim was silent, but the expression on his face let me know he thought the same as Amty. Faisal and I spoke deep into the night. We had plans to make, connections to forge, and little time. There was a palpable sense of urgency.

"*Erees*, before I meet you in New York, I want to see my mother in Amman and renew my Jordanian passport."

I grew alarmed. "Isn't it dangerous to cross the Allenby Bridge?"

Faisal reassured me, as he always did. "Thousands of Palestinians are leaving. The Israelis are letting them go." The bridge, built by General Allenby in 1918 to allow British troops to enter the West Bank, was destroyed in 1946 by the Palmach, a Jewish militia, and rebuilt by Jordan, who called it the King Hussein Bridge. During the recent war, the bridge spanning the Jordan River had once again been destroyed. While we spoke, entire families, weighed down by possessions, were trudging across its mangled remnants.

We said goodbye with our bodies; curved arches of ancient walls matched our nakedness. My clothes and books were piled neatly in a corner. The exotic had become familiar and dear. A wanderer found a hearth in this stone dwelling in the Old City of Jerusalem.

Like a farewell song, the *muezzin*'s call to prayer echoed through the streets as Faisal and I walked to the Damascus Gate. Outside the Old City walls, we caught a taxi to the West Jerusalem depot, and from there the morning bus to Haifa. Faisal accompanied me to the port city where I had booked passage on a boat sailing to Venice. From there, I planned to take the Orient Express train to Luxembourg, and then a plane to JFK. It would have been easier to fly directly from Tel Aviv to New York, but the transition seemed too abrupt. I needed time to digest all that had happened. Staring out the window at the passing landscape, all I saw was my reflection in the glass. We arrived at the dock an hour before the ship's departure.

"*Habibti*, I promise we will be together before the trees bloom in New York," Faisal whispered. I held his hand and promised I would be waiting. Had I been religious, I would have prayed that the Israelis had the wisdom and the will to welcome the people whose ancient villages and towns had hugged the hillsides and *wadis* for thousands of years.

The Palestinians remembered a past I knew little about. In 1948, their world had been destroyed, erased, expunged, and bulldozed. In Jaffa, Haifa, Acre, Ramleh, Lydda, and more, Palestinian homes filled with their owners' belongings were given to homeless Jewish immigrants. Palestinians watched their villages and cities be taken over or buried, while new cities, villages, apartment buildings, *kibbutzim*, *moshavim* were built for the ingathering of Jews from around the world, mainly Jewish Holocaust survivors. The creation of the Jewish nation-state of Israel spelled doom for 700,000 people not identified as Jewish. If the Palestinians knew for certain what they were about to endure, they would have sat beneath their olive trees and wept.

Immediately following the Six-Day War, Israel annexed 18,000 acres around Jerusalem, including 28 Palestinian villages, with a population of about 69,000. The battle for demographic domination was beginning. Just as Pharaoh had feared that the Israelites would become "as numerous as the stars," the Israelis worried about being outnumbered by the Palestinians.

I should have brought my mother a bouquet of wild flowers from the Promised Land—pink rock rose, fragrant plumeria, wild iris, Persian cyclamen, hollyhocks, gladiolus, buttercups, and almond blossoms, but even had they survived the trip, U.S. Customs would have blocked their entrance. Instead I returned home with fresh figs, gifts from Cousin Meyer, a handful of seeds from Yusra's loofah vine, and the story of my welcoming.

BACK IN THE U.S. OF A.

half expected State Department officials would meet me at JFK for a debriefing. I was bursting, yearning, for someone to ask, "How did you come to stay with a Palestinian family during the war? What information can you share?" After all, I may have been the only Jew hiding with a Palestinian family on the West Bank. Customs *did* stop me upon discovering suspicious-looking black seeds resembling watermelon pits in my backpack. I tried to tell the official they came from a loofah vine growing beside a stone house in a small village near Jerusalem, and that I hoped to tell friends about the miracle of this plant:

Scrape off dead layers of skin with this fibrous gourd and anoint yourself with olive oil. Your skin will be left shimmery and rejuvenated.

The customs official never identified the seeds, except to confirm they were not illegal.

"Welcome back to the USA," he declared before ushering me into the terminal, where my mother and grandma were waiting. Grandma looked frail. Short wispy white hairs barely covered her scalp, and her shriveled lips were threatening to disappear. Mom's green eyes were underlined with dark circles. I fell into their welcoming arms. I had been so resistant to returning, but here I was—home at last!

I moved into the finished basement of mom's two story home in

Queens, waiting to hear from Faisal, but the State Department contacted me first. A week after returning home, a telegram arrived informing me I'd been accepted into the Peace Corps—destination: Ankara, Turkey. Ironically, this was the city where Faisal would have gone to complete university—had we not met and gotten married. I turned down their offer.

Trying to pick up the threads of my former life, I contacted friends who listened to my stories with shock, awe, and disbelief. I had become a fascinating social anomaly. A college boyfriend phoned to tell me he'd made it back from 'Nam. Via my mother, our letters had crisscrossed the world when I was living in Paris. Many women had found his bad boy image irresistible, but not me. During college, I'd been a committed virgin afflicted with wanderlust, which had caused us to become friends instead of lovers. Curious to see his transformation from long-haired renegade to crew-cut uniformed soldier, I was disappointed when he showed up in civvies. We shared a bottle of wine and spoke about love and war and choices and dreams. I was surprised to find out he'd never even considered resisting the draft. After dropping out of college, he had no clear direction and had actually enlisted. I told him about Paris and introduced him to my alter ego, Karen Trotsky. We were having a wonderful time until he bent over and kissed me hard on the mouth. For a moment I returned the kiss as if welcoming home a war hero. Then I caught my breath and told him I was in love and waiting for my husband to arrive from Jerusalem. Before I could tell my war story, he cursed me under his breath and left. During his year of hell in Vietnam, he had held onto an image of me as one of the last virgins waiting to be claimed.

Not wanting to face my mother's hurt, I procrastinated telling her I had gotten married. Living the bohemian life in Paris, hitch-hiking across Europe and the Middle East, experiencing a *coup d'etat* in Greece, falling in love, getting married, and surviving a war were events that seemed to have happened to another woman. I irrationally reasoned that because the marriage happened in a court with no jurisdiction in the States, the certificate was in Arabic, the court thought I was a Christian converting to Islam, and no one in my family knew, perhaps the union was not legal. But someone in the family did know. Aunt Edith, my mother's sister, worked for Immigration and Naturalization. She told my mother that if an Arab received a Green Card in a matter of months, it meant he was married to an American. Confronted with these inconvenient facts, I admitted the truth.

"Someday, we'll have a formal ceremony and celebration," I said, not believing my own words. Mom stoically endured her disappointment.

My brother was still Stateside. Army recruiters had falsely promised Aaron training as an airplane and helicopter mechanic, skills he'd begun to acquire in Aviation High School. In his soldier's uniform, Aaron bore an undeniable resemblance to our father in his police uniform. I wanted to tell my brother about Dō Hu Tai, the Vietnamese man who'd saved my life in Paris, so he wouldn't be brainwashed into believing all Asians were the enemy, but I never had the chance. The year Aaron was gone, I grew hoarse shouting at antiwar rallies. "Bring the troops home!" was a personal invocation.

Job-hunting kept me busy. I read the want ads and went into Manhattan every day. Receptionists with long, polished fingernails sat in sterile offices lined with file cabinets. Marble lobbies and crowded elevators in skyscrapers made me feel alienated and trapped. To my relief, no jobs were offered. "Maybe you should apply to graduate school," Mom suggested. I entertained fleeting thoughts of applying to NYU film school, where I might have met Martin Scorsese or Robert De Niro.

One day an offer came. "Honey, if you're willing to take the train to 125th Street, you're hired. No elementary teaching certificate? No problem. We'll give you one." My 40-year teaching career began as a storyteller for black children in Harlem. I ignored our principal's warning not to walk through Mount Morris Park across from the school, where junkies were almost as common as children jumping rope. My daily sojourn to Harlem took me to a world as different from suburban Queens as Jerusalem had been.

Faisal's postcards and letters arrived with the same regularity as Mom's had when I was traveling. Chock-full of romantic yearnings, they reassured me we would be together soon. He and Farid were learning to speak Hebrew from young Israelis hanging out in Old City cafés, which was where they met Yuri Avnery, a peace activist searching for like-minded Palestinians. Avnery had once been a member of a Jewish militia fighting to create Israel; he went on to become a member of the Knesset and founder of *Gush Shalom*, a well-known Israeli peace group.

In November of 1967, the United Nations passed Resolution 242, calling for the *"withdrawal of Israeli armed forces from territories occupied in the recent conflict."* The resolution emphasized *"the inadmissibility of the acquisition of territory by war and the need to work for a just and lasting peace in which every State in the area can live in security."* Faisal hoped that the Israeli military would leave the West Bank and the UN would find a just solution for the refugee problem created in 1948.

At breakfast one morning, Mom told me she'd had an unsettling dream. "You were married to a Chinese man who spoke no English and was hopelessly foreign." In her attempt to Americanize Faisal, she suggested we call him Fred or Philip, which I firmly vetoed.

The weekend before Faisal's expected arrival, I celebrated the end of an exhausting work week with a fellow teacher who invited me to dinner at her Harlem apartment. The streets were alive with people hanging out, gambling, laughing, playing music, and making deals. Posters of Malcolm X, African-American Muslim minister and civil rights activist, were plastered on storefronts and abandoned walls. Martyred in 1965, Malcolm X was shot to death at a nearby civil rights rally. The smooth sounds of Motown playing on the radio went well with the collard greens, fried plantains, and pork chitlins sizzling on the stove. Sipping beer, I explained to my black soul sister-teacher-friend that Jews do not eat pork. On the subway ride back to Queens, I imagined telling her on Monday, "Guess what? Over the weekend, my Palestinian husband showed up." I could already hear her loud, disbelieving laugh.

Faisal arrived at JFK on a cold day in February, during President's Day weekend. The tall swarthy man walking toward me was my husband. He carried one suitcase, a renewed Jordanian passport, and a Jerusalem identity card that he hoped would allow him to return home. He had been one of the lucky ones counted in the Israeli census after the war. I stepped back to take him in. He wore a navy blue suit with a white shirt. Tinted glasses hid dark eyes. His mustache had become a neatly trimmed goatee. We'd been apart five months—longer than we'd been together. If he was anxious about meeting my family, he didn't show it. I had been so welcomed by his family; he just assumed the welcome would be reciprocated.

From the moment they met, Mom called him Faisal, and he called her Mama Janet. She confessed relief when she saw his honey-colored skin matched her own. His English had improved, but he still said endearing things like "the fingers of your feet" for toes and "breast socks" for brassiere. That he was a gifted storyteller was immediately evident.

Faisal and I lived together in the wood-paneled basement of my mother's house, but we did not live in sin. Mom ordered 100 wedding announcements from a neighborhood printer and mailed them to every known relative and friend. They simply said the groom was from Jerusalem, Israel, leaving people free to assume whatever they wanted. Palestinian was not a word that had entered the American lexicon. My mother was the first American Jew to have openly annexed East Jerusalem to Israel.

At family weddings and bar mitzvahs, relatives would invariably ask for wardrobe consultations to help plan their trips to Israel. "What's the weather in Jerusalem this time of year? What kind of clothes will I need?" Politics, facts on the ground, the occupation, and fear of Arabs were never mentioned. Faisal politely answered all their questions, as if "next year in Jerusalem" referred to him as much as to them. And it did: Jerusalem was his birthplace and his home.

Long after his arrival, Faisal reluctantly told me about his experience of renewing his Jordanian passport.

"Leaving was easy," he said. "I showed my Jordanian passport to Israeli border guards, and they let me pass." But re-entering the West Bank had been dangerous.

"For two *dinar*, about five dollars, I hired a taxi in Amman. The driver took me to a wide, shallow place by the Jordan River where the Bedouin lived. Israeli helicopters patrolled the area every few hours. The Bedouin warned me to keep my clothes dry when I crossed the river in case soldiers searched me on the other side. I rolled my pants above my knees and carried my shoes in my hands and a suitcase on my head. The water wasn't deep. If I walked toward Jordan, the helicopters left me alone, but if they saw me head toward Israel, they fired guns. I hid in the thick bulrushes and when I got to the Bedouin tents on the other side, they quickly told me their names and the names of their cousins. 'If Israeli soldiers come, tell them you're married to my cousin so-and-so.' A taxi took me to Jericho and another to Jerusalem. I walked home, packed my things, said goodbye to my family, and came to New York."

Fortunately, Faisal got to visit his mother in Amman because when Israel finally allowed her to return to Jerusalem, he was already living in the States.

Faisal had risked his life to be with me. Memories came rushing back—falling in love, getting married, the sweetness of living with his family in the Old City and their village, the terror of war, and the aftermath. All those things had really happened.

Mom, Faisal, and I watched the news every evening. When the broadcaster announced, "There's heavy fighting in the DMZ," we looked at the map hanging on the kitchen wall and pretended Aaron was in Hue or Khe Sanh, anywhere far from the fighting, which was everywhere. We heard Walter Cronkite declare that the Vietnam War was "a stalemate that could only be ended by negotiation. There would be no military victory."

"So bring them home," I shouted to an unresponsive TV that showed pictures of a Vietnamese police chief shooting a suspected Vietcong in the head. My brother's letters sounded as if he were a tourist in Southeast Asia. Aaron was in Vietnam during the 1968 Tet Offensive, named for the lunar New Year holiday. A surprise attack launched by 70,000 Vietcong forces on more than 100 towns in South Vietnam marked a turning point in the war. It was hard to believe that last year at this time, I had been celebrating Tet with a Vietnamese family living in Paris.

Every Friday night, Mom lit Sabbath candles, walked to the synagogue, and prayed for the safe return of her eldest son. Aaron survived his tour of duty and came home with a thousand and one slides of monsoon clouds, rice paddies, and tea leaf fields, as well as shrapnel in his right shoulder and nightmares to last a lifetime. He'd been a helicopter gunner perched precariously over dangerous jungle, but there were no slides of that.

When my teaching year was finished, Faisal and I had time and money to go apartment hunting. Faisal was a reluctant hippie. He would gladly have stayed in the brick house on the tree-lined street in suburban Queens, but I was inexorably drawn to the Lower East Side, where hippies roamed the streets preaching revolution, and roach-filled rent-controlled apartments were plentiful. We found a one-bedroom apartment on the corner of Avenue A and St. Mark's Place that cost $86 a month. Our only additional expenses were telephone and electricity—a manageable overhead. The dining and living room windows overlooked Tompkins Square Park, one of the epicenters of the counterculture. We listened to the Fugs perform original poetry, watched the Hare Krishnas dance in saffron robes, and cheered for Dick Gregory, whose inspiring speeches promoting his presidential candidacy were fiery enough to ignite the sycamore trees in the park. Blocks away, psychedelic music blasted in the Fillmore East. We decorated our slum dwelling on a minimal budget using outdated Chinese newspapers to cover the crumbling wall in the dining room. Amber shellac sealed the plaster, hid the decay, and forced the roaches to relocate. Faisal studied English at New York University and got a job as a librarian in the *Herald Tribune Media Morgue,* part of the university library that contained every edition of the paper ever printed.

Grandma barraged us with questions when she found out we were living on Avenue A. After passing through Ellis Island, her family's first home in America had been a three-room railroad flat around the corner. "Are the Turkish baths still on Ninth Street? We used to go there for a *shvitz* on Friday afternoons before *Shabbos*."

"Yes, they are," I said, without adding that the baths were now frequented by homosexual men.

"Do they still have lectures at Cooper Union college? That's where I heard about moving pictures that could talk and carriages that ran without horses. I saw the first horseless carriage drive through Central Park. Thousands of us ran cheering and screaming behind it." My grandmother had been a witness to the advent of the Industrial Age. If she'd had enough money to eat out, she might have met Charlie Chaplin, Leon Trotsky, or Isaac Bashevis Singer. Actors, writers, revolutionaries, and journalists hung out in the Lower East Side, known then as the Yiddish Tin Pan Alley.

Faisal and I visited Grandma in Far Rockaway, but our visits were never reciprocated. Trains, buses, and four flights of stairs were impossible obstacles, not to mention our kitchen was not *kosher*, though we ate no pork. Grandma never could remember Faisal's name although he sang kudos to her *gefilte* fish, stuffed cabbage, and apple *strudel*. She never got over the fact that her only granddaughter had married an Arab *goy*.

Luckily Faisal was an exceptional cook, because I had never bothered to learn. About once a week the scent of lamb simmering with onions, eggplant, pine nuts, and garlic filled our apartment. Faisal cooked sumptuous feasts for motley crews of hippies who sat on our imitation Persian rug while getting stoned and waiting for the moment of "upside-down." Entering the room as if carrying the Holy Grail, Faisal would flip the casserole onto a communal platter, leaving the lamb on top, just like Amty had done. After each feast, Faisal played the *oud* he'd carried from Jerusalem, his nimble fingers dancing along the neck of the big-bellied fretless guitar. Everyone joined in when he broke into a personal rendition of "Going Up to Cripple Creek." I once dreamed of gatherings like this, but they took place in Faisal's grandfather's stone house in Jerusalem, not a tenement on the Lower East Side.

Events in the Middle East were temporarily overshadowed by one of the most turbulent years in American history: 1968. Six million draft-age American men waited to see what number they'd drawn in the lottery. We mourned the death of Martin Luther King, and were devastated when the TV showed Robert Kennedy's bloody body on a hotel kitchen floor, shot and killed minutes after declaring victory in the California Democratic primary on a peace platform. The loss of these leaders, who had galvanized the Civil Rights and antiwar movements, was immeasurable.

We went through a roller coaster of emotions—hope, anger, grief, despair, and back to hope. Thousands of people boarded chartered buses in Union Square on 14th Street—destination: the Chicago Democratic Convention. As he was not yet a U.S. citizen, Faisal decided to stay home, but encouraged me to support the nomination of Senator Eugene McCarthy, poet, philosopher, statesman, and our greatest hope for ending the war. When Chicago's Mayor Daley refused to grant permits allowing a legal protest, the Festival of Life became a police riot. Ten thousand anti-war demonstrators in Grant Park were met by 23,000 armed police and the National Guard. Many got their heads bashed in while shouting, "The whole world is watching!" "Hell no, we won't go!" and "Join us!" We spilled onto the streets in front of the Hilton Hotel, where the police assault was broadcast live, including an on-air assault of Dan Rather, the CBS News anchor. The world watched, but little changed. When Hubert Humphrey won the Democratic presidential nomination, many gave up on the political system as a vehicle for change. In a foolish act of rebellion, I cast my first vote for Pigasus the Pig, the 145-pound porcine protest candidate paraded around by the Youth International Party (Yippies) during the convention.

Faisal's trimmed goatee became a thick mustache reaching his chin. Frizzy black hair framed his face like a dark halo. He wore bell-bottoms, a fringed leather vest and a black and white *keffiyeh* around his neck. This wild-looking man who cooked, sang, played music, recited poetry, and told amazing stories was my own Scheherazade—well, maybe not exclusively mine. We always wore the gold wedding bands his mother had given us, but

our *joie de vivre* communicated as "I'm available." Birth control pills and antibiotics allowed everyone to become a potential lover. Ambivalence about monogamy shone like a beacon to women who were inexorably drawn to Faisal. Although reveling in the possibilities myself, I felt possessive and jealous when women aggressively pursued Faisal—a dangerous elixir for a marriage.

But we never forgot that his family in Jerusalem was waiting to learn what was going to happen to them. UN Resolution 242, promising a "just and lasting peace with security for all," showed no sign of being implemented. Upon orders from the Israeli military commander of East Jerusalem, Amty and Ibrahim were evicted from their home in the Old City along with about 5,000 others. The Jewish Quarter was being modernized as an exclusively Jewish enclave. Before 1948, boundaries between the quarters had overlapped, allowing for an ethnic mix. Jewish properties in the Jewish quarter tended to be religious institutions like synagogues and yeshivas. Arab properties were also public trusts like mosques, schools, and hospitals. Private trusts held by families could be leased but not sold, which explained how the Khatibs held a 100-year lease at an affordable rent. After the war, Israel bought their lease for $300, a paltry sum considering Amty and Ibrahim were planning to live in their home the rest of their lives. They rented a house in Samua. Others less fortunate relocated to refugee camps, some for the second time in their lives.

Faisal and I pursued personal peace based on our belief in joy to the world. We bought a Ford Galaxy station wagon for $250, threw a mattress in the back, and drove across the country to visit his aunt, a literature professor at the University of California, Berkeley. Gas cost 29 cents a gallon. The highways were crowded with young people driving vehicles hand-painted with psychedelic landscapes and swirling designs.

When I met Aunt Diana, there was no doubt that she was Yusra's sister. They had the same fair skin, black curly hair, and sapphire blue eyes—except Diana's eyes flickered without focusing. A childhood illness had left her blind. She lived with her Sri Lankan husband and their three children in a comfortable home within walking distance of the university. Faisal and I drank exotic health elixirs in whimsical cafés, browsed in bookstores along Telegraph Avenue, and hung out with war protesters in recently liberated People's Park. One afternoon, after absorbing enough kinetic street energy and revolutionary fervor to keep us buzzing for hours, we went back to Diana's house where Faisal cooked a Palestinian feast. He invited his aunt to the movies to see *Yellow Submarine*. Aunt Diana's peals of laughter, heard throughout the theatre, were a testament to the fact that Faisal had managed to translate this psychedelic animation into Arabic. Between themselves, they spoke in Arabic while telling endless stories about their lives in Jerusalem. When we left Berkeley, Faisal was insanely homesick.

As a diversion, we drove to New York via the Sonoran Desert in Mexico. Big detour. Big mistake. Blistering heat almost melted the rubber hoses on the old Ford Galaxy. Sweat dripped from every pore, leaving us little need to urinate. We decided to take the next road heading north, which led to Albuquerque, New Mexico. The sidewalks on Central Avenue were hot enough to fry an egg, so we kept heading north. Dusk found us sitting in the Santa Fe Plaza, where a passing hippie handed us a newsletter with maps to all the local communes. I convinced Faisal we should visit one.

A two-lane highway meandered through a narrow gorge, past orchards and sleepy towns nestled on the Rio Grande. At the crest of Pilar Hill, the canyon walls opened into a broad valley bathed in transparent light. Jagged mountain peaks to the East looked nothing like the soft round Judaean Hills that surrounded Jerusalem. Expanses of semi-arid desert were dotted with twisted cedars and piñons. We followed the map to the New Buffalo Commune ten miles north of Taos.

The deeply rutted driveway led us into the counter culture. Who were these bare-breasted women sauntering by? Lunch was rice, beans, and vegetables. So was dinner. The denizens of the commune were already aligned with the mysterious *yin-yang* forces I'd heard about in Paris. Tuned in to the desire to create a balanced universe, they chose not to exploit the earth for the love of hamburgers—or so I thought. Faisal, who carried his culture like a turtle shell, ignored the prevailing macrobiotic ideology. He fired up our camping stove in the shadeless dirt courtyard and announced, "I am an Arab from Jerusalem. I must eat meat."

In less time than it took to smoke a joint, succulent odors of *shish kabob* wafted through the air. I expected our makeshift kitchen to be quickly shut down but learned that when one is culturally intact, as in "*shish kabob* is my native diet," one is respected. Doors opened as Faisal threw spices on the sizzling meat, and with typical Palestinian hospitality, he shared the *kabobs.* After dinner he played the *oud*, sang, and told stories. The next morning, we were offered a tipi. My dream of living in a village was rekindled here, but Faisal was not impressed with mud homes lit by kerosene lamps and four-seater outhouses filled with flies and torn newspaper. As we drove down the rutted driveway heading back to NYC, I knew I was on the threshold of heeding Timothy Leary's advice: "Turn on, tune in, drop out."

The rift between Faisal and me had begun before visiting the commune, before I fell in love with spectacular New Mexico sunsets, breathtaking moonrises, soaking naked in hot springs, watching thunder clouds spout rain that often never touched the desert floor—and before the benefit.

In New York, Faisal had become a lightning rod for Palestinians in exile and peace activists, particularly Jewish women activists inexorably drawn to handsome Arab men. A benefit to help Palestinian refugees was held in a downtown church. Faisal, a culture carrier of Middle Eastern music, poetry, and food, was swarmed by the organizers. A group of women mobilized in our tiny kitchen to bake chicken, roll grape leaves, roast eggplants, and boil chickpeas. In the middle of their never-ending ideological chatter, I burst forth like a broken dam.

"Palestinians long for their lost towns and villages. They hold keys to homes that have been destroyed or given away. That is their sorrow and their tragedy. I am a second-generation American Jew born in Brooklyn, but I have little attachment to this concrete-and-steel world. I belong nowhere."

The women watched in silence, not sure how to respond to my rant.

"I too dream of my village, but I have no idea where on earth it is."

I mourned for an elusive dream and for my tenuous marriage.

The night of the benefit, Faisal played the *oud*, sang, and recited poetry. We raised almost $2,000, a small fortune at the time; all the money was given to a refugee camp near Jerusalem. I found myself at the heart of a human rights movement that grips me to this day.

In 1970, Faisal and I returned to the West Bank, traveling together for the last time. My youngest brother Paul came with us, perhaps as Mom's insurance for my timely return. That year, President Nasser died of a heart attack while mediating between King Hussein and the Palestinian resistance movement. With him died the dream of a united Middle East.

Faisal's mother welcomed us with open arms. The last time I saw Yusra was before the war. I would have welcomed the opportunity to talk with her about our marital discord. My mother-in-law was one of the wisest women I've ever known. She now lived in a cozy vine-covered cottage in Abu Dis, a bucolic Palestinian village, very close to the Old City. After several days of showing my brother around Jerusalem, we went to Samua to visit Ibrahim and Amty. The village still loomed in my mind as an impossible ideal.

We stopped in Hebron long enough to catch the bus. Although Israeli soldiers were a visible presence, the streets were filled with traffic, commerce, and shoppers. The occupation was in its early stages. Omar the bus driver welcomed us as if he'd seen us yesterday and gave my brother Paul an Arabic name that stuck for the remainder of our trip: *"Ahlein Boulos!"*

Amty was standing by the door of her house as if she'd been waiting. Her bright smile clouded over when she understood that Faisal and I had returned for only a short visit. I was happy to hear that Nyfeh had married her beloved cousin, and they were living in Damascus. I wondered what she had worn on her wedding day. Faisal's father slaughtered a lamb in honor of our return, but a sadness filtered through the feasting. We didn't ride donkeys to check water levels in the well on their land. Ibrahim's thoughts were transparent. The future he'd hoped for—Faisal and his family living in the village—was never going to happen.

When my brother came down with dysentery and high fevers, Faisal's mother took him to Hadassah Medical Center, certain he would be cared for because he was Jewish. She was wrong. Paul's insurance card was not good enough. The admissions clerk said, "No cash, no treatment." Yusra took him to an Arab doctor who was a friend of hers. The doctor refused payment. "You are a guest in our country," he said. Yusra cared for Paul until he was well enough to travel. Mom was not shy about expressing her outrage with the Sisterhood in her synagogue. "I've worked for years to raise money for Hadassah Medical Center—but never again."

Mom made her first trip to Israel the following year. For two days and one night Mom and her friend Ida Mintzer left the safety net of their B'nai B'rith tour and kept her promise to visit Yusra, her *machatunim*, Yiddish for her daughter's in-laws. English lacks a word to describe this relationship.

"We were the only tourists on the bus that was full of Arabs," Mom told me. "We felt self-conscious but not afraid." Luckily the driver spoke English and knew where the Khatib family lived because Mom and Ida had no idea where to get off. Mom knocked on the door of a stone house in Abu Dis, identified herself as Iris's mother, and was embraced by Yusra, who had prepared a kosher meal for her Jewish guests. They were given the master bedroom that had a huge east facing window. Yusra had to work the night shift at the hospital but left Mom and Ida in Samira's capable hands. Yusra returned in the morning, cooked breakfast for her guests and showed them around Jerusalem, very different from B'nai B'rith's tour. Yusra had been unable to secure permission for non-Muslims to enter the Dome of the Rock Mosque, so the three women strolled the esplanade on the Temple Mount above the Wailing Wall. After a shopping spree, during which Yusra made sure her friends got the best deals, the trio ended up at Zalatimo's for carrot juice and *knafeh*.

"We visited a place that was so overcrowded we hardly had room to walk in the alleyway. No one spoke English. I could tell the people were very poor, but the women offered us coffee, tea, and cookies, and Ida never refuses sweets," Mom laughed. Her friend's extravagance in eating and shopping more than balanced my mother's stoic restraint. Faisal's mother had taken them to the refugee camp where Ahmed's family lived. At the end of the day, Yusra walked her guests to the bus depot in West Jerusalem so they could rejoin their tour group.

"Did you ever tell your B'nai B'rith friends where you'd been?" I asked.

"No. It was none of their business."

I was glad my mom had visited Faisal's mother but questioned why she never told her friends where she'd been. Was she ashamed to admit she was visiting her Palestinian extended family? If mom had told them about the hospitality, warmth, and generosity she'd just experienced, perhaps their fears would have been alleviated, so they, too, could someday enjoy the legendary Palestinian hospitality. Back in New York, Mom declared Yusra to be "a very gracious lady." Masada and the day in Jerusalem with Faisal's mother were the highlights of her trip.

Our weekly gatherings in the apartment on Avenue A were never declared over. Faisal just stopped cooking, and the ragtag assortment of people stopped showing up. He wrapped his *oud* in a red velvet cloth and placed it on a high shelf in the bedroom closet. Life in the counterculture on the Lower East Side lost its allure. It was hard to admit we were preparing to go our separate ways. Our unlikely union, solidified by the chaos of sustaining each other during a terrifying war, had lasted three years, longer than many had predicted.

We decided to cheer each other up with a farewell celebration in the neutral territory of Christmas, where the perils and pitfalls were equally unknown. Neither of us had ever celebrated the birth of Jesus. Watching the day-glo colors of an industrial sunset, we wondered where to start.

"With a tree," Faisal suggested.

We dragged a poor evergreen along St. Mark's Place and up four flights of stairs, not sure Christmas was worth the effort. Pine needles from the shell-shocked tree littered the wood floor. What we lacked in experience we made up for with ingenuity. Perched on a stool, Faisal hammered metal hooks into the plaster ceiling, looped ropes around the heaviest branches, and pulled. Suspended in midair, the tree swung like a pendulum in search of its arc, threatening to knock down anything or anyone in its path. The tree had the same problem as our marriage. We couldn't figure out how to stabilize it. Neither tinsel, twinkling lights, a popcorn necklace, nor dangling dreidels, bubble gum, and bags of chocolate kisses could lighten our sadness.

Georgia O'Keeffe painted lower Manhattan as a cityscape of graceful geometric buildings bathed in lamplight, but all I saw was concrete, steel, and plenty of garbage, but not enough dirt to plant a garden. In the spring, tiny flowers defied all odds by bravely poking their heads between sidewalk cracks before being rudely trampled by a thousand oblivious feet. In the midst of a Christmas shopping frenzy, I spoke the words hidden in my heart.

"Listen, Faisal, I want to live simply. I can no longer pretend a herd of goats lives on our tenement roof. All I will miss from Western Civilization is toilet paper and hot showers." I could not stop thinking about the commune in New Mexico.

I questioned what he wanted. A slice of the American pie? The freedom to explore the sexual freedom of the counterculture? He wanted both.

On Christmas Eve, we went to St. Patrick's Cathedral for midnight mass. Chestnut vendors huddled near charcoal braziers. Thousands gathered in the Gothic cathedral, where wooden carvings of the Via Dolorosa and the Stations of the Cross reminded us of Jerusalem. Stained glass windows of the crucifixion and resurrection rose to high stone ceilings. *"Ave Marias"* echoing off stone walls offered little comfort. Instead of a frigid carriage ride through Central Park, we opted for dinner in Chinatown, where we knew the restaurants would be open.

Driving along Broadway, we passed the Bowery and saw people standing at the edge of darkness around crackling flames leaping out of a metal dumpster. We joined the homeless, the winos, the derelicts, and those with nowhere else to go. Translucent hands reached out to gather the warmth, reminding me that no matter what I did—stay in or leave my marriage—the light in the world was returning, and some of it was for me. The present seemed to have already vaporized into a puff of memory, and I was looking back at this moment.

When the slings and arrows of life caused Faisal and me to divorce, and the crying, screaming, disappointments, betrayals, and hurt lost their heat, we forged a lifetime friendship. I moved to northern New Mexico and fell in love with mountains, starry skies, walking rain clouds, adobe homes, cedar-scented fires, chopping wood, gardens—and a handsome Jewish blacksmith from New York. We transformed an adobe ruin into a comfortable home for our two children. When the realities of motherhood found me home alone, sleep deprived with two babies, and a husband working hard to support us, I imagined myself sitting in the sun weaving rugs and rolling grape leaves with other women. Those memories made me smile.

PART TWO

RETURN: 1998

When I was 20, time was mine to spend lavishly. Thirty-two years later, time was far more precious than money. Even so, three movies, a snooze, and several meals on a jet plane went by too fast to digest the enormous distance between Albuquerque, New Mexico, and Tel Aviv, Israel. The middle-aged couple sitting next to me spoke quietly to one another, seemingly determined to maintain their wall of privacy. The woman's headscarf and dark, loose-fitting dress let the world know she was Muslim. Perhaps they were going home. I longed to tell them I was returning as well. Hours of endless ocean below left much time for reflection.

If I had not met Gabi, I might never have gone back to Jerusalem; I was not Palestinian and had too much personal history to visit Israel as a Jewish-American tourist. Gabi was a Jewish Israeli who grew up in West Jerusalem. In 1976 he and I were teachers in a Taos private school, often referred to as "the hippie school." When he told me he had been among the first Israeli soldiers to enter the Old City during the 1967 Six-Day War, I knew he could have been one of the soldiers who greeted Faisal and me when we walked through the streets of postwar Jerusalem. Gabi was unexpectedly forthcoming.

"My platoon was among the first to reach the Temple Mount."

"I was hiding in Ramallah with a Palestinian family," I countered. We compared war stories.

"My platoon hid in a dump on the edge of East Jerusalem listening to the screech of incoming mortar bombs retaliating for our attacks. During the night our ammunition ran out, so we dug foxholes and waited. Enemy mortars kept exploding. At first light, Israeli planes silenced all bombs in minutes. Half the squad next to us died from bombs ricocheting off stone buildings. The soft dump saved our lives. It was the most terrifying night of my life. When our platoon slowly walked toward the Old City, the streets were running with blood. Bodies littered the ground. It was my first time ever in Arab East Jerusalem. We heard random gunshots and dropped to the ground. The snipers were found and immediately executed. I was shocked."

In 1986, Gabi's sister, Dina, came to New Mexico as an emissary for a mythical-sounding place—the Oasis of Peace, *Neve Shalom* in Hebrew, *Wahat al-Salam* in Arabic. The fair-skinned woman with a thick Hebrew accent told us about a unique village in Israel where Jews, Muslims, and Christians lived as neighbors.

But while Dina painted an irresistible vision of coexistence, an entire generation of Palestinians had grown up under occupation. They lived in political limbo with limited civil rights, their despair increasing as they watched the growth of Jewish settlements on land stolen from them. The First Intifada in 1987 was a spontaneous popular uprising triggered when an Israeli army truck plowed into a line of civilian cars in Gaza. In response, Israel closed Palestinian universities, colleges, and schools, demolished homes, and installed a curfew. Palestinian civil disobedience included strikes, boycotts, and refusal to work in Israeli settlements or pay taxes. More than 150 Palestinians were killed that year, and more than 10,000 were wounded. Thirty thousand

Israelis demonstrated in Tel Aviv to protest the harsh actions of their government, but on American television, all we saw were mobs of angry Arabs throwing rocks at Israeli soldiers. The death rate for Palestinian rock-throwers during the first year of the popular uprising was six times greater than the annual death rate of American soldiers in Vietnam.[10]

Claiming security reasons, King Hussein renounced Jordan's claim to the West Bank in 1988. Israel did not fill the void by offering citizenship to millions of Palestinians who had just become officially stateless. Nor did Israel accept the Palestine Liberation Organization's (PLO's) declaration to recognize the State of Israel alongside an independent Palestinian State in the West Bank and Gaza with a government "based on principles of social justice, equality, and non-discrimination." These noble sentiments received no press, and the Palestinians received no state.

During most of the '80s and '90s, my attention shifted from political realities in Israel and the West Bank to being a mom, wife and teacher in Taos and Albuquerque, New Mexico. The Middle East became a cultural touchstone but not a human rights imperative. I studied belly dance, enjoyed Arab music, served hummus to appreciative friends and shared stories about living with the Palestinians.

In 1997, Gabi introduced me to another emissary from the Oasis of Peace, this time an Israeli Muslim named Abdesalaam. "His name means 'slave of peace,' and don't worry, he travels with his own prayer rug," Gabi joked. Abdesalaam was invited to speak in an Albuquerque synagogue at a Friday night Shabbat service during Sukkot, a time when many Jews build temporary dwellings in their backyard to commemorate the former Egyptian slaves wandering in the desert for 40 years. Abdesalaam told the congregants, "Life in the Oasis of Peace is not without problems, but it is without soldiers, barbed wire fences, weapons, and fear." Abdesallam joined the cantor from the pulpit in singing the final Hebrew prayers.

[10] Bickerton and Klausner, *A Concise History of the Arab-Israeli Conflict,* 226-232.

After the service, he was welcomed into the *sukkah* to share the bounty of the fall harvest. A few months later, a letter arrived from Abdesalaam inviting me to travel to the West Bank and Gaza with a delegation organized by the Oasis of Peace. I was ready.

Wing lights flickered in the darkness as I tried to imagine the world that awaited me. Sleep was impossible. No one in Faisal's family was left living in Jerusalem. Ibrahim had watched his sons and daughter leave one by one. Their visits became the highlights of his life. One day he took a bus to the Allenby Bridge at the Israeli/Jordanian border crossing to welcome Marwan, who had written from Kuwait to say he was coming home. Ibrahim had no way of knowing his youngest son had been denied a visa to enter the West Bank. All day he waited by the bridge before catching the last bus to the village. Ibrahim died three weeks later from a brain hemorrhage.

Ibrahim, born under Ottoman rule, became a policeman during the British Mandate, and saw his homeland partitioned by the United Nations in 1947. When the armistice lines were drawn, 78 percent of Palestine had become the Jewish State of Israel, the rest divided between Egypt and Jordan. A citizen of the Hashemite Kingdom of Jordan until Israel conquered the West Bank in 1967, Ibrahim died living under occupation, a citizen of no country. The Palestinian state he dreamed of, with a constitution committed to the principles of the Universal Declaration of Human Rights, had yet to be created.

Upon Ibrahim's death, Amty moved to the Shu'fat refugee camp, six miles north of Jerusalem. By then, Faisal was living in Buffalo, New York, with his wife and growing family. Whenever he visited Amty, which was every few years, she asked the same question: "When are you coming home?" Although it never happened, Faisal said the words Amty longed to hear: "I'm moving to Samua with my family." Amty died soon after that visit in the refugee camp, a faithful wife and beloved mother.

After a 12-hour flight, we landed in Ben Gurion International. I walked past signs in Hebrew, English, and Arabic, duty-free shops, and soldiers carrying Uzis and M16s. Originally built by the British in the Palestinian town of Lydda, now called Lod, the airport was named to honor Israel's first prime minister. Passport control took less time than expected. Abdesalaam was waiting for me near the luggage carousels.

"*Shalom, salaam, Erees*! I hope you had an easy trip."

After 32 years, I was welcomed to Israel by an Arab Muslim.

The Oasis of Peace, near the Latrun Junction, was midway between Tel Aviv and Jerusalem. The no-frills but comfortable room in their guest house, my home for the next two weeks, included a balcony overlooking green-and-gold checkered fields and flocks of sheep guarded by local Bedouin. I woke to the sound of birds chirping what sounded like *boker tov, boker tov*—good morning" in Hebrew. The sky was growing light as I walked along the only road looping through the village, past modest homes surrounded by low stone walls and gardens dripping with roses, bougainvillea, honeysuckle, and other blooms.

At the end of the road was a white-domed structure called the Doumia, the House of Silence. Unlike other towns and villages in Israel, the Oasis of Peace did not have a synagogue, mosque, or church to mark the religion of its inhabitants. Only non-denominational prayers echoed inside the circular dome with a concrete floor covered in places with scattered rugs. I walked inside the unlocked building, faced the huge windows overlooking the valley, raised my arms in a gesture of thanksgiving, and broke the silence with an irrepressible "OM."

Dina was unable to be our guide as planned. She was mourning the recent death of her 21-year-old son, Tom, who had been killed when two military helicopters collided in midair near the Golan Heights. It was his last mission before completing military duty. I offered my condolences and reminded her that we'd met through her brother ten years ago in New Mexico. She offered to meet after the tour and take me to the Street of the Prophets, where she and Gabi had grown up.

Joyful noises reached our ears as we approached the primary school in the heart of the village. There were no security guards protecting the children who were busy painting murals, working in gardens, playing music, and learning to count in Hebrew and Arabic. Dina's husband, one of the principals, welcomed us into his office. Tall and fair, possibly from a German-Jewish background, he explained the school also had an Arab administrator and that every classroom had an Arab and a Jewish teacher. "This is the first bilingual, bi-cultural school in the country," he proudly declared.

Abdesalaam's wife taught kindergarten. During the morning circle, her students sat cross-legged on the floor sharing stories in their language of choice. To the chagrin of the teachers, who strove for egalitarian language use, all the children gabbed in Hebrew during recess. Without linguistic differences, it was impossible to distinguish the ethnicity of a child—and who cared? A sandbox filled with children at play, whose imaginations could turn a gas mask left from the Gulf War into a sand toy, was the hope in this oasis.

Our eclectic group, ready to witness and report on the military occupation, included a Palestinian-American filmmaker from Los Angeles, a female journalist, a Quaker family, a brash New York Jewish woman who professed to being on first-name basis with every leftist leader in the Knesset, a bilingual Spanish-English teacher from Massachusetts, and two members of the Oasis of Peace.

Before crossing the Green Line, the former international border between Israel proper and the occupied West Bank, we met with an "absent-present" man, an Orwellian term that every Israeli seemed to understand. In 1948, thousands of Palestinians became second-class citizens and internal refugees in the newly created Jewish state. The Muslim-Israeli, showing us the crumbling walls of a mosque ringed with coils of barbed wire and several "No Trespassing" signs posted by the Israeli military, was risking arrest. He lived a few miles up the road but was forbidden to restore or pray in the mosque that had once been the center of life in his village. The internally displaced man looked longingly at the rock piles and wondered why they were not allowed to care for their mosque or rebuild their village.

Our first stop in the West Bank was Hebron, the bustling town where I once ate camel *kabob* sandwiches with Faisal's family. In 1995, the Oslo Accords had given people hope that the tragic conflict would be resolved, but when Hebron was sliced into areas of control with barbed wire and concrete barricades, hope dwindled into cynicism, despair and anger. The larger area, H1, 18 square kilometers, was home to about 115,000

Palestinians. Nominally administered by the Palestinian Authority, the Israeli army could enter at will. H2, the smaller quadrant, only four square kilometers, included Hebron's commercial center, the main traffic artery, the historic Old City, and the Tomb of the Patriarchs, known to Muslims as the Ibrahimi Mosque. Jews called it the Cave of Machpelah. Abraham, Sarah, Jacob, and Leah lay buried in the fortress-like structure built by King Herod. About 2,000 Israeli soldiers guarded 500-plus Jewish settlers in an area that was home to about 30,000 Palestinians.[11]

Led by an orthodox rabbi, religious Jewish settlers began moving to Hebron soon after the Six Day War. They rented rooms in Hebron's main hotel, and refused to leave. The Israeli government moved the group to an abandoned army camp on the edge of the city and supplied them with weapons. The makeshift encampment grew into house trailers, which became apartment buildings offering hundreds of housing units for Jews, which became the settlement of Kiryat Arba, approved by the Knesset in 1970. But Jewish settlement in the heart of the city didn't start until the eighties, when a yeshiva was built in the old Jewish Quarter and two small settlements were established near the Tomb of the Patriarchs.[12]

When Israel first gained control of the Tomb of the Patriarchs in 1967, they established a complex schedule of worship. Officially, Jews and Muslims had exclusive use of the Ibrahimi Mosque/Cave of Machpelah on their respective holidays. On rare occasions, they prayed together, a unique sharing that ended on February 25, 1994, during the holy month of Ramadan. Dr. Baruch Goldstein, a Jewish-American settler, entered the mosque with an assault rifle and killed 29 worshipers. More than 100 were wounded. Prime Minister Rabin described Goldstein as "a shame on Zionism and an embarrassment to Judaism." A shrine built by the

---

[11] Bickerton and Klausner, *A Concise History,* 299-311.

[12] Gershon Gorenberg, *The Accidental Empire: Israel and the Birth of the Settlements, 1967-1977* (New York: *New York Times* Books, Henry Holt and Company, LLC, 2007), 137.

settlers to honor Goldstein was later dismantled by the government, but the epitaph on his tombstone remains: "He was a martyr who gave his life for the people of Israel, its Torah and land."[13]

After the massacre, Israel closed over 500 Palestinian businesses, welded shut their homes, and forbade Palestinians to walk on Shuhada Street, the main commercial center. Only settlers and internationals were allowed to walk throughout the city. The mosque was closed to allow time for repairs and to replace the blood-soaked carpets. Nine months later, the shrine reopened with separate entrances and security checks for Muslims and Jews.

The Palestinian mayor of Hebron invited an international group of unarmed volunteers, the Christian Peacemakers Teams (CPT), to patrol the streets of the stricken city. He hoped their presence would help stop violent confrontations, especially on Friday afternoons, the Muslim Sabbath, when Israeli soldiers often prevented young Muslim men from entering the mosque. "Restrictions change minute by minute, soldier by soldier," explained our Dutch CPT guide. She pointed to Israeli military outposts on the rooftops of Palestinian homes. From the ground they looked like makeshift wooden shacks, but "temporary" things in this land have a way of becoming permanent. Local Palestinians hung netting and chicken wire across open courtyards and passageways to protect themselves and their produce from garbage and debris thrown down by settlers and soldiers, but there was no protection from urine, eggs, and human feces.

A former Israeli soldier who had served in Hebron told me, "Our orders were to protect the settlers—not to protect Palestinian families from settler violence. Soldiers are combatants, not police." As if to excuse the inexcusable, he added, "Rooftop shifts could last twelve hours— without bathroom breaks. To keep myself awake I sang at the top of my

---

[13] Joel Greenberg, "Israel Destroys Shrine to Gunman," *New York Times*, December 30, 1999.

lungs." He helped me understand that young soldiers sometimes found themselves in positions of power and authority over civilians who had been living under occupation longer than the soldiers had been alive.

Before entering the Ibrahimi Mosque, women in our tour group were handed hooded robes to wear, but once inside, we were free to wander and admire the exquisitely inlaid wood and the ornate colorful mosaics that surrounded Quranic inscriptions running along the walls. Through an iron lattice, I could see the marble tombs covered with gold-embroidered tapestries.

I had always thought of Abraham as the first Jew, a notion once

challenged by a Muslim friend who claimed that the Prophet Ibrahim (known to Jews as Abraham) was the first monotheist, revered equally by both religions. What would Abraham, our common great-grandfather, say if he saw his descendants poised to hurt or kill each other in a house of worship devoted to his memory?

When Faisal's father had welcomed me as his daughter-in-law, perhaps he hoped our union might be signaling a new era of Jewish-Muslim coexistence. For centuries, the two communities had once lived side by side. A Jewish cemetery, dating back thousands of years, testified

to the fact that there had once been a thriving Jewish community here. Ibrahim died before the 1994 massacre in the mosque but was a child during the 1929 riots. This seemingly ideal world had come unraveled with a vengeance.

History books offer vague and sometimes conflicting reasons: the 1929 riots were a reaction to rumors that Jews were killing Arabs and seizing control of Muslim holy sites; or the riots were a response to Muslims praying and building near the Wailing Wall; or they were the result of conflicting promises made by the British. The clashes seemed to have started in Jerusalem and spread to Safed, Tiberias, Jaffa, and Hebron. More than 100 Jews and slightly fewer Arabs were killed. The British quelled the riots, forced the Jews to leave Hebron, and limited Jewish emigration from Europe at a time when a worldwide economic depression and anti-Semitic outbreaks were prompting a flood of Jewish immigration to Palestine. Despite British restrictions, by 1936 Jews living in Palestine numbered almost 400,000.[14] The indigenous population, including Jews who had been living in Hebron for generations, feared being displaced economically and politically by the incoming European Jews.

A more personal version of history was told to me by a 20-year-old woman, Sahar M. Vardi, whose family had been living in Hebron during the 1929 riots: "My great-grandfather was a rabbi who traveled from Iraq to the Holy Land in 1860 with a camel caravan. He observed the Sabbath for the duration of a difficult journey and chose to settle in Hebron because it was an ethnically mixed city. Generations of rabbis followed him.

"My great-grandmother, 16 at the time of the riots, left an eyewitness account in a handwritten journal. Certain her entire family was about to be killed, she wrote about her terror when an Arab man entered their home with a drawn sword. Her father calmed the cowering children. 'Don't be afraid. This man has come to help us.' Slashing his sword, the Arab made a pathway through streets littered with bodies. When they got to his home, they found other Jewish families had also found sanctuary there. Survivors of the massacre later created two lists—

---

[14] Bickerton and Klausner, *A Concise History of the Arab-Israeli Conflict*, 52.

naming those who had saved Jewish lives and those who had not."[15]

The soft-spoken, blue-eyed, fair-skinned Israeli women telling me this story looked more European than Iraqi. She had been arrested and put in prison on several occasions for refusing to serve in the Israeli army and for being part of weekly vigils to open Shuhada Street to Palestinians. Some of the families currently being harassed and dispossessed by the settlers were descendants of families who had risked their lives during the 1929 riots to save Jewish families, including hers. She knew this because their names were on the list created by the survivors.

I was relieved to discover that despite 32 years of military occupation, Hebron pulsed with a life force that barbed wire, concrete barricades, harsh curfews, and armed soldiers could not entirely repress. A blacksmith labored in front of a fiery forge, transforming iron rods into window grills, building ornamentation and utensils. Flying feathers and squawking chickens announced stalls where you could buy fresh eggs. Shoppers walked through an open-air market overflowing with produce grown in nearby villages—tomatoes, apricots, figs, dates, grapes, watermelon, almonds, and squash. In the covered part of the casbah, racks of clothing with American logos hung alongside embroidered dresses, colorful scarves, *keffiyehs*, shawls, shoes, jewelry, hand-blown glassware, olive wood carvings, and more. Old men played backgammon around tables in front of cafés while drinking Turkish coffee, tea, and smoking tobacco on their *narghiles*.

Our itinerary did not include a visit to any of the outlying villages in the South Hebron Hills. In the din of a noisy restaurant, our overwhelmed

---

[15] Sahar M. Vardi, one of the Israelis responsible for the broadcast "Jerusalem Syndrome," lives in Jerusalem, and is an independent activist with the American Friends Service Committee (AFSC). Micha Kurz, who has moved to the U.S., is the cofounder of Breaking the Silence: Israeli soldiers speaking out about the occupation (www.breakingthesilence.org.il) and Grassroots Jerusalem (http://www.grassroots alquds.net).

guide never responded to my request to stop in Samua. Faisal had warned me that the village of my dreams was now beset with traffic jams, overcrowding, and pollution, but I wanted to see it for myself. We were so close, but armed soldiers, checkpoints, and roadblocks could

turn even the shortest excursion in the West Bank into an ordeal. We boarded our air-conditioned tour bus, headed to a Jewish settlement called Tekoa.

We sat on uncomfortable benches on the woman's side of the synagogue listening to Rabbi Menachem Froman lecture on the history of Tekoa Settlement. Founded in the mid-1970s, the Jewish settlement was a short bus ride to Jerusalem or Bethlehem. An older Arab village by the same name existed down the road. Standing in front of the ark that held the sacred Torah, the rabbi started with Biblical scripture. I braced

myself for what I thought would be an act of endurance as he shuffled back and forth in leather shoes worn like slippers, the strings of his *tallit* visible under a suit. A long beard, more black than silver, came to a point in the middle of his chest. Rabbi Froman, born and raised in Galilee, told us that most of the settlers in Tekoa had emigrated from Russia. A goat herd, vineyard, mushroom farm, and carpentry shop gave this settlement the feel of a traditional village. The elementary school welcomed secular and religious children, which was highly unusual in Israel. As if on cue, a group of children, including the rabbi's own, entered the sanctuary to decorate the ark with greens for the Jewish holiday of Shavuot, so we went outside.

The rabbi loomed large as he stood over us. He looked like a Patriarch from the Bible as he raised his voice and issued a stern warning: "We will never leave Tekoa. We would give our lives for it. The question is how we will live, in peace or at war with our neighbors?"

We respectfully sat straight-backed on the grass as he stressed the importance of winning battles through spiritual power, not military might. "The *Gush Emunim* movement to settle the West Bank was founded in 1974 by a group of yeshiva boys. I am one of them. We believe God commanded us to live in Judea and Samaria, as it is called in the Torah." Referring to the West Bank by its Biblical name, the rabbi invoked God's promise to the Jews, which was non-negotiable.

To secure their settlement, built on the Palestinian side of the Green Line, the rabbi had traveled to Gaza and visited with Sheikh Ahmed Yassin, a quadriplegic cleric and leading member of the Palestinian branch of the Muslim Brotherhood, which later became Hamas. Born in al-Jura, a small village in British Mandate Palestine, Yassin's family fled to Gaza after the village was captured in 1948. The sheikh opposed the peace process and supported armed resistance against Israel. He was arrested in 1989 and sentenced to life in prison. Eight years later, with the help of Rabbi Froman, the sheikh was released in exchange for two Mossad agents.

Sitting in the warm sun made us lazy, and soon many of us were reclining on the soft grass. The rabbi joined us. "For the first hour, the sheikh and I praised God. We continued this praise for hours, and in our last five minutes together, we worked on political problems. The sheikh assured me that Jewish Tekoa was welcomed to become part of a Palestinian state in the West Bank. I believe you cannot make peace in the Holy Land without attending to the issue of holiness." The rabbi was a strong believer in interreligious reconciliation. After a long pause, he offered a solution and a warning. "We must create two states with one capital—Jerusalem—as soon as possible. Otherwise there will be ongoing bloodshed. We must look at Israel from a post-Zionist view."

The rabbi seemed unconcerned that the movement he helped to found had opened a Pandora's Box to a messianic movement that quickly became a militant movement to colonize the West Bank. The victory of the religious right in 1977, in partnership with ultra-nationalists, brought to power people who opposed trading "land for peace." Since my visit to Tekoa in 1998, Jewish-only settlement blocks in the West Bank have continued to grow exponentially, panicking those who hold onto the belief that two states are possible.

In 2004, the sheikh was killed when an Israeli helicopter gunship fired missiles at him and his bodyguards as he was being wheeled out of an early morning prayer session. Twelve bystanders were killed including two of Yassin's sons. Hamas called for retaliations against Israel as 200,000 people in Gaza took to the streets to celebrate their latest martyr. Some Israelis saw him as the Palestinian Bin Laden, while others warned that his assassination could lead to an escalation of terror. The United States Representative to the United Nations stated that his country was "deeply troubled by the actions of the Israeli government."

To remain living in Tekoa, the rabbi was willing to become a citizen of Palestine, but his viewpoint was unique among members of *Gush Emunim*, the "Bloc of the Faithful." The rabbi's final words to us: "According to Hillel, the essence of Torah is to treat your neighbor like yourself. The world exists because of 36 hidden *tzaddikim*, or wise men, who may or may not be Jewish. I am not one of them." He smiled. "As spiritual advisor to the Israeli Knesset, I am not so hidden."

☙

Yitzhak Frankenthal made an important condolence call to Dina and her husband on the day their son died. He was also a bereaved parent. When his own son Arik was killed by Palestinians, Frankenthal spoke on national Israeli television. With the power of the bully pulpit he could have shouted, "Death to Arabs! We have no partners for peace." His compatriots would have been sympathetic. The nation was mourning with him. Instead, he transformed his unimaginable grief into a cry for compassion, forgiveness, and reconciliation.

Frankenthal's informal dress and short hair obscured the fact that he was an Orthodox Jew. Our delegation met Frankenthal at an East Jerusalem hotel where he welcomed Muslims, Christians, and any form of Jewish identity. We laughed. "I welcome all who seek a just peace. We can talk about pain. We can talk about anger, repression, conquest, or hope. We can talk about lost opportunities, or we can talk about our family. We can talk about everything. It is essential to talk, because foremost we are human, and words make a difference. My son Arik tried to warn me about the rising violence in our country, but I was too busy to listen."

In 1995, Frankenthal founded The Bereaved Families' Forum, a group that unites families on both sides of the Green Line who have lost loved ones to the violence. Politically he wanted to see a Palestinian state in the West Bank and Gaza and for Jerusalem to become a shared city. Personally he wanted an end to the violence. I understood why Dina and her husband took such comfort from Frankenthal's bereavement call. They were standing in the same circle of hell.

Rivka, the manager of the Oasis of Peace guest house, did not want to become one of Israel's bereaved parents. The death of Dina's son had affected her greatly. I discovered this when she invited me to celebrate Shavuot on a *kibbutz* in the Negev. This 2000-year-old festival dated back to when people offered their first ripened fruits, wheat, barley, grapes, figs, pomegranates and olives to the temple in Jerusalem. A country fair atmosphere on the *kibbutz* included craft and game booths and home-cooked food. The greenness of the land defied the fact that we were in the desert. Towards dusk, hundreds of people sat on hay bales lining the hillside, listening to live music and watching dancers spotlighted by a full moon.

Rivka worried for the safety of her only child, an 18-year-old about to begin his obligatory three-year army duty. She was trying to get him military exemption, but only yeshiva students and "Arabs" (Palestinian-Israelis) were automatically excused. The original military exemption of 400 Talmudic students by Israel's first prime minister had swelled to over 6,000 by 2012. The tax burden for full-time yeshiva students fell on the bulk of Israeli citizens. The High Court of Justice ruled this draft discrimination unconstitutional, but little had been done.[16] And even if her son managed to obtain an exemption, Rivka was concerned he could become an outsider in Israeli society. The camaraderie and networking that took place during military service were crucial when applying for jobs, university, and other Israeli institutions. "It's not fair. My son who grew up with Arabs as friends and neighbors is being asked to raise arms against them or risk being alienated in his own society." She was caught in a "catch-22."

Abject fear made me reluctant to enter Gaza, a tiny coastal enclave five miles wide and 25 miles long where about 1.5 million people, including 900,000 refugees, lived in one of the most densely populated places on earth. Media reports would have us believe that Gaza was a hotbed of terrorists, Yasser Arafat clones without his hope of becoming a prime minister.

Going through the Erez checkpoint in Israel tested our will, stamina,

---

[16] "Talmud and Cheesecake," *The Economist,* July 28, 2012. www.economist.com

and determination. Our water bottles were almost empty, and no one offered us a drink as we sat in the sun for hours waiting for passports to be processed. Several members of our group were suffering from diarrhea, and the one filthy chemical toilet available to our group barely sufficed. American passports were a definite plus—unless you were an Arab. Hana, one of our guides, was a Palestinian-Israeli-American filmmaker born in the Galilee. Although he had a U.S. and an Israeli passport, soldiers ordered him to go through a separate checkpoint for Palestinians. We

kept in touch via cell phone. "I want you all to go into Gaza, even if I'm not allowed," he insisted. As Hana spoke, we heard voices echoing as if inside a tunnel. They sounded like distressed chickens in an overcrowded pen. Our other guide, a Norwegian resident of the Oasis of Peace, could speak three languages, but not Arabic. Everyone agreed—we did not want to enter Gaza without someone who knew Arabic. Anxiety mushroomed. When Hana was finally allowed to rejoin us, our relief was palpable. He never spoke about his experience.

On the Gazan side of the checkpoint, a smiling driver waited next to an old bus adorned with a red, black, and green Palestinian flag. Gaza City was not what I expected. Modern concrete structures rose up alongside traditional stone houses. We drove past camels and donkeys who had learned to share the road with buses, cars, and taxis. Electric lines and telephones poles crisscrossed busy streets. Shoppers in outdoor markets were dressed in modern clothing as well as in traditional *keffiyehs*, *jelabiyas*, and *hijabs*.

Curious students surrounded us in the lobby of Al-Azhar University, decorated with a wall-size mural of the Dome of the Rock. Few of them had ever had the opportunity to visit this iconic world-renowned mosque, a few hours drive by car. Friendly escorts led us into a spacious office, where we were served coffee, tea, and cookies at a long shiny black conference table. Dr. Al Khoudary, the university president, entered the room wearing a grey suit and white shirt. A geologist by profession, he lectured about the politics of water in flawless English.

"Whoever controls the water in Gaza and the West Bank controls life. Israelis have gardens and swimming pools while Palestinians are forced to ration water for drinking and bathing. When Israel captured the Golan Heights and the West Bank, they gained control of the headwaters of the Jordan River and the aquifers in the Jordan River Valley." Control of water may have been the actual trigger for the '67 War. Living in the high desert of northern New Mexico, I too understood that water was life.

Dr. Al Khoudary continued. "At the beginning of the Oslo Peace Accords in 1994, Japan offered us a grant to start a university. We began with 700 law and education students. Our curriculum has since expanded. Despite poverty and overcrowded conditions, literacy rates in Gaza are in the mid-nineties. We accept all students who complete high school. If they didn't go to university, there would be nothing to do. A young person with nothing to do is dangerous. To train our young to become scientists, teachers, pharmacists, and engineers is to give them a stake in the future. That is the solution. However, most of our students cannot afford to pay $600 per semester. We are interested in student exchanges, scholarships, books for our library, and a printing press."

Simple needs, I thought, for a university with a mission as ambitious and noble as peace and prosperity in Gaza.

Several students joined us for lunch in a downtown restaurant, where enticing smells wafted through an elegant dining room echoing with snippets of conversations in Arabic and English, laughter, and clinking glasses. I struck up a conversation with the 19-year-old English literature major sitting next to me. Slender with curly dark hair and a light case of acne, the young man told me he was entering his third year of college. We spoke about the pleasure of reading Thomas Hardy and Shakespeare, as well as day-to-day realities. He hoped to continue his education outside of Gaza, but traveling anywhere was difficult. Visits to his family in Amman were rare. Checkpoints, visas, and the expense made such journeys difficult and dangerous. The sheer normalcy of enjoying lunch in a downtown Gaza City restaurant was not the stuff of headlines.

But life in a Gazan refugee camp was a stark contrast. Children played along a dirt road amidst blowing trash and open sewers. I visited a home where three generations lived in one cramped room with intermittent electricity and no running water. Mattresses were the only furniture, family photos the only decoration. A woman in a black embroidered ankle-length dress offered me hot tea. I accepted with a polite thank you in Arabic and secretly hoped the water had been well-boiled. A toddler crawled onto my lap and began pulling my hair—hard. I picked up the child, who was ignoring the reprimands of a nearby adult, put her on the floor, and walked outside where children were swarming, begging, beseeching us for shekels, dollars, anything. As their numbers grew, they became more insistent. Our guide ordered us to walk quickly toward the bus. Shaken and overwhelmed, we knew we had to tell the world about the plight of descendants of the refugees who had been expelled from villages that were now on the other side of the Green Line inside Israel.

Our Gaza tour included sitting in the cramped office of the Secretary-General of the Cabinet of the Palestine National Authority. Created as part of the Oslo Accords in 1993, the Palestinian Authority was tasked with administering the Occupied Territories, but ultimate control remained with Israel.[17] Handsome, with a thick black mustache, Ahmed Abdul Rahman chain-smoked for two hours while telling us his version of the Palestinian tragedy.

"My father was killed in 1948 defending the holy shrines in Jerusalem. We, the Palestinians, are facing a diaspora not unlike the Jewish Diaspora. Not a day goes by without innocent blood being spilled. The West Bank is sliced by checkpoints and highways for Israelis only. Israel keeps raising the price of water for us. Our fishing boats are not allowed in deep waters. We are forbidden to use our new airport. Checkpoints are the only way to enter or leave Gaza. I have spoken all over the world as a representative of Fatah and have faced several assassination attempts. Palestinians have come to accept the unacceptable—we must give up land we believe is ours." He was referring to the fact that Israel exists on 78 percent of land that was formerly Palestine. "I tell you this frankly: What we demand is the right to live. I believe the majority of Israelis are ready for peace. Palestinians want peace as well, but extremists on both sides hold the power. I say this to you today: We denounce terrorism and announce tourism." He made eye contact with each one of us as he shook our hands and gave us his card.

---

[17] Josh Ruebner, *Shattered Hopes: Obama's Failure to Broker Israeli-Palestinian Peace,* (New York: Verso Books, 2013)

The multi-million-dollar airport Ahmed Abdul Rahman had referred to was in southern Gaza near the Egyptian border. Every aspect of the airport—paid for with funds from Japan, Egypt, Saudi Arabia, Spain, and Germany, and designed by Moroccan architects—was approved and supervised by Israel. Upon our arrival, bored Palestinian soldiers were guarding priceless Palestinian treasures in a ghostly airport, using guns as props to keep themselves awake. Excited by our presence, they showed us around as if they were docents in a world-class museum. Two-

story arch-shaped glass windows allowed the light to stream into the spacious main terminal decorated with Moroccan tiles. We were standing in the embodiment of the future Palestinian state. Months after our visit, President Clinton stood next to Yasser Arafat for the official opening ceremony. The airport, designed to handle 700,000 passengers per year, was planning to be open every day of the year except on *Yom Kippur*, the Jewish day of atonement. But the hum and bustle of world travelers and the sound of jet planes flying over Gaza International was short-lived.

Israeli warplanes destroyed the control tower at the start of the Al-Aqsa Intifada in 2001, and in 2002, they destroyed the runway.[18] The *intifada* was triggered by Ariel Sharon's provocative visit to the Temple Mount accompanied by a unit of police. The Palestinian symbol of coming statehood in the West Bank and Gaza was destroyed just after they had reluctantly postponed a declaration of statehood. Their international airport became another footnote in a long, tragic history.

On our last day in the Oasis of Peace, I walked to the cemetery and sat next to Tom's grave, my fingers tracing the Hebrew letters carved in stone. Born: March 5, 1976. Died: February 4, 1997. Fresh flowers adorned the site; a tiny blue-and-white Israeli flag fluttered on a breeze. Did he die for that symbol of the Jewish state? Tom was about to complete his military duty, return to his family, find a sweetheart, and plant seeds. Every home I visited in the village—Jewish, Muslim or Christian—displayed the same photo: a young man wearing an Israeli army uniform who exuded optimism for a glorious future. Tom's death was felt by everyone. As Jewish tradition required, I placed a stone on his grave and walked to Diana and Rayek's home. The village mayor and his wife had invited our group to a farewell barbecue.

I sat with friends in the shade of a fig tree under a trellis of grapevines eating bread, cheese, olives, shish kabob, figs, and watermelon, wondering why anyone would study war. A well-known verse from the Bible came to mind: *They shall sit every man beneath his vine and fig tree. And none shall make them afraid anymore.*

---

[18] Bickerton and Klausner, *A Concise History of the Arab-Israeli Conflict*, 339-343.

WELCOME HOME, SISTER

For two weeks I had resisted the impulse to rush to Jerusalem. I stood in front of the Ottoman towers and Crusader-built revetments of the Damascus Gate waiting for Farid, wondering if we would even recognize each other. We had not seen each other for 32 years. "I'll be wearing beige pants and a pink flowered shirt," I told him over the phone. New buildings and roads threatened to obscure the familiar skyline until you were quite close. The Old City used to appear from great distances as if floating on a ridge top.

Faisal had encouraged this visit. "Farid will be so glad to see you. I told him you were coming." I was worried that both time and perceived religious and political differences might have created a rift between us. Exhaust from cars, taxis, and buses on Saladin Street mingled with the scent of a thousand spices, especially Arabic coffee with crushed cardamom and freshly baked sesame rolls. Broad curving steps shaped like an amphitheater led to an unfamiliar bustling market outside the Old City walls. Pilgrims, tourists, and shoppers scuttled every which way among a myriad of vendors. I promised myself to buy an Umm Kulthum CD from the booth near the moneychangers. People wearing T-shirts sporting American logos walked among those in traditional dresses and desert robes. Head coverings were as varied as humanity.

When Farid asked where we should meet, the only landmark I could think of was the Damascus Gate. I had no idea that most Israelis and international tourists entered the Old City through the Jaffa or Dung Gate, closest to the Wailing Wall. This gate was mainly used by local Palestinians. Separation had become the norm.

I returned to Jerusalem as a teacher, writer, mother, and wife—married, but not to Faisal. My husband Marc joined me for this leg of the journey. On his 13th birthday, Marc's grandparents had offered him a free trip to *Eretz Yisrael* for his bar mitzvah, which he turned down. This was his first visit to the "holy land." With a black mustache, olive skin, and large nose, Marc blended in this part of the world. Standing amidst the swirling crowd, listening to the babble, an almond-complected man approached me.

"*Erees, ahlein, ahlein. Salaam aleikum*. Welcome home, sister."

After traveling throughout Israel, the West Bank, and Gaza, Farid was the first person to welcome me home. My eyes welled with tears. His hair had become salt-and-pepper, his complexion darker than I remembered, and his smile warmer. We were unsure of protocol. How does a Muslim man greet a long lost Jewish-American friend, standing alongside her husband?

"Farid, it's so good to see you. I hope you and your family are well." Years fell away as we spontaneously gave each other a hug. He was expecting my visit, but I was not expecting his welcome.

"*Hamdulillah*, thanks be to God, we are well." A slight shrug of his shoulders offered a hint that all was not rosy. It would take more than two weeks of travel in Israel/Palestine for me to understand his reality. Farid was pleased to introduce us to his sons, who worked in a nearby office. Over several cups of coffee, he explained to them how we had met 32 years ago. To mark the occasion, we posed for a group photo. I stood beside Farid, who proudly stood behind his two sons—the elder, serious looking, his clasped hands resting on a desk; the younger, leaning back in a swivel chair and smiling. I promised to share the photo with Faisal.

Other than his five children, Farid was most proud of his library. On Nablus Road, we walked past the Garden Tomb, where Faisal had kissed me for the first time. Beyond the new East Jerusalem bus depot, we came to an enticing-looking fish restaurant. Behind the restaurant was a steep flight of stairs leading to a windowless room with stacked shelves from floor to ceiling. We were looking at periodicals, old newspapers and magazines, scholarly treatises on Islam and archeology, novels, histories of Palestinian families, and unpublished manuscripts. Cigarette cartons glued together served as bookends to secure the 45,000 volumes, which had taken over 40 years to collect. Many Palestinians, including Faisal, had donated their personal collections to this library. Farid's memory was the only organizing tool. This was his domain, a family library that had become a national treasure.

Marc and I were introduced to the chain-smoking gentlemen gathered around a long metal table. "These are my friends from America," Farid told them. "*Erees* used to live in the Old City with the Khatib family." Another round of coffee in the smoky basement firmed our welcome into this community of intellectuals, journalists, poets, writers, and scholars determined to survive—with their culture. I thought of Shakespeare and Company, the Paris bookstore and library, that had been and still is a gathering place for generations of Americans.

Since we'd last met, Farid had learned to speak, read, and write in English and Hebrew. He had written books on Palestinian culture and history and was now a respected teacher. Walking with him through the streets of the Old City was like having a living encyclopedia by our side. He pointed out remains of past civilizations—a Roman arch, a tower built by King Herod, Ottoman walls, a medieval Russian church with onion-shaped domes. Farid laughingly explained that centuries of bickering between different Christian denominations about who should open and lock the Church of the Holy Sepulchre was resolved by giving the responsibility to a Muslim family.

To avoid passing near the security-laden Wailing Wall, forbidden to

Muslims, Farid took us to the Temple Mount through back streets that led to an entrance for local Muslims. Words carry political and religious agendas. Jews call this raised plateau the Temple Mount and believe it to be the site of their two lost Temples, the first destroyed by the Babylonians in 587 BCE, when a portion of the Jewish population went into exile, the second by the Romans in 70 CE. Muslims call it *Haram al-Sharif* or the Noble Sanctuary. Two mosques, *Al-Aqsa* and the Dome of the Rock, have been standing here since the Muslim conquest in the seventh century. I decided to call this coveted piece of real estate—the "Sacred Plateau."

As Faisal had done 32 years ago, Farid secured permission for non-Muslims to enter the domed shrine that protected a black granite boulder upon which Abraham almost sacrificed his son Isaac, if you're Jewish; or Ishmael, if you're Muslim. The color blue dominated the intricate mosaics and calligraphic designs adorning the walls. Like Judaism, Islam required religious art to be symbolic, decorative, and without human images. Standing in the pitch-black cave in the underbelly of the boulder, Farid, an anthropologist, historian, writer, and teacher, told us this cave had likely originated when an old well went dry, not when the Prophet Mohammed rode his steed to heaven, a belief held by devout Muslims. His comments revealed him to be a man of science as well as faith.

After leaving the mosque, we walked on nearby Chabad Street in the Jewish Quarter, where Farid wisely ignored a storefront with a cardboard model of the third Jewish Temple standing alone on the Sacred Plateau. That archeology has found no physical evidence to prove the existence of the First Temple built by King Solomon shocks many Jews like myself, who grew up believing this was factual history. Architectural remains of sanctuaries built elsewhere in the region during the same era have allowed people to imagine what it may have looked like. Many ultra-Orthodox Jews believe the two mosques must be destroyed so the third Jewish Temple can be built—an idea that creates anxiety in the Muslim community. Until the sovereignty of East Jerusalem was at stake, Palestinian historians and archaeologists did not dispute the existence of this temple. Today there was the illusion of peace—or was it quiet despair? There appeared to be enough physical space for two mosques and a synagogue to stand on the Sacred Plateau—but was there enough spiritual space?

Back in the *souq*, merchants called out to Farid, "Welcome, my teacher!" saying the word *teacher* with reverence. When they discovered Marc and I were friends of the teacher, prices dropped. Farid clicked his tongue in disapproval if he thought we were not getting a great deal. Taking advantage of this, I bought belly dancing pants and a lapis necklace for our daughter, an inlaid chess set for our son, a silver mezuzah for my mother, and a hand-embroidered shawl for myself. Marc bought carved olive wood Sabbath candlesticks for his mother, and in no time, we were weighted down with packages and buzzing on Arabic coffee.

Farid and Dina might have grown up a few blocks apart in the same city, but they lived in different countries on opposite sides of a hostile international border and never would have met by chance. Dina had admitted to me that her visits to the Old City were rare. She loathed being looked upon as a conqueror walking through the streets. She looked tiny sitting on the broad, curving steps outside the Damascus Gate. A delicate strand of white pearls around her neck, which I couldn't see until we were close, made her look as if she had dressed for an important occasion. Farid invited the three of us to lunch at his favorite restaurant in the Muslim Quarter. The owner, a former student, treated us like honored guests. Plates of food kept coming—hummus, baba ghannouj, tahini salad, lamb kabobs, tilapia, pita, olives, pickles. English was our common language. When Farid told Dina about his library, it surprised me to learn she'd already heard about it from Jewish scholars at Hebrew University who researched there.

Politics was not mentioned until Marc and I told them about our upcoming road trip to the Galilee, the Golan Heights, the Jordan River Valley, Jericho, and the Dead Sea, with stops in Ein Gedi and Masada. We planned to rent a car in East Jerusalem, where the prices were cheaper. Farid clicked his tongue disapprovingly. "You must rent in West Jerusalem so your car will have yellow license plates. Otherwise, you could be stopped and held up at checkpoints." Dina agreed. Until that moment, I had no idea that license plates in Israel were color-coded. The guidebook neglected to warn thrifty travelers that driving in Israel with Palestinian plates could be problematic. Israelis and Jewish settlers living in the Occupied Territories drove cars with yellow plates; Palestinian cars had green plates. The meal ended with a cup of Arabic coffee. Farid refused any help with the bill.

"Please, you are my honored guests."

I wondered if he could afford such generosity.

At my request, Farid led us on a pilgrimage to my past. We followed him through a warren of streets in the *souq*. Butcher shops were curtained with hanging carcasses, although the actual butchering was now forbidden inside the Old City. Donkeys had been replaced by golf-cart-sized tractors belching exhaust in their wake instead of dung. Farid jokingly referred to them as iron donkeys. Much had changed, but Zalatimo's Sweet Shop stood the test of time. The baker didn't remember me, but I thought back to the day when Faisal and I sat on his rooftop eating *knafeh* and toasting with carrot juice. It was here that we first spoke of getting married. I made a mental note: return to Zalatimo's when hungry. After a cup of freshly squeezed orange juice, we left the congested part of the market and followed a slightly uphill secondary street that unexpectedly curved to the right and became broad steps.

Farid pointed to a quiet courtyard. "That is where you lived with the Khatib family."

I stuck my head through the locked iron gate that prevented any entrance into the courtyard. Flowering geraniums indicated someone lived here, but I couldn't crane my neck enough to see the stone steps hugging the outside of the two-story building, or the well that had been the water source for the families living here.

"Are you sure this is the house?"

Farid nodded his head in affirmation. I rang a bell, hoping to get permission to enter the courtyard, but no one answered. My past, present, and possible future merged in that moment—Iris Devinsky, Jewish girl collecting *tsedukah* (charity) to plant trees in Israel; existentialist Karen Trotsky, moving through life like a rolling stone; Umm Ibrahim Khatib, married woman living with a Palestinian family; Iris Keltz, counterculture idealist, remarried, raising children and living in New Mexico. I knew that even if I made *aliyah* to Israel, became a citizen, moved to Jerusalem, and rented this house, the courtyard where I once rolled grape leaves in the morning sun with Amty no longer existed. That reality had been erased. My sense of loss and dispossession was nothing compared to Faisal and Farid's.

We walked to the juncture that had once divided East and West Jerusalem, a boundary Farid would not cross.

"*Salaam aleikum*, my friends," he said. "It's time to return home."

"*Aleikum al salaam*, Farid. Be safe until we meet again." I watched him grow small as he walked away.

The three of us continued walking to Rehov HaNevi'im, the Street of the Prophets where Dina and her brother Gabi had grown up in West Jerusalem. From the Jaffa Gate to this tree-lined street with signs printed in three languages and three alphabets was only a few blocks.

"That's where we lived," Dina said, pointing to the second floor of a flat-roofed stone building with iron bars covering arched windows that faced the street. "On warm nights, all the kids living here would play on the rooftop patio." Thick foliage hanging over a protective stone wall prevented us from seeing into the yard. Her family paid an affordable rent to an Israeli government agency, but as soon as her family had saved enough money, they moved. Everyone in Israel knew homes like this belonged to an Arab family forbidden to return.

Dina continued. "It was so quiet on Shabbat you could almost sleep in the street. My brother and I loved to play outside, but our mother forbade us to go past the huge dilapidated building at the end of the street. Neighborhood kids called it 'The Castle.' Beyond this building, Moroccan and Yemenite Jews lived in decrepit and abandoned homes along with Israeli-Arabs. The closer you got to the border, the more run-down the neighborhood. Our block ended with a wall of rolled barbed wire, concrete cones, and a sign that read Danger! Stop! Frontier Ahead."

In 1967, an identical sign had been posted near the Youth Hostel in East Jerusalem, Jordan—on the opposite side of the border.

"My brother told me about an incident that happened when I was three and he was five. We were playing on the sidewalk in front of our house wearing only underwear. It was a hot summer's day. An Orthodox Jew from the Mea She'arim District a few blocks away spat in our faces as he walked by and started to pray for us because he thought we looked indecent. We ran inside to tell our mother. She came outside to scream at the man, but he was gone."

Dina and Gabi's parents left Poland in 1936—three years before the Nazi invasion and more than a decade before the creation of Israel. They chose a secular life in a non-religious neighborhood of Jerusalem and sent their two children to the nearby public school. Their family originated in the same shifting borders of Europe as mine, but their family immigrated to Palestine while mine chose America.

"That was 'The Castle,'" declared Dina, pointing to an upscale apartment building on the corner. A steady stream of traffic made it hard to imagine Rehov HaNevi'im had ever been a quiet street on the edge of their world.

Secure in our rental car with yellow license plates, Marc and I set off on a whirlwind road trip. He drove. I planned the route. We headed north along the Mediterranean coast, stopped at the Roman ruins in Caesarea, bypassed Haifa, and spent the night in the Crusader town of Akko. Although this coastal city was known as an ethnically diverse town, Arab citizens lived in segregated neighborhoods known as "the ghetto" because of economic stagnation. Oblivious to all but this exquisite moment, Marc and I walked along the seawall promenade and dined in a café overlooking a fleet of sailboats while a full moon rose behind the slender minaret of a green-domed Ottoman mosque. An increasing number of Jewish families had become inspired to settle in this beach town, inflaming and challenging the tenuous coexistence.

The streets of Safed were full of artisans selling trinkets to awestruck tourists. We bought hand-dipped braided *havdalah* candles from a white-robed man sitting beside his outdoor stall, but left the city without seeing a hint of Safed's famous Kabbalistic sages studying the Jewish book of mysticism.

Needing a break from driving, we stopped to walk in an olive grove visible from the highway. No signs or fences indicated that this was private property. Marc and I wrapped our arms around the trunks of gnarled old trees, trying to guess their age. Our hands never touched. This ancient grove held trees that might have been a thousand years old. I have seen photos of leathery old men with calloused hands caressing torn limbs, sobbing after the trees had been uprooted by the Israeli army. To kill a tree is to destroy a life.

In the Golan Heights, we hiked alongside streams, past waterfalls and archaeological landmarks up to a rock escarpment that had views of the Sea of Galilee (also called Lake Tiberias or the Kinneret) and the Jordan River. Before Israel conquered this strategic 690-square-mile plateau from Syria in 1967, there had been frequent exchanges of gun fire. On the day we visited the nature reserve, there were no armed soldiers, and there was no sense of danger. Rain and winter snow sustained the natural springs and rivers, including the Jordan, as it flowed through the Rift Valley into the Sea of Galilee and on to the Dead Sea. The Golan Heights, which Israel officially annexed in 1981, supplied the country

with about 14 percent of its water. I remembered the words of Dr. Al Khoudary, the water engineer and president of the university in Gaza: "Control of this watershed was a trigger for the 1967 War. Water is life."

There was nothing rustic or primitive about the *kibbutz* we visited on the edge of the Sea of Galilee. No suntanned, virile-looking young men or women sweating in the fields or caring for animals. Modern capitalism had transformed many of the socialist *kibbutzim* of history into tourist destinations. Marc and I enjoyed the comfortable guest house and swam in the lake where Jesus was said to have walked on water.

Until we entered the Jordan River Valley and crossed the unmarked border into the West Bank, we saw no checkpoints. Cruising at top speed on a new superhighway in a car with yellow license plates, Israeli soldiers waved us on. The four-lane blacktop had surprisingly little traffic. No road sign directed us to Jericho. When we realized we had bypassed one of the oldest cities in the world, we circled back and found a secondary, unmarked, pothole-riddled road that brought us into a run-down-looking town. The Oslo Accords in 1994 had given nominal control of Jericho to the Palestinian Authority. They were allowed to issue postage stamps and travel documents, regulate imports and exports, and had an international dialing code; but Palestinians were denied the right to station their police on the Allenby Bridge,[19] and had no control over their borders.

We appeared to be the only tourists in town. No savory scents wafted from restaurants; there was no marketplace full of "must have" trinkets. We stayed in Jericho long enough to discover an adobe ruin standing in the shade of a flowering acacia tree. The structure had no roof to protect the mud walls. In spite of this, the arched doorways and windows showed little signs of crumbling. At first I thought the lovely round tower by the structure's western wall was a fireplace, but upon closer inspection, I realized it could have been the minaret of a future mosque. Having restored an adobe ruin in New Mexico, my husband and I have an affinity with derelict buildings melting back to the earth. The abandonment of this solid adobe structure made me think something terrible must have

[19] Bickerton and Klausner, *A Concise History of the Arab-Israeli Conflict*, 282.

happened to the builders.

As a child, I'd been told the Old Testament story about Joshua fighting the battle of Jericho. After 40 years of wandering in the desert, the Israelites were on the brink of entering Canaan. The tribe's leader, Joshua, sent out spies to find out who lived in the land. They returned with stories of "the Amalekites, who dwell in the desert to the South. [The] Hittites, Jebusites, and Amorites, [who] dwell in the mountains, and the Canaanites, who dwell by the sea and along the Jordan River."

The Promised Land was peopled.

Listening to the story of the Israelites attacking Jericho, I always imagined marching with them. I heard the blare of trumpets as they surrounded the impenetrable protective walls of the doomed Canaanite city. I shouted along with the Israelites when they conquered and killed every man, woman, child, and animal. The walls crumbled because God was on our side. Today, for the first time in my life, I imagined what it might have been like to be inside the walls of Jericho. The cries and screams of people who expected no mercy from a marauding desert tribe pierced my heart. Walls separate, but they also protect.

Before I build a wall I'd ask to know / What I was walling in or walling out / And to whom I was like to give offense. — Robert Frost

Marc and I photographed the abandoned adobe and returned to the highway along the same pothole-riddled road. When we got close to the Dead Sea, Israeli soldiers waved us through. Farid and Dina had advised us well. Yellow license plates were a definite advantage.

We washed the desert dust from our bodies under the waterfall in the oasis of Ein Gedi and hiked to Masada at dawn. On this plateau in 73 CE, 900 Jewish men, women, and children killed themselves to avoid capture by the Roman army. Meditating on this human tragedy while floating on the Dead Sea, and watching clouds dissolve and reform, I questioned the wisdom of martyrdom as a heroic solution.

An Orthodox Jewish family living in the Old City of Jerusalem had rented us a room in their house just blocks from where I once lived with the Khatibs. Marc and I arrived just in time to celebrate the Sabbath. Our hostess welcomed us while glancing nervously at her watch. The scent of baking chicken and challah bread filled her home.

"All work must be finished before sundown. Everyone welcomes Sabbath at the *Kotel*," she said, referring to the Wailing Wall. "Afterward, you're welcome to join us for a holiday dinner." We accepted the invitation and followed her directions to the Wall: "Go stand in the street half an hour before sundown, and you will find your way."

A trickle of people became a tsunami rushing along every street and alley, carrying us in their wake. From a balcony overlooking the *Kotel*, we watched the frenzy. Cacophonous sounds of prayer, both joyful and lamenting, floated over the celebrants. There appeared to be many leaders of different sects practicing a variety of traditions. Some stepped forward to kiss the timeworn stones of the Wailing Wall while others danced alone or in small groups. Some prayed quietly, some held a prayer book, but everyone prayed with an abandon and fervor I had never before seen among Jews.

We followed the stone steps down into the plaza and joined the throng. Dress was as diverse as the Jewish Diaspora. Full-bearded Hasidic men rocked back and forth in long black coats and broad-brimmed black hats. Marc did not have a *tallit* on his shoulders or a *kippah* on his head. I wore a modest calf-length skirt and covered my arms with a shawl, but unlike Orthodox women who hid their hair under matronly wigs, hats, and scarves, my dark waves were exposed. Women stood on plastic lawn chairs watching a bar mitzvah happening on the men's side of the *mechitza*, a divider that separated men and women. Even the bar mitzvah boy's mother had to peer over the divider. The jostling, boisterous crowd intimidated me from getting near the Wall.

Faisal had taken me to the Wailing Wall when it was part of the Mughrabi Quarter, a poor Moroccan neighborhood established as a charitable trust in 1193 by Saladin's son. Ramshackle houses pressed close together left only a 12-foot-wide alley for Jews to pray. On June 10, 1967, the inhabitants of this 800-year-old quarter were given hours to vacate. Israel demolished more than 100 homes and several small

mosques and schools to create the world's largest open-air synagogue. Amidst the joyful frenzy, I thought of the dispossessed.

The mauve-streaked sky darkened while everyone waited for the celestial sign to indicate that the Sabbath had arrived. A crescendo of ecstatic voices rose heavenward when three twinkling stars appeared in the fading light, and then, the people dispersed as if scattered by a divine wind.

The dining room table was covered with a linen cloth and set with porcelain dishes and crystal glasses. Covering her eyes with the palms of her hands, the mother of the family said the blessings and lit the Sabbath candles, followed by the husband's recitation of the *kiddish* over the wine and the blessing for the challah. I told them that in New Mexico, after we blessed the challah, we tore it apart and fed each other. They liked this idea. Before moving to Israel in the seventies, they had been part of the ashram movement. Transitioning from new age spiritualists to Orthodox Jews living in Jerusalem seemed like a quantum leap. The father of the family, a musician and flute maker, sold his instruments in a nearby shop. Their six-year-old son was born in Israel. He attended a nearby yeshiva and studied Hebrew, which he could understand but not speak. Their son's English had a familiar New York accent. According to the family, when the Arabs lived in this quarter (they never said Palestinians), this house had been the neighborhood pharmacy. Did Faisal's family ever buy medicine here, I wondered?

Courses kept coming, familiar foods my grandmother used to cook—chopped liver, matzoh ball soup, roast chicken with soft potatoes, string beans, and apple strudel. If I had not already been a Shabbat lover, this evening would have made me one. After dinner, the father read and interpreted this week's Torah portion, a process he called *dvar* Torah. "My favorite part of Shabbat," he said.

"The Israelites were wandering in the desert after receiving the Ten Commandments. A cloud led them by day and a fire by night. They ate their allotted amount of manna but got bored on this bland although miraculous nourishment. They complained to God. 'We want meat, something substantial, to sink our teeth into.' God answered, 'If it's meat you want, it's meat you'll get, not for one day, or one week, but until you can't stand the stench of it.'" Our host took this to mean the Israelites craved something that was not good for them and didn't appreciate God's offering.

Protected by the thick walls of our room, I lay across the queen-sized bed, my fingers tracing the vaulted arches that met in the center of a domed ceiling to create a star-shaped shadow mandala. There was much to ponder on this Sabbath. We live in a world where fear has caused many of us to close our tents to the stranger. The Torah said the Israelites arrived in the Promised Land filled with manna provided by God. What if, instead of conquering Jericho, the Israelites had pounded on the city walls and asked for sanctuary? Should we place our trust in military might, divine intervention, human compassion, or the belief in ultimate justice?

We left the bedroom window open to the night. Blanketed by ancient stone walls, desert stars, church bells, and calls to prayer, I fell asleep beside my husband, half expecting to receive prophetic dreams.

In the morning our hosts invited us for Saturday prayers. Orthodox Jews are forbidden to shop on the Sabbath, so we hesitated to tell them that on our last day in Jerusalem, we wanted to spend the rest of our shekels in the *souq*. They adamantly warned against this, but not on religious grounds. "It's dangerous for Jews to be in the Muslim part of the market. We never go there." With more bravado than I felt, I said, "The merchants want my money, not my life," but I knew terrible things sometimes happened to innocent people. Marc and I thanked them for their concern and hospitality, wished them good *Shabbos*, and walked into the *souq*, where the world exploded—not with violence, but into a kaleidoscope of colors, scents, and sights.

I never tired of wandering through the labyrinthine streets of the Old City. On a mission to find traditional Palestinian embroidery, I resolutely passed gorgeous rugs and hand-blown glass goblets, but gave in to the impulse to buy a clay drum for our son and gold filigree earrings for our daughter. Fortified on Arabic coffee, we wandered everywhere, as visible as patrolling Israeli soldiers. Shopkeepers vied for our attention. On some obscure side street, away from the main marketplace, we chanced upon an unglamorous, dusty-looking storefront with a display of amber necklaces accessorizing traditional Bedouin dresses. The shopkeeper rushed out.

"Be welcomed. Come inside. Please take a look. Where you from, my friends?" His excessively friendly manner was annoying, and my first inclination was to keep walking, but he kept up a patter with his limited English.

"My name is Mahmoud," he said, reaching out to shake my husband's hand. As a blacksmith and welder, Marc's leathery hands never got soft, no matter how much lotion he used, and the pointer finger on his right hand was missing, sliced at the knuckle, taken by a power tool when he was young. Mahmoud touched Marc's hand and knew this American earned his keep by the sweat of his brow. The stereotype of Americans walking around with pockets full of easy money was broken. He invited us into an apartment behind the shop, where he served tea and cookies. Like Marc, Mahmoud had been a blacksmith and welder before his eyes went bad from lack of protection. He spoke of his wife and five children; his eldest son was studying at the university in Ramallah, and his daughter was pregnant with their third grandchild.

"We are from a small village outside of Bethlehem. When you buy our embroidery, you are buying a piece of our culture and must learn some of our history. Years ago the dresses were plentiful. Now they are expensive and hard to find, so people cut them into small pieces to make skirts, purses, and prayer caps." He reached for a large hard bound book on a nearby shelf that contained photos of Palestinian clothing worn by men and women in different regions and historic times.

"In the old days, thread colors came from natural dyes—indigo from the Jordan Valley, red from sumac growing wild all over Palestine, and yellow from the soil near the Egyptian border." The embroidered dresses lining the walls of his shop took on greater significance. Patterns of orange branches surrounded by green triangles represented cypress trees. Undulating lines of indigo meant the dress originated near the Mediterranean. The stemmed cup of plenty was a centuries-old pattern found in tombs and buildings in Palestine and Syria. Each dress, painstakingly sewn with tiny stitches, took months or even years to finish. I thought of my dress folded in the cedar chest at home—a fruit-bearing grapevine that wound its way from hem to bodice until it reached a fountain where two birds sang as if they were in Paradise. We left the shop with an embroidered *kippah*, several purses, and a shawl.

If only I could have introduced Mahmoud to the Jewish family with whom we had just shared the Sabbath. If they had drunk tea together and touched hands, they would have learned so much about each other. The Torah had been right—hold your faith, and the world will provide nourishment.

We returned to the Wailing Wall in the late afternoon, when the crowd was thinner, calmer, and less intimidating. A young woman wearing a halter top and shorts had an M16 assault rifle slung over her shoulder. Her approach to the Wall was deliberately slow. With the arm that supported her gun, she pushed a paper prayer into a crack between the massive bricks, where it mingled with a thousand other prayers. Keeping her face to the Wall, the woman retreated with tiny backward steps. Only when she had created enough distance did she turn and walk away. I noticed others backing away in the same peculiar fashion. I thought this might be some kind of religious ritual until someone told me the Wall must be treated like royalty. "We never turn our back on royalty."

I defiantly turned my back to the Wall. It was not royalty to me—but I could not resist one more look. That's when I noticed doves flying between

the Wailing Wall and the Dome of the Rock on the Sacred Plateau—flying between those who prayed to Allah and those who prayed to Adonai, one God with different names.

On the plane, soaring over the ocean like a bird, I remembered a Hebrew prayer I could have said:

"The whole world is a narrow bridge, just a narrow bridge. The thing is not to be afraid."

A QURAN IN EXILE: 2006

I had not seen Faisal or his sister Samira for over 20 years. Marwan, the youngest brother, was the first in the family to move to Buffalo, New York. Samira and her family left Washington, D.C. so they could live near her mother and Marwan in Buffalo. By then, Yusra had been living in the States for almost a decade. Faisal uprooted his family, sold his Long Island home and joined his extended family, an irresistible gravitational pull.

When my mother retired and moved to Florida, I stopped traveling to New York, which was where I had an annual reunion with Faisal and his family. Our contact became limited to phone calls and emails. When I gave birth in 1977, Faisal called to congratulate me. "*Mabrook*, *Erees*," he said. "You have chosen a beautiful name for your daughter. Mona means the one wished for in Arabic, and I know how much you wished for her." Named to honor the memory of my grandmother, I was pleased to discover her name also carried echoes of another culture close to my heart. The following year, I congratulated Faisal after his wife gave birth to their first child, fulfilling the family's dream of a son named Ibrahim. Two years later, my son Eli arrived; then, Faisal had two more daughters and another son. Our children met once when they were toddlers and Faisal was still living in Queens. After a lovely afternoon in the park, Eli innocently asked, "Was Faisal almost my father?"

Spring of 2006, I retired from a teaching career spanning 40 years. The sense of loss surprised me. In the first autumn of my new freedom, my body felt it was time to get back to work. I called forth everything that had been on hold—writing, activism, and travel.

Before the plane landed in Buffalo, I looked in the mirror and felt a need for eyeliner, lipstick, a face lift, a skin peel—anything to wipe away the slings and arrows of time. A restless night's sleep had left dark circles under my eyes. It was easier to look back in time, before this flesh fell victim to gravity, before arroyos crossed smooth cheeks, when auburn highlights glinted against black, not salt against pepper. People passing me in the airport saw an older woman. They had no idea that inside I was twenty-something and about to visit my former husband, sister-in-law, their spouses, and children whom I'd never met. When I called Faisal to confirm the date and time of my arrival, a deep male voice had answered the phone: "I'm his son, Ibrahim, and I look forward to meeting you. I have heard a lot about you." Faisal and I had woven each other into our family stories.

As if preparing me for the passage of time, months ago, Faisal said, "Maybe you should remember me as I used to be. I'm bald and fat now." Decades had passed since I fell in love with a charismatic young poet and musician, but to affirm our lifelong friendship, we had to face each other.

"How is Mama Janet?" he'd asked. "I love that lady. I wish I could see her again."

I told him Mom had turned 91 last summer but still bounced out of cars as if late for a marathon. "She sends her love and best wishes. I'm bringing a surprise from her."

"Oh?" was all he'd said.

Decades ago, when Faisal and I moved out of her home in Queens, we'd carelessly left behind his grandfather's Quran. When Mom sold her house and moved into a Florida condo, the Quran went with her. For years, no one thought about the sacred book that had been through wars, occupation, a transatlantic flight, and another unintentional abandonment. I'd once considered the possibility of giving the Quran to my Taos friend, Gabi, who had become a devout Muslim, prayed five times a day, fasted on Ramadan, and had built a mosque in his backyard. The white-domed structure was crowned with a minaret from Jerusalem. Surrounded by willows, wild flowers, and grass, the mosque faced the Sangre de Cristo Mountains to the East. When I asked Mom for the Quran, she swore she had no idea where she'd hidden it. "I'm so forgetful," she said apologetically.

I imagined combing through her possessions someday and finding the Quran on some shelf in her walk-in closet. "Mom, please take one more look. I'm going to visit Faisal and Samira, and if you find the Quran, I will give it to them." That was when she craftily confessed that the sacred book had never been lost. In her opinion the Quran belonged to Faisal's family, not in some mosque in Taos, New Mexico. After wrapping the Quran in bubble wrap and brown paper, mom showed her package to a postmistress who inquired as to the contents. Afraid to admit it was a Quran, Mom simply said, "A book."

"We have the right to open and search this package," threatened the postmistress. Mom stood her ground and got the cheapest rate.

When the package arrived in New Mexico, I slipped the sacred book out of the faded red cloth bag and rubbed my fingers along the front and back covers, tracing the intricate red-and-gold design. Had Faisal and I not retrieved this precious volume from his grandfather's house, the brittle paper would have already turned to dust.

Samira was alone when she met me at the airport. I was disappointed, and a little relieved. The hood of Samira's white woolen coat framed her unlined face. Had the olive oil treatments worked, or was it her Mediterranean-skin genes? After a warm embrace, she explained, "Faisal couldn't come because of a heavy snowstorm but he'll be at the house tomorrow. He lives an hour and a half from here."

Snow-laden tree boughs surrounded her two-story house in a wooded area outside of Buffalo. Once an industrial center on the Canadian border, this affordable but economically depressed city had become a gathering place for the Palestinian-American community. With his familiar rolling "r" Faisal had once told me on the phone, "*Erees*, this is no place for an Arab from Jerusalem. It's *frrrrreezing.*"

A plush couch, two overstuffed chairs, large lamps, and an Oriental rug filled the spacious living room, but I quickly discovered that the real life of the family happened in the den. We sat on a well-worn L-shaped leather couch in front of a coffee table facing a large-screen TV, eating buffalo wings and pizza. The Middle East feast I was hoping for came the next day. Samira lived with her husband of 30 years who was also from Jerusalem, their adult son and daughter, the son's fiancée, two cats, ten colorful caged birds, and a free-roaming ferret.

Samira took me to Niagara Falls. The bracing air and roaring falls formed the backdrop of a conversation that leaped through time. Samira had dreams of moving to California but complained about the high cost of living there. I invited her to visit me in the sage-scented mesas and mountains of New Mexico, where "the landscape and climate will remind you of the Middle East," I added.

She told me that Marwan, her younger brother, was living in Cairo and had recently gotten married—again, "to a much younger woman." Her big-sisterly tone sounded disapproving. She also expressed concern for Faisal's health. "He's very changed." The more she spoke, the more apprehensive I became.

"Both my kids are engaged," I told her. "Eli teaches children's theatre in Seattle, and Mona—we call her Minka—teaches third grade and lives in Florida near Mama Janet." I complained about my children living on opposite sides of the continent. She sympathized. Palestinian families tended to cluster together. Samira's gorgeous dark-eyed 20-year-old daughter had recently moved back home from Los Angeles, where she had become a cosmetologist licensed to perform rejuvenating facials, an experience I volunteered for immediately. Her daughter loved malls, new clothes, and expensive makeup. Samira's son, a budding filmmaker, had just gotten engaged. Neither of us had grandchildren to brag about.

"I'll never forget all those wonderful dinners in Mama Janet's home. She was so welcoming to our family." Samira echoed Faisal's sentiments.

"And I will always be grateful to your mother, who welcomed me into your family when I was a stranger." In my mind's eye, I saw Yusra's robin's-egg-blue eyes, moon-shaped face, and beaming smile and could hear her high-pitched sweet voice. She had succumbed to cancer 14 years ago, her extensive knowledge of midwifery buried with her in Buffalo, N.Y., far from the home of her heart.

Samira and I imagined traveling together to Jerusalem with our daughters. My sense of justice was offended by the fact that I had the possibility of becoming an Israeli citizen and receiving government subsidies in the form of an affordable home in an illegal West Bank settlement for Jews only. Samira, born and raised in a family who had lived in Jerusalem for generations, did not even know if her identity card was still valid. Current Israeli law prohibited her from returning as a resident, and even if she was allowed to return, economic opportunities for educated Palestinian-Americans were limited.

Politics is personal when talking about the Middle East. History books described an attack in November 1966 on villages in the South Hebron Hills, including Samua. Around 400 Israeli soldiers crossed the Green Line, the internationally recognized border between Jordan and

Israel. When the Israeli military unexpectedly met a 20-vehicle Jordanian convoy with soldiers, a battle ensued that left 18 Palestinians dead and 54 wounded.[20]

"Samira, this attack happened six months before I visited the village. Do you know anything about this?"

"Yes, I clearly remember that day. Faisal was traveling in Africa. Just hours before the soldiers entered, Marwan, my father, and I left the village to go to a birthday party in Jerusalem. A friend called my father and told him the Israeli army was forcing people to gather in the town square. One poor woman who lived alone because of a recent divorce got scared and started running. She was shot and killed. People from Yatta, a nearby village, came to protect us with the guns they traditionally used for weddings. The soldiers scared the hell out of everyone and left 48 hours later. The Jordanian army finally arrived and asked everyone to turn in their guns, but we knew no one would defend us except ourselves."

The attack destroyed 100 homes, a police station, a clinic, and a school. The aggression was condemned by the UN Security Council and the United States, who assured King Hussein of Jordan's territorial integrity. Major demonstrations broke out across the West Bank because King Hussein refused to deploy troops to protect the villages.

"Israel claimed they were retaliating for guerrilla attacks by Fatah, and Samua was their stronghold. Was that true?" I asked.

"I swear there was no Fatah in the village back then. I would have known if there was a political movement. Now Samua has traffic jams, crime, overcrowding, pollution, police—and militants. But back then it was quiet."

From the first day we'd met, Samira's family had known I was Jewish and on my way to Israel, yet they unquestioningly welcomed me. They never said a word about an invasion that had happened six months before

---

[20] Bickerton and Klausner, *A Concise History of the Arab-Israeli Conflict,* 147.

I entered their lives. The attack may have been a trial balloon to the 1967 War. Israel discovered that Jordan would not or could not protect Palestinian villages in the South Hebron Hills—invaluable information.

The roaring falls sprayed icy water on our backs as we posed for a photo, arms resting around each other. That evening, much to my delight, Samira cooked *mansaf*. Every morsel of lamb simmered in yogurt and garlic, served on a bed of rice, proved she had acquired Amty's culinary gift. Faisal still had not come over. The roads were too icy, Samira said. Or maybe he was procrastinating.

Samira was grocery shopping when a rotund man entered the house without knocking. Strands of silver hair swept across his forehead covered baldness. If I'd met Faisal in the street, I might have walked right past him. But his voice was reassuringly familiar. We gave each other an awkward hug.

"*Erees*, sorry I couldn't meet you at the airport. You look great. How long will you be staying?" We laughed, remembering this was the first question he'd asked me 40 years before. I gave him the same answer as I had then.

"Three days," I said. This time we knew it was true.

Samira came home, arms filled with grocery bags. Brother and sister spoke Arabic to one another as we put away the food, allowing me time to collect my roiling emotions. Faisal leaned against the kitchen table, perusing the album I'd put together. Photos in chronological order: Faisal standing in front of a grass hut in an African village; our wedding portrait—I'm wearing the silver dangling earrings he'd just given me and the blue-and-white cotton dress from his mother; we're holding hands in a West Jerusalem park after picnicking on falafel sandwiches; bike riding in Queens on a cold winter's day; Faisal in bell-bottom pants, a fringed leather vest, his hair in a wild Afro; visiting with Aunt Diana in Berkeley, me on Faisal's lap wearing an African-print minidress. Faisal closed the album, pushed his glasses onto his forehead, and sighed. The past was present.

"This is from Mom," I said, handing Faisal the Quran. He slipped the book out of the red cloth sack, gently rubbed his fingers on the inside covers, and announced to no one in particular, "This Quran is at least a hundred years old. I can't believe Mama Janet took care of it for so long." The sacred book now included blessings from his former Jewish mother-in-law. Faisal carefully put the book back in the red cloth bag and began to speak about his youngest son. "Nazar was born and raised in the States, but he has the soul of a Palestinian. At 23 he plays the *oud* better than I ever did, and he learned to speak Arabic in Amman from his cousins."

Faisal never mentioned the Quran again. The sacred book was a symbol of everything his family had lost. He would never forget the day we found his grandfather's stone house in No Man's Land, and he would never forget that a day later the home was bulldozed. The West Bank had become a land marred with checkpoints, separate roads for Jews and Arabs, illegal Jewish settlements, land confiscations, home demolitions, illegal detentions, a hideous separation wall, and the destruction of ancient olive groves. Faisal believed he would live in exile forever and be buried in Buffalo alongside his mother. The return of a Quran could not compensate for such loss. If anything, it underscored the tragedy.

That evening was the first and only meal we ate in the formal dining room. I looked around the table at Samira, her husband, their adult daughter and son, the son's fiancée, Faisal and his married daughter and my nephew Joseph, who happened to live in Buffalo. Samira and Faisal had known Joseph's father, my brother Aaron, when we all lived in New York. Marwan had, in fact, introduced Aaron to his future wife, who became Joseph's mother.

"My parents never told me how they met," said Joseph incredulously.

Faisal signed all this to his blue-eyed daughter, Aisha, who was born deaf. We ate tilapia with rice, pine nuts, tahini salad, hummus, olives, and pita bread as we reminisced.

After dinner, Faisal and I moved into the living room, where we sat side by side on comfortable chairs drinking Arabic coffee and eating baklava. I told him I was returning to Jerusalem in the spring to commemorate the fortieth year since the war, and that I was writing about our time together. While Faisal perused the manuscript, Aisha and I passed notes between us because I did not know how to sign. He emerged from reading, put his hand on my shoulder, and spoke the words I'd hoped to hear: "*Erees*, you are the perfect person to tell this story. My blessings and good wishes are with you."

I wanted Faisal to tell us a story so we could all laugh, like we used to, when laughter and stories were abundant. He tried. We never managed to laugh, but we did cry together.

"It's not right for one people to be chosen by God for the real estate deal of the millennium," Faisal said. "This is the time for all God's creatures to be chosen. The Israelis will never be able to kill every Palestinian, and as long as there is one left alive, the truth will come out. Someday the world will ask forgiveness for turning a blind eye to the suffering of the Palestinians, whose main sin was trying to survive." These words, released like a torrential rainfall, clearly had been locked inside him for a long time.

"I'm old now and might die without ever seeing the streets and alleyways of my childhood. I wandered through Africa and attended university in Turkey, but always believed I would return to Jerusalem to raise my family. I would have been the happiest man on earth, sharing Palestine with my fellow Jews, Christians, and Muslims. My children have grown up in America. They will never know Palestine." Faisal's voice broke at the idea.

"The day Yitzhak Rabin was killed was the darkest day of my life. When Rabin and Arafat shook hands, I dreamed that Jews and Arabs would become friends and I could return home, or not, as I wished, and the pain of my life would stop. When Rabin was shot, I lost all hope, even worse than after the war."

Holding back my own tears, I told Faisal, "On the day Rabin's death was announced across the world, I was certain Israelis would be shocked into seeing the danger of extremists." Rabin's land-for-peace deal was anathema to right-wing conservatives represented by the Likud Party, and by the messianic Gush Emunim movement who claimed to be on God's mission to settle Judea and Samaria, as they called the West Bank. Provocative posters of Rabin dressed in a Nazi SS uniform were held high at their rallies.

The Israeli prime minister who desperately tried to bring peace to his country was assassinated on November 4, 1995, by a Jewish zealot. Yigal Amir believed his action was sanctified by God because Rabin had betrayed traditional Jewish values by his willingness to trade land for peace. Along with 100,000 of his fellow countrymen, Rabin had just finished singing a well-known song of peace in the Kings of Israel Square in the center of Tel Aviv. Ironically, the song dwelt on the impossibility of bringing the dead back to life. Rabin, a military commander who once advocated breaking the bones of rock-throwers, had come to understand that depriving freedom and human rights to millions of Palestinians was dangerous for Israel, militarily and morally. That Israel, the most security-minded country in the world, had failed to protect their own prime minister was unfathomable.

King Hussein of Jordan delivered a moving eulogy at Rabin's funeral. *"You lived as a soldier. You died as a soldier for peace. We believe our one God wishes us to live in peace, for these are His teachings to all the children of Abraham... As long as I live, I'll be proud to have worked with him, as a brother and as a friend... He had courage; he had vision, and he had a commitment to an honorable and lasting peace.* [21]

The day I left Buffalo, Samira and her family were getting ready to attend a local Palestinian wedding. In the United States, where the cost of a wedding was determined by head count, there were no unexpected guests. Samira promised to visit me in New Mexico, but I knew this was unlikely. Faisal and Samira would again become disembodied voices and sporadic emails. I looked at the two-story house on the edge of the woods knowing I might never pass this way again.

[21] Israel Ministry of Foreign Affairs, quoted in Bickerton and Klausner, *A Concise History of the Arab-Israeli Conflict*, 307-308.

FRIENDS CANNOT BE DIVIDED: 2007

My decision was irrevocable. You can't jump off a jumbo jet plane zooming relentlessly toward southwest Asia, aka the Middle East. So I sat back and tried to relax. Weeks before leaving home, I was agitated, couldn't sleep well, and had an unsettling dream:

I'm standing on the stage in a crowded theatre surrounded by men, women, and children running from pursuing soldiers. Someone warns me to stand still because running makes you look guilty. The pulsing crowd is perilously close to the edge of the stage. A human chain is formed in a group effort to lower everyone safely to the ground. Those not strong enough to hold on fall screaming into an abyss. I'm trying to stay away from the edge.

The geography of my dream was so real it jolted me awake. Military experts refer to "the theatre of war" as if war were a spectator event. Friends think I'm brave for going to the Middle East. "Be our ears and eyes and come home safely," they tell me.

"And may you survive the weapons of mass destruction near Albuquerque Airport," I respond defensively.

We expected to land in Ben Gurion Airport at 2 am. I was traveling with Rita, a fair-skinned, redheaded fellow activist who sat beside me reading a manuscript written by a mutual friend about his transition from Zionist Jew to universalist evangelical Buddhist. Layers of belief, including his Jewish identity, were shed like a snakeskin—or so he claimed. I knew from experience that identity was not easy to shed. Rita's chatter calmed me, but her willingness to share the details of our itinerary with anyone on the plane was disturbing. We were going on a tour of Israel and the West Bank with Sabeel, a Christian ecumenical organization based in Jerusalem with supporters around the world. Their mission was to seek peace with justice in the Holy Land. We also planned to visit Rita's older sister, Lois, who lived in the West Bank with her Palestinian-Israeli-American husband.

"You never know who's on board this plane—maybe the Israeli Mossad. Someone might turn us in for questioning," I warned Rita. Everyone on this flight had been subject to additional security. Suspected peace activists, even Jewish ones, had been detained, searched, questioned, and even deported. My paranoia eventually gave way to boredom and restlessness.

This direct flight from Newark to Tel Aviv held an amazing cross-section of American and Israeli society, but there were no Arabs, at least none whose dress revealed their ethnicity. In the seat behind us, a young woman with an olive complexion identified herself as a Mizrahi Jew. "Not to be confused with Ashkenazi," she emphasized. "My grandparents come from Yemen in the Arabian peninsula, not Europe."

"Do you speak Arabic?" I asked, admiring her dark unruly curls.

"A few words." She unapologetically confessed a lack of interest in learning Arabic, the mother tongue of her family, even if that meant not understanding her grandmother.

"I regret not learning Yiddish," I said, "the language my grandparents spoke when they arrived on Ellis Island. I don't even know the name of their Austrian village. It's important to learn the *mammeloshn* (mother tongue) of your grandparents," but I knew my advice was as lost as her grandmother's stories.

In line, waiting for the toilet, I met a woman traveling to Jerusalem for her daughter's wedding. "My daughter is an Orthodox Jew. When she goes out in public, not one strand of her hair is allowed to show." The woman seemed surprised and amused by her daughter's religious devotion. I wondered what the daughter thought of her mother's dyed-blonde hair, visible to the world.

"Does your daughter live in East or West Jerusalem?" I asked, knowing about the generous real estate deals offered to Jews willing to live in West Bank settlements. The woman looked confused. I restated my question: "Does she live in the part of the city that belonged to Israel before the 1967 War?" I was glad to find out the daughter lived in the Mea She'arim, the Orthodox Jewish Quarter in West Jerusalem. This American Jewish woman seemed unaware that Jerusalem was a divided city—or had East and West truly merged?

I strained to overhear a heated conversation between two young men seated across the aisle. Both were Jewish. One, a playwright from New York City, was challenging the other to admit the immorality of the occupation and the Separation Wall, which inspired the Israeli to defend the actions of his country. "Suicide bombers gave us no choice. We deserve to feel secure in our own country."

"Security does not come from a wall, the barrel of a gun, or an occupation," responded the playwright. The men argued until attendants darkened the cabin and everyone settled down.

I woke to the smell of fresh coffee, breakfast being served, and the twinkling lights of Tel Aviv below. The cosmopolitan city on the edge of the Mediterranean gave no hint of the struggles happening on the ground.

The modern-looking international airport was decorated with rows of Israeli flags and Stars of David. Signs in Hebrew and English directed new arrivals, but there were no longer signs in Arabic. The absence spoke volumes. Ben Gurion Airport was the gateway for Israelis and international tourists. Most Palestinians entering or leaving the West Bank flew to Amman and crossed into the West Bank at the Allenby Bridge international border, controlled by Jordan and Israel. Rules of border crossings connecting Israel with the West Bank, Jordan, and the world seemed arbitrary, changed regularly, and were not applied consistently. Even Palestinians with American passports were subject to humiliating interrogations and sometimes denied entry.

An officious customs person asked me, "What is the purpose of your trip? Where are you staying? How long will you be here?" She looked up from her paper-shuffling long enough to compare my passport photo with the face in front of her. I lacked the guts to say, "I've come to witness the effects of a 40-year occupation, and I have a morbid fascination to see the Separation Wall."

I simply said, "A tourist, here to see the holy sites."

Nobody was waiting for us. Rita and I passed a man holding a sign that read, "Checkpoint." Exhaustion was greater than my guilt about being a privileged Jewish-American who did not have to worry about going through a checkpoint in the middle of the night.

"I can't believe I'm in the Promised Land," shouted the young playwright to anyone he recognized from the plane. "I've heard about this place my entire life."

"Tell me when your play is showing in New York," I shouted back before Rita and I caught a taxi to the Oasis of Peace.

The sound of pounding rain and chimes from the nearby Latrun Monastery woke us at dawn. Rita and I walked along the road looping through the village, inhaling the rich earthy scents. Except for the extravagant growth of bougainvillea, Spanish broom, honeysuckle, and roses, the Oasis of Peace looked very much the same. The village cemetery was at the end of the road. I remembered where Tom was buried and went to sit beside his grave, which was adorned with fresh flowers. He had not been forgotten.

Dina was expecting us. She stopped by the guest house to invite us for dinner in her split-level home that had been under construction during my last visit. The living room window opened onto the same expansive view of the valley as her son's grave. Dina's daughter, on weekend leave from the army, leaned affectionately into her mother as they sat on the couch. Her daughter taught Hebrew to new Russian immigrants, a low-risk military assignment offered to sons and daughters from families who had suffered a death.

"My husband is now head of the Bereaved Parents group. I volunteer there as well." Dina and her husband had become grief experts. "We're not involved with daily life in the village anymore, although we try to attend community meetings," she added. The ecumenical community they helped to found was still home to an equal number of Palestinian and Jewish Israelis, with a waiting list of over 500 families. I once wondered that if Faisal and I had remained in Jerusalem, could we have lived here? But according to Israeli law, Palestinians from the West Bank are not allowed to live in Israel proper. Faisal was born on the wrong side of the Green Line.

After dinner, Dina showed us the book she had written honoring her son's short life from infancy to young adulthood. "Tom was special," she said, caressing the pages as if they were alive. Transparent tissue paper protected each image. The final photo showed a young man standing tall and proud in a soldier's uniform. Text was in Hebrew, but the pain of a mother navigating through unrelenting grief was apparent. Anger and sorrow filled my being. Tom should be living in this Eden his parents helped to create. He should have had the chance to raise a family, send his children to the village school, and encourage his fear-filled compatriots to understand the only solution is coexistence.

Eye-catching lanterns sat on a shelf near the couch: two doves cut out of white paper were flying toward each other under a shawl printed with Arabic and Hebrew letters. "What do they mean?" I asked. Dina lit a candle and placed it inside the lanterns. Radiant letters rose from the shadows.

"They say, 'It won't be over until we sit down and talk.'"

The congested intersection in West Jerusalem, surrounded by buses and cars spewing exhaust, seemed more than an hour's taxi drive from the tranquility of the Oasis of Peace. Men and women stood on a triangular pedestrian island holding large black signs with eye-popping white print. Each sign was shaped like a hand and carried the same message in English, Hebrew, or Arabic: *Stop the Occupation*. A tall, rather large woman with short wavy hair was handing out black shirts and welcoming internationals who had come to show solidarity. Gila Svirsky had been sending me informative emails for years. I let her know I was coming to Jerusalem. She replied, "I can't invite you to a Sabbath dinner as you mentioned, but I look forward to schmoozing at the Friday vigil. We do not stand in silence."

Israeli Women in Black had been standing on this corner every Friday afternoon in blazing heat, rain, or cold for over 20 years. A spontaneous vigil, started in 1988 by a group of Israeli Arab and Jewish women to protest violence, grew into an international movement against ethnic conflict, militarism, and racism. Gila proudly notified the international community when Women in Black was nominated in 2001 for a Nobel Peace Prize.

I put on a black *Stop the Occupation* T-shirt, grabbed a sign, and was enjoying the long-anticipated chat with Gila when a pedestrian began screaming at us, "What the hell occupation are you talking about? You anti-Semites. You Israel haters will never drive us into the sea!" Before walking up to the man, Gila pointed to armed Israeli soldiers across the street and explained. "They're here to protect us. Sometimes we're spit upon. Occasionally we're attacked." She spoke to the angry man in a calm voice filled with conviction. "We stand against the occupation of the West Bank, East Jerusalem, and Gaza. We are committed to peace with justice and a world without violence."

"Jewish whore," he cursed, before continuing on his way, possibly to get ready for the Sabbath. After all, it was Friday afternoon in Jerusalem.

Rita and I sat on a bench inside the Jaffa Gate near a breach in the Old City wall. The opening, one of the only places where cars could enter the city, was created in 1898 on the occasion of a visit from Kaiser Wilhelm II and his wife, Augusta Viktoria. A yellow Jetta pulled up next to us. It was Rita's sister, Lois. We quickly loaded our luggage in the trunk, but not before the sisters shared a warm hug. Lois was endearingly maternal.

"You've gotten too thin, Rita," she said before turning to welcome me. Unlike her younger sister, Lois wore no makeup, and her hair did not look coifed.

This would be my first visit to Ramallah since the Six-Day War. I sat in the back seat half-listening to the sisters' chatter. A 20-minute bus ride on the two-lane highway that had once passed through an expansive landscape dotted with cyprus and olive trees surrounding occasional villages had become a chaos of new highways, buildings, checkpoints, barriers, and walls. All roads seemed to lead to a massive, ugly concrete structure surrounded by lines of traffic spiraling off in different directions. Nothing looked familiar.

We passed a warning sign in English, Hebrew, and Arabic: *Palestinian Authority Territory: Area A Ahead: No entry for Israelis.* Amidst blowing dust and trash, in a landscape devoid of trees and shrubs, my eyes locked onto the Separation Wall for the first time. It rose out of the earth like a gateway to hell. Words can barely express my horror. From that moment, I obsessively photographed words and images on the massive barrier. Throughout the West Bank and Gaza, Banksy, an internationally known European graffiti artist, used the barrier wall as his canvas. I stared at one of his more iconic images—painted in black silhouette, a pigtailed girl in a knee-high skirt held onto the strings of a balloon bouquet that floated up and over the wall. It was a picture of innocent hope.

Armed Israeli soldiers stopped the car, asked to see our passports, looked at our faces, determined we were settlers, and waved our vehicle with yellow license plates on to a settler-only road. We had just passed through the Hizma checkpoint connecting the West Bank Jewish settlements with Jerusalem. After driving a short distance, Lois turned off the smoothly paved settler road onto the side entrance of a refugee camp. We had just driven around the Qalandia checkpoint and could see a long line of backed-up cars, minivans, taxis, and buses with green license plates waiting, waiting, waiting to pass into Israel through the concrete bottleneck. Children from the nearby refugee camp were selling gum, trinkets, and cold drinks to the anxious commuters.

Lois explained. "Most vehicles entering Israel have yellow license plates. Palestinians, traveling in cars with green plates, need a permit, and even having one is no guarantee of entry. Sometimes ambulances

have trouble getting through checkpoints." Palestinians were vulnerable to unpredictable detentions, their freedom of movement subject to the whims of soldiers. Identifying ethnicities through license plates had been going on during my visit in 1998, but it seemed the occupation had become more entrenched, institutionalized. Separation had become normalized. I wondered why Israelis chose to self-identify with yellow plates. They reminded me of the yellow arm bands Jews were forced to wear in Nazi Germany. Why not blue, the color of their flag?

Lois skillfully navigated her Volkswagen Jetta around potholes, concrete rubble, barricades, and deeply rutted roads. I searched in vain for Kafr Aqab, the Palestinian village where Faisal's mother had once lived in a stone house on a lonely hillside. Perhaps we had passed it on the other side of the checkpoint?

After driving less than a mile, a modern city began to emerge from the wasteland around the checkpoint. At the leading edge of Ramallah—Area A, according to the Oslo Accords—blocks of modern apartment buildings stood alongside traditional stone houses overlooking terraced hillsides sprinkled with olive and fig trees. On a pedestrian-filled street, Lois bought us a pizza-to-go at Ramallah's highly successful pizza joint. Close to the city center was a defunct movie theatre, near Al-Manara Square where Faisal and I had once watched a John Wayne western. And before heading home, we stopped at a well-known specialty shop to buy some roasted nuts.

Lois pulled into a reserved parking spot in the shadow of a modern five-story building in a quiet residential neighborhood. The spacious apartment was decorated with Lois's original drawings of wild flowers and seedpods, ready to spawn the next generation. As a botanical artist, she strove for anatomical accuracy. In this region of sparse rainfall, every flower was struggling to survive, much like the people.

Lois's husband Khalil, a cultural anthropologist, had written several books. With dark curly hair, olive skin, a prominent nose, and modern clothes, it would have been difficult to identify his ethnicity had I met him in the street. Lois and Khalil had met and fallen in love while attending neighboring Catholic colleges in Minnesota.

Before dinner, the four of us washed down salty nuts with cold beer on their well-tended rooftop garden, home to an impressive variety of thriving succulents. We could see for miles in every direction. Pointing to black barrels lining most rooftops, Lois said they were filled with water, "as a precautionary measure because during the summer and fall, the bulk of our water is routed to the surrounding Jewish-only settlements."

After learning the Latin name for each plant, we listened as Lois and Khalil spoke about their traumatic experience during the 54-day siege of Ramallah in 2002. Khalil directed our gaze to the Palestinian Authority headquarters: "That's the *Muqataa*. From our living room window we could see Arafat's compound surrounded by helicopters and being pounded by explosives. The night sky was lit-up like the Fourth of July. In the morning, tanks began rolling in the streets and voices on loudspeakers demanded the surrender of all arms. People were warned to obey curfew. The price of leaving home was to risk being shot on sight."

"Every five days there was a four-hour break. People scrambled to buy whatever food was left in the stores. We had no idea when the siege would end, or when we would be allowed to go out again," Lois added.

The army retreated, leaving hundreds of water tanks shot full of holes, disabled beyond repair. Streets were littered with shell casings, broken glass, twisted cars, rubble, and dead bodies. For two years after the invasion, Yasser Arafat was held under house arrest, isolated in the compound that had been partially demolished by the Israeli military. The courtyard of the compound, still Palestinian Authority headquarters, became his final resting place.

I thought about Micha, a former IDF soldier, who told me about his experience during the siege. Ordered to empty an apartment building of all people, he pounded on doors and waited for the terrified occupants to open. In the chaos of entering one home, a confused toddler ran up to him. Micha gently picked up the sobbing child. The mother stared at the Israeli soldier as if he were a fire-breathing monster, when in fact his heart was breaking. "Go to your mama, little one," he said in Hebrew. Unfortunately, the child only understood Arabic, and the soldier had his orders.

Khalil grew up in a Christian Arab village in the Galilee in northern Israel. As a child, all he knew about Palestine was that his mother received permission from the Israeli military to pass through the Mandelbaum Gate on Christmas and Easter so she could worship in the churches of East Jerusalem and Bethlehem. He and his friends aspired to be Jewish so they could help in the creation of a modern state where nothing had existed—although they knew better. As part of their indoctrination, they memorized *Hatikvah*, the Israeli national anthem about hope for the new state, and studied Jewish writers and poets. Khalil had been a child when his village was occupied in 1948 by the Israeli army, an event he never forgot. Unlike nearby villages whose lands were taken to build a *kibbutz*, the inhabitants of Rami were allowed to return. They watched the electric lights twinkle in nearby *kibbutzim* while their village remained in darkness. And they were helpless when Israel channeled water from their village spring into the Israeli water system.[22] Khalil, along with 150,000 other Palestinians, became second-class citizens in the Jewish state. His frustration, anger, and pain about the unfair course of history was palpable.

While Lois and Khalil described their terrifying experience during the siege of Ramallah, my mind shifted to a basement apartment in this city where I had hidden with Faisal 40 years ago. Wars happened in *wadis*, on terraced hillsides dotted with trees, on crowded streets filled with traffic, to mothers shopping for groceries, to students on their way to school, to newlyweds planning their honeymoon, and on rooftop terraces on midsummer evenings. Cool desert winds penetrated my thin jacket when the sun plunged below the horizon. I stayed on the roof long enough to enjoy the ever-changing colors billowing toward darkness while a crescent moon rose over buildings topped with satellite dishes and black water tanks.

---

[22] Khalil Nakhleh, *In Search of a Palestinian Identity: A Personal Odyssey* (Jerusalem: Palestinian Society of International Affairs, 2005)

I promised Hyam that if I ever went back to Ramallah, I would visit her family. We'd met in a Taos health food store at the launch of her catering business. A beautiful dark-eyed woman wearing a headscarf was offering free samples of her homemade hummus, tabouli, baba ghannouj, and pita bread to shoppers. I helped myself to seconds and thirds of her delicious food while we spoke as if in the privacy of her home. Hyam was stunned to hear about my war experience in the city of her birth. Since that day more than 15 years ago, we have broken fasts for *Ramadan* and *Yom Kippur* and celebrated her daughters' high school and college graduations, my son's and daughter's weddings, and my mother's ninetieth birthday.

Cell phone to cell phone, Lois called Hyam's family and got directions to a stone house on the edge of a *wadi*. Lois, Rita, and I were welcomed by three women and two children. "Hyam sends her love," I said, not sure to whom I was speaking. "She has often spoken about her home and family." I pronounced each word slowly, as if it would make English more intelligible. Every detail of this visit would be shared with Hyam when I returned to Taos.

At first we were polite, self-conscious, cordial and somewhat awkward—six strangers sitting on couches and soft chairs in a formal living room. A language barrier made for a stilted conversation. The women sat straight-backed wearing long black dresses that looked much too hot for a hot summer's day. Scarves covered their heads and necks. Lois, who had lived in the West Bank for over ten years, heroically attempted to translate, which encouraged one of the younger women to do the same.

"I am Hyam's niece, N'amati. My name means 'grace.' I study English in college," she said before leaving the room. A few minutes later, a young woman in blue jeans, with black hair cascading down her back, entered, carrying a tray of mint tea, freshly cut watermelon, and salty black seeds.

I extended my hand and introduced myself. The women began to laugh at my confusion. "It's me, N'amati." Her transformation into a modern-looking woman was stunning. Since no men were present, she was free to remove her head scarf and heavy dress. Determined to make the most of our visit, N'amati unearthed her electronic translator and asked how to pronounce the word *thyme*.

"It is pronounced like *time*," I said. "Thyme is one of the spices in *zaattar*." Her question pointed to the difficulties of learning English. Between Lois's ungrammatical Arabic and N'amati's imperfect English, their confidence growing as the afternoon wore on, the conversation became infinitely more personal. One woman admitted to being a 56-year-old widow but never said what happened to her husband. The other woman's spouse worked in the States. He sent money to his family, but travel costs and visa restrictions made his visits a rare luxury. We felt a sense of abandonment among them. The men who these women depended upon were gone.

Nineteen-year-old N'amati had never visited Jerusalem or been to the sea, but on clear days, she could see the Mediterranean shimmering on the distant horizon. N'amati boldly seized the opportunity, and asked Lois to drive her to the American Consulate in Jerusalem and vouch for her character. She was trying to get a visa to visit family in America, but a special permit was needed just to get to Jerusalem. Palestinians living in the West Bank hold Palestinian Authority passports, from a country that does not yet officially exist. Their freedom of movement is a maze of confusing and ever-changing restrictions.[23] Lois silently considered the seemingly simple request before turning N'amati down. Current Israeli law forbade Israelis and foreigners from transporting Palestinians if they were not related. Lois was not prepared to risk

---

[23] Marian Houk, "Humans of Palestine," *Newsweek Middle East*, September 2, 2016. http://newsweekme.com/humans-of-palestine/

arrest or deportation. Frustration and anger over the unfairness of the situation precipitated a hot flash. N'amati brought her a glass of cold water while the rest of us fanned Lois with pieces of paper.

When things calmed down, Rita asked the women how they fastened their head scarves. "They're so graceful-looking," she declared. That was when N'amati led us to a back bedroom with a view of the *wadi* Hyam had so often spoken about—and a dresser filled with a tangle of colorful scarves. Quicker than I could have imagined, six strangers sitting on a couch became six women playing dress-up. "I should have been a nun or a Muslim," Rita said, admiring how the rust-colored scarf offset her green eyes.

"It's too damned hot for a scarf," Lois complained before reluctantly allowing one of the women to frame her moon-shaped face with mauve. They chose spring green for me, which had the undesirable effect of emphasizing my bloodshot hazel eyes. We returned to the living room wearing the headscarves, an equalizer that made us look like an extended family. After more coffee and chocolate cake, we posed for a group portrait. An onlooker would have been hard-pressed to identify each person's ethnicity, nationality, or religion. With typical Palestinian generosity, the women gave us the scarves, but their gift came with a request:

"Please remember us. *Salaam aleikum.*"

"Until we meet again. *Aleikum al salaam.* We will not forget you."

Mornings in Ramallah were ideal for walkers and joggers. Khalil left at dawn and returned home with fresh hummus, falafel, and pita bread. The next day I overcame my laziness and joined Khalil and Rita on a morning jaunt. We walked past modern apartment buildings, traditional stone houses with wraparound porches, stairways leading to hidden gardens, and an abandoned construction site with a sign posted: *Future*

Mövenpick Hotel. This well-known Swiss chain seemed to be waiting for Ramallah to become a world-class tourist destination like Tel Aviv. The detritus of war mixed with the mundane plastic-dominated garbage in makeshift dumps on open lots. Postal workers, garbage workers, and teachers had not been paid since Hamas won the 2006 election, because Israel was withholding the Palestinian Authority tax revenues. Without revenues, dumps proliferated, mail was undependable, and the civil government had little chance of success.

On the surface, everyday life in Ramallah looked amazingly normal and, compared to the rest of the West Bank, it was prosperous. People went to work; shopped; tended gardens; celebrated marriages, new babies, and graduations; and enjoyed outings to the pizza joint, bakery, and movie theatre. Lois feared that upon completion of the Separation Wall, Ramallah would become an urban island of "enemy territory," according to Israel. I held onto the hope that the doors of N'amati's prison would someday be flung open, and I would be among those to welcome her into the wider world.

A few days later, Lois drove us back to the Jaffa Gate. Rita and I met our Sabeel delegation at the Lutheran Guest House on St. Mark's Road, where the Christian Quarter meets the Jewish Quarter in the Old City. Tall protective walls and locked heavy wooden doors at the entrance made the guest house feel as secure as when it had been a Crusader fortress. The delegation sitting around wooden tables under stone arches in the dining room consisted of middle-aged and older men and women, including three ministers, a priest, a former nun, and three young adults. They hardly looked like radicals ready to bear witness and change the world. One of the young people identified herself as a Christian-Jew. Did that mean she was a Christian Zionist? Did she believe Jews must return to the Holy Land and accept Jesus as Savior, or be damned in eternal hell fires?

That night there was a knock on our door. "I hope you're still awake," said a soft voice. "I need to talk." An ethereal-looking young woman with curly brown hair and glasses so thick she was probably almost blind without them let herself into our room. Molly was the self-identified Christian-Jew. We began a heartfelt conversation about Jewish identity that continued for the duration of our two-week journey. Molly's torn loyalty came from having a Jewish mother and Christian father. I cavalierly told her, "Your mother's Jewish lineage makes you Jewish," but that simplistic answer felt like a betrayal of her father.

Who is a Jew? A descendant of a tribe exiled from Canaan 2,000 years ago? An accident of birth? By the classic definition, I'm purebred—Jewish mother, father, and grandparents on both sides in an unbroken chain. I never exercised my "birthright" to live in Israel, but I had the choice. If Faisal and I had had children, would a Palestinian father have canceled their birthright to return to the "Jewish homeland?" Are my two granddaughters, born to a gentile daughter-in-law, Jewish? What about Jewish converts from "unapproved rabbis?" Israel's Chief Rabbinate was constantly debating what constituted a legitimate conversion, including which rabbis were approved to oversee conversions.

My Jewish identity has been forged by family, culture, food, and intellectual pursuits—Mom's chicken soup, grandma's apple strudel, *knishes,* pastrami on rye, the writings of Sholem Aleichem and Isaac Bashevis Singer, who described the European *shtetl* of my grandparents. As a young adult, I devoured Holocaust novels until I personally felt hunted. I've always appreciated Judaism's concern with the treatment of our fellow humans and never worried about burning in hell, nor did I expect eternal rewards in Paradise.

Christian friends on the tour assured me that belief in the Rapture and the final Battle of Armageddon were militaristic distortions of their faith, as is the accusation that the Jews killed God. Although Christian Zionists profess to be friends of Israel, their ideology is deeply anti-Semitic and considered by many scholars to be heretical to the teachings of Jesus. In the company of my new Christian friends, I listened to

inspiring hymns echo and bounce off stone walls in ancient churches. We sailed in wooden boats on the Sea of Galilee, where Rabbi Jesus is said to have walked on water. They came with me to the Wailing Wall, where we waited for three stars to appear in the darkening sky, signaling the arrival of the Sabbath. And we stood together in the shadow of the Separation Wall, documenting the horror. Our mutual belief in human rights trumped any religious differences.

To satisfy our ever-present thirst, we bought bottled water in a dilapidated grocery store next to a defunct gas station within walking distance of the Old City. These buildings stood as ghosts of a prosperous past when this was the main road to Bethlehem, rather than a dead end next to the concrete behemoth. Twice the height and almost three times the length of the Berlin Wall, this wall snaked through the West Bank like a viper feeding on virgin land. In places it looked like a fence surrounded by trenches, barbed wire, thermal imaging scanners, video cameras, and access roads. Upon completion, it will leave many Palestinian towns and cities isolated and unable to reach farmland, water resources, schools, hospitals, or holy sites. Claiming the need to deter suicide bombers, the Israeli government began building the Wall in 2002. Sniper towers every 300 meters overlook everything, yet most Israeli military experts agree that the meandering route of the Wall, which juts deeply into the West Bank, is not defensible.

Israel's Shin Bet, the Internal Security and Intelligence Service, admitted that "flawed inspection procedures at checkpoints, gaps, and uncompleted sections enabled suicide bombers to enter Israel." Hundreds of Palestinians working inside of Israel managed to cross the Wall without a permit. The drop in attacks was not because of the so-called security wall. The bombings were not supported by the Palestinian public.[24]

In 2004, the International Court of Justice ruled that the route of the Wall violated international humanitarian law and called on Israel to dismantle it—or relocate it to the Green Line. Israel has done nothing to

---

[24] Amos Harel, "Shin Bet: Palestinian Truce Main Cause for Reduced Terror," *Haaretz*, January 2, 2006.

implement the ruling. The concrete blocks are not as permanent as they appear. They hold the possibility of squeezing people into ever-smaller spaces—or they could be removed overnight.

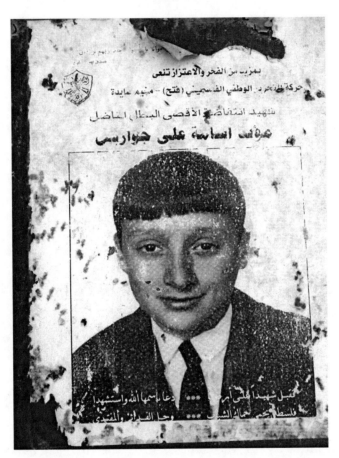

Aida Refugee Camp near Bethlehem was home to about 5,000 people living in the shadow of the Wall. Our guide, a middle-aged man wearing a shirt printed with 1948, the year of the Palestinian Nakba, met us at the camp's entrance under a concrete arch that supported a giant metal key, the symbol of lost Palestinian homes. *"Ahlein.* Please be welcomed," he said before guiding us through the camp. Except for a few shrubs adorning the UN compound, the 15 acres were unrelieved by trees, grass, or flowers. Our guide apologetically explained, "Palestinians love to grow things, but water must be saved for drinking, cooking, and washing. Sometimes we only get water once a week." Water insecurity for the most basic needs was a recurrent theme among Palestinians.

A poster plastered on a green metal door of a run-down building across the road from the Separation Wall read: *This nine-year-old child was killed while playing soccer, shot by a sniper from a watchtower in the Wall.* Did the boy's smiling face capture the moment of scoring a goal? We

were told that the bereaved father donated his son's heart to the son of a Jewish family, who later visited the refugee camp to thank the family for this priceless gift. A healthy young Palestinian heart still beats inside a Jewish body.

We climbed a stairwell to the roof of the tallest building in the camp. Many doors were ajar, giving us an opportunity to peek into apartments that were little more than concrete shells. Electricity, running water, stoves and heat were luxuries. Mothers caring for children looked curiously at us. "We may look like tourists, but we have come to bear witness so we can tell the world," I said in a language they could not understand. Most of these people were from villages now inside of Israel.

The rooftop offered panoramic views beyond the run-down buildings of the camp, beyond the potholed road, and into the olive groves on the other side of the Separation Wall. The opposing hilltop was sliced flat at the top to accommodate a new Israeli settlement. Traditional Palestinian villages originated in valleys, leaving open land for grazing, orchards, groves, and agriculture, but open land is vulnerable to being claimed by the ever-expanding settlements.

"Only our eyes can touch the olive trees whose branches welcomed us as children," said our poetic guide. Afraid to play in the street, children were flying kites on a nearby balcony. I listened to a toddler cry inconsolably when a bag of potato chips fell to the street below, lost to an unexpected breeze. How simple it would have been to ease the hurt—buy a bag of chips, run up the stairs, and deliver them. Another child took a hard fall on her one roller skate with only three wheels. I imagined telling her, "Don't cry, little girl, I'll buy you new skates." But the potato chip godmother did not come to the rescue, and there was no nearby toy store.

A celebration was happening in the streets as we were leaving. People were singing and lighting candles. One of the residents had just been released after four years in an Israeli prison. The former prisoner had been accused of taking donations from a tourist group with suspected terrorist connections. In spite of this, we gave our guide a dangerously generous tip.

The feasibility of Jewish settlers living as law-abiding citizens or foreign residents within a Palestinian State as suggested by Rabbi Froman from Tekoa was dashed during our visit to Efrat, a Jewish settlement founded in the '80s. An easy commute to Jerusalem or Bethlehem, this modern gated community with tree-lined streets shading red-tile-roofed houses even had a swimming pool for the 8,000 people who called this home. A lone olive tree in the middle of a roundabout at the settlement entrance looked as misplaced as the verdant lawns. A bulletin board outside the synagogue held announcements of upcoming events: "Lecture tomorrow entitled '*Halachic* Adjustments in the Face of Living Realities.'" *Halachic* referred to Jewish law. Adjusting Jewish law to suit living realities sounded like a slippery slope.

Wearing Bermuda shorts and a summer jersey, our host, a settlement resident, met us outside the sanctuary of the synagogue. Surrounded by beautiful stained glass windows, we sat on comfortable wooden benches in a sanctuary that reminded me of the Conservative temple I'd attended as a child. There was no separation between men and women.

Born in Chicago, Artie had been living in Israel for ten years. With an assured smile, he offered a very polished, hour-long presentation and left little time for a response, which made us quite frustrated. Over the years, I've had an extensive imagined dialogue with him.

His presentation began with American history: "The U.S. is responsible for the attempted annihilation of the Native population. Americans have no right to point the finger at another country. America set the precedent." Words I never got to speak:

Point taken. With some exceptions, the indigenous population of North America lost their ancestral lands and way of life to colonists who believed in "Manifest Destiny"—that the continent of North America from the Atlantic to the Pacific was destined for the settlers arriving from Europe. I was not alive during the genocide against Native Americans, but I am witnessing the ongoing human rights violations of Palestinians. The fact that America got away with ethnic cleansing is no defense.

Artie said, "Jews have the right to return to the land that God promised us in the Torah."

My thoughts: *The myth of God's chosen people is as audacious as it is perplexing. Abraham, originally Abram, a seemingly ordinary man from Mesopotamia, and his descendants were promised a land flowing with milk and honey, known as Canaan in the Bible. Both Jews and Muslims claim lineage to one of Abraham's sons, either Isaac or Ishmael. Coming on the heels of the goddess cultures in Mesopotamia, Judaism is the most ancient of the Abrahamic religions. Palestine is believed to be the birthplace of Jesus and the departure point of the Prophet Mohammed when he ascended to heaven. Narratives blur, converge, and eclipse one another until they become a diadem with a thousand facets. The Divine Deed means that the Promised Land has been promised to humankind.*

History offers another response to religious mythology. Early references to Palestine come from the Greek historian Herodotus in the fifth century BCE, and again when the Romans crushed a Jewish revolt in the second century CE. For thousands of years, Palestine has known a succession of rulers and conquerors. Moving backward in time, this coveted real estate currently controlled by Israel has been ruled by the British, Ottoman Turks, Mameluks, Crusaders, Ayyubids, Fatimids, Abbasids, Umayyads, Persians, Byzantines, Romans, Jewish Hasmoneans, Greeks, Seleucids, Egyptians, Macedonians, Babylonians, Kings of Judah, and so on. What if every civilization that ever conquered or lived in Palestine-Canaan-Judeah-Samaria demanded the right to return?

Documented historical evidence shows that the nucleus of Eastern European Jewry may have originated in Khazar, a kingdom north of the Caucasus Mountains between the Caspian and Black Seas. The empire's conversion to Judaism around 740 CE was pragmatic resistance to surrounding Christian and Muslim Kingdoms.[25] Upon the demise of this Empire in the thirteenth century, Jews dispersed to Poland, Lithuania, Hungary, the Crimea, and the Ukraine. According to this, I may be genetically closer to the tribes of Central Asia than to the seed of Abraham, Isaac, and Jacob. But the heart of

---

[25] Arthur Koestler, *The Thirteenth Tribe: The Khazar Empire and Its Heritage* (New York: Random House, Inc., 1976).

this conflict is not about genetic differences or similarities; it is about settler-colonialism and human rights.

The Declaration of the Establishment of the State of Israel clearly states an intention to "ensure the complete equality of social and political rights to all its inhabitants irrespective of religion, race, or sex."

Artie spoke of Jewish pride: "We have done what no other people have done. Jews were a vanquished people; then we got strong and took over."

My response: *From the ashes of the Holocaust, European Jews created a modern nation state with the strongest military in the Middle East, a sovereign nation with nuclear capabilities. Why pretend to be eternal victims? Our suffering should have taught us to be compassionate to the suffering of others.*

"We are not an occupying power. This is disputed territory," Artie proclaimed.

My response: *That sentiment conveniently ignored UN Resolution 242, which reiterates the inadmissibility of the acquisition of territory by conquest. Even former Israeli Prime Minister Ariel Sharon admitted, "To hold 3.5 million Palestinians under occupation is terrible."*

Artie said, "The West Bank was not considered occupied when it was controlled by Jordan."

Jordan was the only Arab country to offer citizenship to the Palestinians. Political limbo is a difficult state to live in.

"The occupation was the result of Palestinian terrorism," Artie asserted.

The occupation was the result of colonialism and war. Land confiscations, home demolitions, separation walls, targeted assassinations, torture, and illegal detentions are also forms of terrorism. If Chicago were under a repressive military occupation, would Artie defend his home?

"We were willing to trade land for peace when there was no precedent for this in civilization."

Wise Jewish elders, including Judah Magnes, Martin Buber, and Albert

Einstein, all believed that Israel should have been created as a bi-national state from its inception. In 1967, Israel's demographic fear stopped them from offering citizenship to Palestinians living in the conquered territories. Jewish-Israelis worried they would eventually be outnumbered by non-Jews in their Jewish State. Twenty-two Arab countries offered full recognition of Israel in 2002, in exchange for withdrawal to the internationally recognized 1967 borders, but Israel did not respond. How could Artie have forgotten that Prime Minister Rabin was assassinated because he was willing to follow the path of trading land for peace? Lost opportunities abound.

"We are infidels in the eyes of extremist Muslims," he said.

I am a self-hating Jew in the eyes of extremist Jews.

"They shoot Qassam rockets into our towns," he volleyed back.

Lacking a modern well-equipped army with the latest military hardware, Palestinians resist occupation with stones and homemade rockets. The number of Palestinians killed or maimed is far greater than the number of Israelis, but behind each statistic is an irrevocable loss to a family and community.

"They teach their children to hate us."

Growing up, I was taught to hate and fear those "damn Arabs" who wanted to drive us into the sea.

"Israelis were living in Gaza for 30 years when the Israeli Defense Force made our people leave."

In 2005, the Israeli government offered Jewish settlers huge compensation packages to relocate on the Israeli side of the Green Line. Packages ranged between $150,000 and up to $400,000 and included two years of free rent depending on house size, number of children, and years spent in Gaza. Some of the 8,000 settlers left voluntarily, while others were dragged from homes destroyed behind them so Gazans would not be able to take possession. Israeli taxpayers who had shouldered the cost of settler infrastructure, bypass roads, *and army units to defend them, were now paying to relocate them.[26] Had Artie accepted a government subsidy for his villa in Efrat? How much money would it take for him to start a life on the other side of the Green Line?*

"The difference between us and them is that we regret killing civilians."

Accusing an entire population of being bloodthirsty murderers is a deeply offensive and racist statement. Members of the Bereaved Families Forum understood that grief was greater than ethnic or religious differences.

Did Artie know that Israeli peace activists, including Uri Avery who had fought with the Irgun and was a former Knesset member, had been detained in Efrat's police station with other Israeli-Jewish activists? They were on their way to stand in solidarity with the villagers of Al-Khader who were trying to save their land from encroaching Israeli settlements.

Had the rabbi from Efrat Settlement ever discussed "Halachic adjustments" with Rabbi Froman from Tekoa, who declared that "the essence of the Torah was to welcome the stranger and treat our neighbors as we want to be treated." Rabbi Froman never said the Golden Rule applied to Jews only.

Although I never had a chance for a personal conversation with Artie, moments before he left the synagogue in Efrat, I stood up, took a deep breath and announced to my Christian friends, "Jews come in all sizes, shapes, colors and opinions. This man does not represent me, or millions of Jewish Israelis and Americans." Molly stood in support.

Photos of Efrat in 2014 show a thriving city. Temporary outposts and quaint red-tile-roofed cottages have become seven-story apartment buildings to accommodate the increasing numbers of Jewish settlers. Open hillsides have been carved into roads, villas, schools, and synagogues for Jewish settlers who do not need expensive permits to build or expand

---

[26] Amira Hass, interview by Amy Goodman, *Democracy Now!* August 8, 2005. Hass is an Israeli-Jewish journalist with *Haaretz Newspaper* who reports on events in Gaza and the West Bank. www.democracy now.org/2005/8/16/jewish_settlers_receive_hundreds_of_thousands

their earthly home in the Promised Land.[27] From 2009 to 2013, a huge network of U.S. nonprofit organizations have raised more than $220 million to expand illegal Jewish settlements in the occupied West Bank. Donors often have no idea their tax deductible donations are being spent to promote and support a military occupation designed to suffocate the Palestinians.

Farid came to the Lutheran Guest House soon after I phoned. Except for an occasional email, we'd not been in touch for twelve years. His hair had become silver. A trimmed goatee, tinted glasses, a pinstriped cotton shirt, and dress trousers made him look quite dapper. "*Alhamdulillah,* thanks to God, my family is well."

As we walked side by side through the streets of the Old City, Farid reminded me that my personal history was written in the stones, and that's why I always longed to return. We had a trust and ease that came from having known each other for many decades. In the past, Farid had no problem securing permission for me to enter the Dome of the Rock, but today Israeli soldiers guarded every access to the holy shrine: only Muslims allowed. Security was tight and tensions were high ever since Israeli archaeologists had begun excavation near the Wailing Wall and Temple Mount. Muslims worried the digging could undermine the mosque's foundation. The archaeologists were searching for remnants of Solomon's Temple—shards, carvings, tiles, mosaics, anything to prove the existence of the ancient Hebrew Kingdom which would, in their eyes, further legitimize the Jewish state.

Farid and I contented ourselves with a leisurely stroll on the broad esplanade of the Sacred Plateau. Statuesque palms and cyprus trees

---

[27] Uri Blau, "Why is the U.S. Subsidizing Israeli Settlements?" *Washington Post*, December 12, 2015. www.washingtonpost.com/opinions/why-is-the-us-subsidizing-israeli-settlements/2015/12/21/407c3558-a781-11e5-9b92-dea7cd4b1a4d_story.html

exuded a sense of serenity. I noticed details I'd never seen before: an ancient sundial mounted over a carved doorway; a granite mosaic of a stylized sun embedded like an eternal welcome mat in front of a minor entrance; school children studying with their teacher in the shade of a gazebo.

Shops on Chabad Street leading to the Wailing Wall were filled with Jewish artifacts—prayer shawls, *yarmulkes*, *menorahs*, candlesticks, and *mezuzahs*. Pregnant, kerchief-clad women pushed carriages trailed by toddlers holding hands with older siblings. Responding to the Biblical injunction to "be fruitful and multiply," Orthodox Jewish families tended to be large. We passed a shop with an eye-catching display of Persian rugs, traditional and modern jewelry, and exotic curios and artifacts. Farid told me the shop was owned by a distant cousin to Faisal.

Stepping inside the shop, Farid introduced me to Khalid, a charming middle-aged man with a friendly face and ready smile. Whenever I dropped by, which was as often as I could, I met journalists, writers, filmmakers, art collectors, and travelers from around the world who gathered here to discuss what was foremost in everyone's mind—the painful realities of occupation. We sat on colorful rugs and hassocks drinking Turkish coffee served by Khalid, who introduced me as his long-lost ex-sister-in-law, a title I relished. A consummate businessman, he had the uncanny ability to speak the appropriate language to any tourist who showed the slightest interest in his merchandise. Code-switching between Hebrew, German, French, New York hipster, and the Queen's English, Khalid reminded me of my grandfather, a multi-lingual Brooklyn grocer who had learned to speak to his customers in their native tongues.

Near the Church of the Holy Sepulchre, in the Aftimos market where I had met Faisal's cousin Ahmed almost 40 years ago, Farid told me that many of the shops here were being sold to Israelis. He shook his head back and forth, as if to say, woe is me. The ancient buildings in the Christian, Muslim, and Armenian Quarters were clearly in need of maintenance, but the Jewish Quarter sparkled with new synagogues, modern apartments, shops, cafés, restaurants, and comfortable squares that enticed people to gather. Much of the development was built on remnants of old structures. The municipality planned to build more than 1,000 new homes in East Jerusalem—for Jews only, which meant Palestinian homes would have to be demolished. Under the guise of religion and security, a demographic

battle was raging. Every historic hotel, shop, or building sold to an Israeli made it harder to believe that East Jerusalem would ever become the capital of a future Palestinian state.

We ate lunch in Abu Taher's unglamorous restaurant on some back street in the Old City. With a generous portion of delicious hummus, baba ghannouj, and a cucumber-yogurt salad, I understood why this affordable eatery was so popular with locals. After we finished eating, I showed Farid the photos of Faisal, Samira, and their children from my recent visit in Buffalo. "Samira looks wonderful, but Faisal must lose poundage," Farid admonished. "You both should have stayed in Jerusalem." His comment surprised me. In 1967, Farid had been the only person to question the wisdom of Faisal marrying a foreign woman he had known for such a short time. It made me wonder if our marriage would have survived in a traditional Muslim society. Would Faisal have continued to write poetry, play the *oud*, become an activist? Impossible questions to answer. Although neither of us was hungry, we went to Zalatimo's for *knafeh*, as if dessert could invoke a lost past.

Farid invited Rita and me for dinner at his home in Al-Azaria, a village near the Old City. We met at his library and drove together. A trip that used to take minutes took over an hour. Road closures, checkpoints, bottlenecks, and the Separation Wall created a horrible traffic jam.

The house faced breathtaking vistas of the Mount of Olives and the Kidron Valley. The last time I'd visited here, I was a young bride sitting next to my groom in the cool shade of a white-tiled courtyard. The two-story house built by his grandfather was shared by Farid's wife, four of their six children, five grandchildren, his four unmarried brothers, an unmarried sister, and a pet gerbil. Functioning as kitchen, dining room, living room, library, and study, the cramped but cozy room where we gathered to eat had a couch and two easy chairs next to a low wooden table. The once spacious house was bursting at the seams. Palestinians are not allowed to repair or add rooms to their homes—or build new ones—without obtaining difficult-to-acquire Israeli permits. Permission to build a modest home on land they owned could cost more than the building itself. Even if a family had the tenacity, patience, and money to go through a process so fraught with red tape, permits were typically denied, which explained why many Palestinians built "illegally," risking expensive fines and the possibility of their home being demolished. The destruction might not happen for years, but once an order was issued, it was never annulled. To avoid paying fines, Palestinians have been known to destroy their own home.

Farid's wife, Inaz, who I was meeting for the first time, was a petite, soft-spoken woman who worked as a social worker in Jerusalem, the city where she was born and raised. Their daughter lived with her husband and three children in nearby Abu Dis, on the other side of a checkpoint. From a security perspective, separating the Palestinian villages of Al-Azaria and Abu Dis by a wall was absurd.

With typical Palestinian hospitality, Rita and I were offered a feast. Remembering how it used to be, I helped myself to the stuffed zucchini and grape leaves using my fingers, until I noticed everyone else was using forks. Farid's oldest daughter, a special education teacher, spoke about her frustrations and challenges—large classes, over-reliance on tests, and the need for more family involvement and a relevant curriculum. As a veteran educator, these problems were familiar. The family hoped their youngest daughter, attending college in the States, would return home after graduation, but they worried about her limited work opportunities. Farid's family lived within Jerusalem's administrative boundaries, and as such, they did not need a special permit to work in Israel. Their identity cards granted them residency status, and they were allowed to vote in local elections, but they did not have the rights or protection of citizenship. And if Farid's family left for any reason, their home could be seized under the Israeli Absentee Property Law, and they would have no right to return. Many *dunams* of land have been lost through such so-called legal means.

"You can see Al-Quds University from the living room window," Farid said, pointing toward the valley in the distance. "My son used to walk to school. Now he has to drive to the checkpoint in Abu Dis, and he never knows how long it will take. But what can you do?" Raising his eyes heavenward, he stoically accepted the hardship as a divine decree. "*Hamdulillah*, thanks be to God, we are fine."

Farid never mentioned the large-scale archaeological dig happening in nearby Silwan. About 55,000 people live in this ancient village in the

Kidrun Valley. Around 700 BC, the Jebusites carved a tunnel from an ancient spring in Silwan so they could bring water inside the Old City. In 1986, archaeological control was given to a religious organization called the *Ir David* (City of David) Foundation. Their goal is to create Jewish communities in Arab neighborhoods of East Jerusalem. The digging had created cracks in the foundations of nearby homes and caused roads to collapse, but had not produced definitive evidence of the historical kingdoms of David nor Solomon. And even if a cornerstone with their imprint were to be discovered, the ethnic cleansing of Palestinian neighborhoods and the violation of their human rights would not be justified.

After dinner, Inaz made tea from mint growing in a window flowerpot. All evening Rita and Tariq, Farid's youngest son, enjoyed the endless antics of the pet gerbil, whose diminutive size guaranteed the pet more freedom of movement than anyone in the family. Wanting to practice his English, Tariq showed us his schoolbooks. I surreptitiously searched them for anti-Israeli, anti-Zionist, or anti-Jewish propaganda, but all I found were essays on literature, science, art, and history. There was not enough time for an in-depth analysis to decide which historical narrative was being presented—that the Jews arrived in an empty land waiting for a people, or that the creation of Israel had resulted in catastrophic dislocation for the indigenous non-Jews of Palestine.

Before we left, Farid's wife presented Rita and me with an array of modern embroidered dresses. "Choose one," she said. The generosity and kindness of this close-knit family was overwhelming. When Farid's oldest son drove us to the Jaffa Gate, we passed near the Separation Wall. I took comfort from the graffiti imprinted there: *Friends cannot be divided.*

From Ramallah and Jerusalem to Bethlehem and Hebron, I recorded images and words with my camera, my pen, and my heart. *From the Warsaw Ghetto to Abu Dis Ghetto* must have been painted on the wall by a student of history. Warsaw had been the site of a violent Jewish uprising during World War II. Most insurgents were killed and the survivors transported to concentration camps. When Jews remember this massacre, sorrow mingles with pride for their incredible heroism. Abu Dis was no longer the bucolic village on the outskirts of Jerusalem where Faisal's mother lived after the war. Surrounded by settlements and sliced by the Separation Wall, this village had become a ghetto, like the one in Poland where the Jews had lived. The graffiti reminded the world that humans will risk everything to be free.

Elsewhere on the Wall was the image of a soldier, his arms raised in a gesture of surrender as he gets a pat-down by a pigtailed girl in a pink party dress. Another image: a diapered toddler sat on the beach playing with his pail and shovel, dappled white clouds floating overhead. This idyll, painted beneath a sniper tower, underscored the human tragedy. The seamless concrete barrier separated Palestinians from each other, from their neighbors, their schools, their holy sites, their land, and from Israelis. There were no cracks for paper prayers like the Wailing Wall, but anyone with a can of spray paint was free to express his or her horror, dream, vision, curse, prayer, or nugget of wisdom.

The lyrics of a Simon and Garfunkel song sprung forth—*"The words of the prophets are written on the subway walls / and tenement halls"*—to which I would add—and the Separation Wall. Snippets of graffiti came hurtling from the Wall to form a message:

This dumb wall is screaming.

Our blood is the same color.

I am not a terrorist.

Sharon + Bush + Blair = 3 Terrorists

Only free men can negotiate.

Seattle supports Palestine!

Scotland supports Palestine!

Hell's Kitchen supports Palestine!

God is too big for one religion.

Friends cannot be divided.

Here is a wall at which to weep.

FORTY YEARS AGO TODAY

May 2007: thousands of celebrants rampaged through the streets of the Old City, singing and dancing in a sea of blue-and-white flags—by the Wailing Wall, on the ancient rooftops, and in every street and alleyway. Loud, boisterous, patriotic songs unlike the sweet, plaintive tunes of Hebrew prayer. Israeli-Jews were celebrating *Yom Yerushalim* (Jerusalem Day), a national holiday commemorating the so-called unification of East and West Jerusalem, "the eternal spiritual capital of the Jewish State." Religious Jews once believed that the creation of a Jewish nation state should await the arrival of the Messiah, but now they were thanking God for their victory in the 1967 War.

For me, remembrance of the Israeli conquest evoked the trauma of war and humiliation of defeat. The sounds of nearby explosions made me want to hide like I did 40 years before. Friends with no memories of war ran to the rooftop of the Lutheran Guest House and confirmed that fireworks, not bombs, were lighting up the night sky. Wanting to remain invisible, Palestinians living in the Old City stayed home. The idea of a united city was a cruel joke. Jerusalem, the heart of religious, political, cultural, and economic life for millions of Palestinians in the West Bank, was deliberately being severed from the towns and villages that had been its historic veins and arteries.

The next day our Sabeel delegation headed to Hebron. We rode in a modern air-conditioned bus on a modern highway built for the exclusive use of international tourists and Israelis—civilians and military. The sweeping desert landscape was marred by views of the Separation Wall which ended abruptly in places as if admitting its uselessness. On a hillside outside of Jerusalem, a huge billboard advertised a future gated settlement called Nof Zion. Printed in Hebrew and English, it read:

Nof Zion's View will have a synagogue, hotel, country club, and public gardens. You can have all this in a harmonious neighborhood with extravagant views of the Old City, the Dome of the Rock, and the Mount of Olives. Next year in Jerusalem!

Israeli condos were being pitched as if inspired by the Passover *Haggadah*. Developers planned to build five-story buildings with 395 condos on 28 acres—for Jews only. Meanwhile the nearby underfunded Palestinian village of Jabal Mukaber had no street lights or sidewalks and was not allowed to hook up to the new sewage system. Bulldozers were permanently altering the landscape in the West Bank. Hilltops once covered with forests; olive groves; and almond, cyprus and fig trees had to accommodate ever-expanding settlement-cities on Palestinian land.

The saddest and most frightening place I visited was Hebron, where the bones of occupation were laid bare. Since 1997, the city had been sliced into two sectors—H1 and H2. Palestinians living under Israeli military control dealt with extended curfews and restrictions on their movement. The lines between the sectors were becoming increasingly blurred as settlers expanded into so-called Palestinian Zones. We stood on a Palestinian rooftop with our guide, a 66-year-old former nun from the States who volunteered with the Christian Peacemakers Teams (CPT). A temporary project that started after the 1994 massacre in the

Ibrahim Mosque had become as permanent as the occupation. From our vantage, we could see the Tomb of the Patriarchs, nearby synagogues, Jewish settlements, Muslim and Jewish cemeteries, the abandoned market, and soldiers on military rooftop outposts who watched us as we watched them.

Shuhada Street, the main commercial thoroughfare, was eerily quiet. Only settlers, soldiers, and internationals were allowed to walk

MAP OF HEBRON CITY CENTER

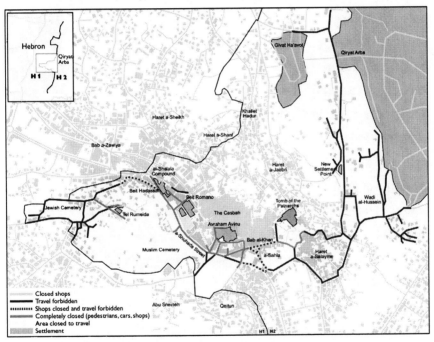

Printed with permission from B'Tselem – The Israeli Information Center for Human Rights in the Occupied Territories. www.btselem.org/download/200705_hebron_center_map_eng.pdf

there. According to *B'Tselem*, an Israeli human rights organization, by 2006 over 1,000 Palestinian homes in the center of Hebron had been padlocked, and almost 2,000 businesses and shops had been welded shut by the Israeli government. Windows were covered with iron bars to protect them from being smashed by settlers. Ancient walls were scribbled with recycled Holocaust slogans: *Arabs to the Gas Chambers, Transfer Arabs, Kill Arabs.*

I was disheartened by the hatred. Gone were the old men playing backgammon and drinking coffee by outdoor tables. Where were the blacksmith bending steel at his forge, the squawking chickens, the bakery, the glass blowers, and the pottery vendors? Jewish settlement in the heart of Hebron had created a ghost town. We passed a Palestinian home recently taken over by settlers. Our CPT guide warned, "Let me speak if we're stopped by soldiers." Defying the Israeli government's order to evacuate the home, settlers had continued to make repairs, claiming their right to remain in the home. The Knesset knew what was happening, but nothing changed. The rift between Israeli law and the implementation of the law is growing.

International law affords all children the right to attend school, including Palestinian children in Hebron who walked to school along rooftops to avoid being spat upon or attacked.[28] The children entered the street through a house near their school, known as the Ladder Lady's house—a mythic-sounding place, but unlike Jacob's ladder to heaven, this one led straight into the jaws of occupation. Our guide told us that when Palestinian children played games, they pretended to be soldiers. They understood that whoever carried guns had real power.

I was reminded several times by activists and soldiers that the army was in Hebron to safeguard Jewish settlers walking between their settlement and the synagogue, not to provide justice or basic security for Palestinians.

---

[28] UN Human Rights Office of the High Commissioner, Convention on the Rights of the Child, ratified by General Assembly resolution, November 1989. "Considering that the child should be fully prepared to live an individual life in society, and brought up in the spirit of the ideals proclaimed in the UN Charter, in particular in the spirit of peace, dignity, tolerance, freedom, equality and solidarity... Article 28: Parties must recognize the right of the child to education..." www.ohchr.org

Tension crackled through the air along with the sound of Hebrew prayer. We were in the synagogue side of the Tomb of the Patriarchs. A soldier, covered by his *tallit*, a prayer shawl, stood before the ark, his machine gun following the sway of his body as if engaged in a macabre

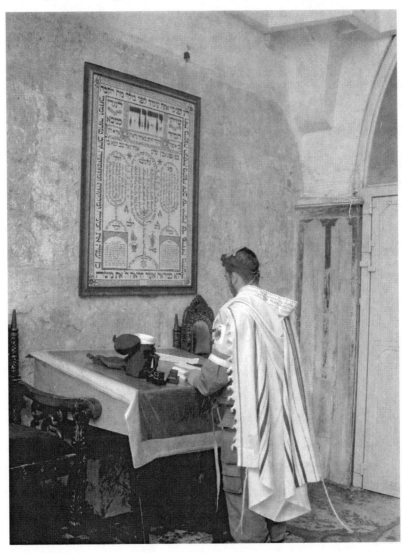

dance. Another soldier approached our group. Speaking to no one in particular, he asked, "Where you guys from? Why you here?" He was checking us out. Clearly, we were not here to pray. The rolling sound of the letter "r" and the missing verbs let me know he was not an American-Israeli. Being the only Jewish member in our group, I took it upon myself to answer the young soldier who had been ordered to guard this synagogue with a machine gun.

After explaining that New Mexico was part of the United States, I volleyed back a question: "You're not Ashkenazi Jew, like me. Is your family from Morocco?"

He looked startled. "How you know this?" Morocco was a lucky guess. His olive complexion, black hair and dark eyes announced his Middle Eastern ethnicity to the world.

"Do you speak Arabic?" I asked. It was my turn to check him out.

"I understand. My grandmother always speak Arabic when she talk about her home in Fez."

"So you are an Arab-Jew," I brazenly declared. Israelis from Yemen, Morocco, Iraq, or Syria, countries that once harbored great Jewish communities, rarely identified themselves as Arab. They were simply known as *Mizrahi*, a Hebrew word meaning "from the East." I started to walk away, but he followed.

"I'm from Haifa," he said, determined to continue our conversation. "When I'm home, I'm not like this. I'm more real." By "more real," I assumed he meant he didn't walk around with his fingers on the trigger of a machine gun. Perhaps this soldier had Christian, Muslim, and Jewish friends in Haifa, known to be an ethnically mixed city.

I looked into the warm brown eyes of this young soldier and said, "You are a bridge. You understand Arabic, know the culture, love the food and music, and share traditions. You can help other Israelis understand their real enemy is fear. Tell them security doesn't come from the barrel of a gun. I hope to return someday when the streets of Hebron are not filled with soldiers." At this thought, involuntary tears welled in my eyes.

"God willing. Let it be so. No one ever talked to me like this."

The Israeli soldier escorted me to the street like a protector, not an armed guard. We never exchanged names. Luckily he didn't walk me to the mosque side of the sacred structure, which was guarded by Israeli soldiers who would not let me enter if they knew I was Jewish. I was upset and baffled when our trusted Palestinian guide told the soldiers that Molly and I were Jewish.

"No Jews allowed," they said, "by order of the Palestinian Authority."

With a sense of outraged entitlement, we waved our American passports in their faces, to no avail. Forced to accept the edict that we were denied access based on our religious identification, we waited in the shade of buildings alongside a concrete road barrier. I thought back to the summer's day in 1967 when I casually walked passed this mosque with Faisal and his family, before there were any soldiers.

American passports allowed us entrance into H1, the area of Hebron administered by the Palestinian Authority. Armed soldiers wearing red berets watched us file through a turnstile inside a cage surrounded by barbed wire. Our Palestinian bus driver and guide were prohibited from going through this checkpoint, but they knew how to sneak around. I couldn't understand why Palestinians were not allowed to enter the Palestinian-administered area. I later realized that our guide had slyly given us a lesson on the humiliation and arbitrary nature of occupation.

On the other side of the checkpoint, the world came alive with shoppers in a vast outdoor market. Nets fastened between rooftops to catch falling debris and garbage thrown by soldiers stationed on top of buildings looked as permanent as the rain gutters on my house.

We ate lunch at the Resistance Café, where the owner limped around while serving falafel sandwiches, sodas, and bottled water. When his work was done, he sat down and spoke with us. We were his only customers.

"This café is a symbol of the struggle to maintain Palestinian life in Hebron. Most Palestinians have made a commitment to stay no matter what. Like many others, I have been tortured in an Israeli prison. We would rather die in our homes than walk away like many did in 1948. My greatest act of resistance is to keep this café open."

He helped us understand the importance of this café which was little more than a few tables under a tarp. With each bite of falafel and sip of water, we became a small part of the resistance.

Walking back to the bus, we listened to vendors cry out, "Help us. We are merchants. Buy something, anything." We passed stalls filled with dresses, scarves, jewelry, glassware, trinkets—including trays of old metal keys. Each key represented the end of a dream to return home. We looked to be the only tourists in town, but we were in a hurry, and all we bought that day were falafel sandwiches, soda pop, and bottled water.

What a relief it was to be sitting in the shade of a forest away from cities, settlements, the Separation Wall, Jewish-only highways, checkpoints—anything associated with the occupation. We were walking through a national park near Jerusalem with Eitan Bronstein, a rugged-looking middle-aged Israeli. At 18, he had unquestioningly joined the Israeli army. Years later, after attending a workshop sponsored by the

Oasis of Peace, he learned a more complex version of history and became passionate about educating internationals and fellow Israelis.

"Canada Park, where we are now, was named for Canadian donors who were unaware their money was being used to annex a portion of the

West Bank. This park was planted in the seventies on the ruins of three Palestinian villages destroyed in 1967—Imwas, Yalu, and Beit Nuba. The 5,000 villagers who lived here became refugees."

These villages located at the strategic Latrun Junction were suspected of supporting Palestinians in 1948 when Israeli fighters failed to secure the corridor between Tel Aviv and Jerusalem, leaving the fledgling country with a narrow bottleneck of land. There was nothing to indicate we were standing on the Palestinian side of the armistice line, also known as the Green Line, the internationally recognized border between Israel and Jordan.

Our guide was the director of *Zochrot*, an Israeli organization whose members traveled all over the country erecting handmade signs in Arabic and Hebrew naming Palestinian villages that were destroyed in 1948. *Zochrot* is the feminine plural Hebrew word meaning "we remember." Typically, these alternative signs were taken down or blackened within hours, like the ones we saw in Canada Park. Official park signs marked a Roman bathhouse, Crusader fortress, and buildings from the Hellenic and Ottoman past. Without Eitan, we would not have understood the significance of the almond trees shading scattered stone blocks that had once been a mosque, a school, and an unmarked cemetery.

The reality of occupation had just invaded the forest.

Eitan explained that the Jewish National Fund (JNF), established in 1901, had bought land all over Palestine. Early Zionists planted pine trees, chosen for their ability to grow quickly and very tall—unlike the slow-growing, fruit-bearing indigenous almond and olive trees. The Legal Center for Arab Minority Rights in Israel petitioned the Israeli Supreme Court in 2004, challenging the prohibition of Arab-Israeli citizens from living on land owned by the Jewish National Fund. They lost. The land was officially declared the collective property of Jewish people around the world.

"Kids across America went door to door holding blue-and-white tin cans, known as a *pushke* in Yiddish, asking for donations to plant trees in Israel."

"I was one of those kids," I chimed in. "I thought we were helping to make the desert bloom."

Months later, while cooking a traditional Passover breakfast of fried matzoh in a batter of milk and eggs, I read an advertisement on the matzoh package. It boasted how the Jewish National Fund had planted over 240 million trees, built over 180 dams and reservoirs, and created more than 1,000 parks throughout the "Jewish homeland." A toll-free number was printed under a picture of a leafy tree with tendrils leading to a quote from Leviticus: *"When you come to the land you shall plant trees."* It didn't say what kind of tree. In 2010, a massive forest fire on Mount Carmel burned over 6,000 acres of these easily ignitable fast-growing pines.

Hiding historical facts in Israeli national parks was not new. Eighty-six Palestinian villages destroyed in 1948 lie buried in other parks. Eitan was frustrated by the denial of painful historic truths among most Jewish-Israelis. A notable exception was famous Israeli war hero General Moshe Dayan. On April 4, 1969, *Haaretz*, Israel's liberal newspaper, printed his declarative statement: *"There is not one place built in this country that did not have a former Arab population."*

Eitan told one last story. "Many years ago, a number of sheep were stolen from a *kibbutz*. It was believed they were stolen by someone from a nearby Palestinian village. Soldiers went to reclaim the lost animals and tried to arrest an old man who was the suspected thief. He begged the soldiers, 'If you make me leave my home, it's like death, so bury me in my home.' The home was destroyed with the old man inside of it."

When Israeli soldiers entered our Ramallah apartment 40 years ago, I could only think of three Hebrew words—*bereshet* (in the beginning), *shem* (name), and *shalom* (peace). I have a new word—*zochrot*, we remember. Like an incantation, I softly repeat the names of the three villages destroyed in 1967—Imwas, Yalu, Beit Nuba. We remember.

An Israeli friend told me she had attended a *Zochrot* sign-raising ceremony. "It was a sunny day in November, 2005. About 100 people were gathered in Nof Yam, the town north of Tel Aviv where I grew up. Israelis were meeting Palestinian elders who had lived in the village before the arrival of Jewish immigrants. My family came from Russia in the early 1900s. Facing the elders, I told them that as a young girl I loved walking to the mosque sitting on a cliff overlooking the sea. Every Friday afternoon, Arab families from nearby villages came to pray in the mosque which was near a Jewish transit camp with small houses and tents. I watched the faces of the elders as they remembered their lost homes and realized my parents' home might have been built on their farm or vineyard. I looked into their eyes and said, 'I'm sorry. Forgive me.' I cannot describe how healing this was for everyone."

The traditional Palestinian system of justice holds an entire tribe culpable for crimes committed by individual members. Revenge is the redress for a wronged family or tribe. Bloodshed can be prevented by a *sulha*, an ancient form of conflict resolution. When my Israeli friend stepped forward that morning to apologize to the Palestinian elders, she took the first step. In an ideal world, this would have been followed by a ceremony with thousands of Israelis accepting responsibility for inflicting unnecessary hardship on the indigenous people of Palestine. All sides would then deliberate until they arrived at a mutually acceptable agreement regarding rights and compensation. Even life-and-death conflicts can be diffused with a dose of honesty, humility, and respect.

As a child of the counterculture, I was hoping the Big Hug would be the mother of all *sulhas*—Woodstock in Jerusalem. On May 21, 2007, thousands of Israelis, Palestinians, and internationals planned to encircle the Old City with a healing love. Part of me was too old and cynical to take this airy-fairy spiritual event seriously, but I did believe in the power of intention. If a critical mass of people held hands around this conflict-riddled city with thoughts of ushering in an era of peace, love, and brotherhood, I wanted to be there. The idealism of the sixties was about to be challenged by the harsh realities of Mideast politics.

When I got to the Damascus Gate, world media was ready to document this well-publicized, possibly world-changing event. TV cameras surrounded an intriguing-looking talking circle. Eliyahu McClain, a self-described Hassidic Highlander with curly sideburns dangling beneath a skullcap, stood beside his peace partner, white-turbaned Haj Ibrahim Abu

ElHawa. Eliyahu spoke first.

"We are here for peace, justice, equality, and unity in the family of Abraham. Jerusalem is the city of God. Let us remember, we are one family!"

Others chimed in.

"I traveled from Holland to be here. I believe together we can create an energetic shift." The woman's words smacked of esoteric knowledge beyond my ken.

"I'm tired of being afraid to get on a bus or sit in a café or restaurant. I want to live peacefully with my Arab neighbors," said an Israeli man wearing a wide-brimmed straw hat.

"Amen," the crowd responded.

"I want to create a vision of inclusion. Everyone must be invited into the circle," said a woman whose English was laced with a foreign accent.

"Amen."

"We must end the tragic cycle of violence and keep hope alive."

"Amen." "Amen." "Amen."

Words seemed to sprout from all around the circle. Even when people spoke languages I couldn't understand, their intentions were clear. Internationals and Israelis—most of whom had once been soldiers—held hands; played flutes, drums, and guitars; and danced barefoot while singing in Arabic, Hebrew, and English. Local Palestinians watched the spectacle from an overlooking sidewalk. When celebrants invited disbelieving Palestinians to join the circle, several young men stepped forward to accept this splendid reality, even if it only lasted for an hour. A palpable hunger for peace and coexistence resonated through the crowd.

The antics of this love-in demonstration threw patrolling Israeli soldiers into momentary confusion. A bronze-skinned woman with curly black hair tamed by hundreds of tiny braids drummed as she moved towards enthralled soldiers who temporarily eased their grip on machine guns. "Dance with her. Be seduced," I silently entreated. The woman's lithe body moved gracefully under a loose fitting saffron tunic. Another woman, dressed in a constricting military uniform, danced as freely as if she too, were wearing a diaphanous robe. Eyes closed and unarmed, she appeared to be performing before an invisible audience. Universal dances of peace were led by a woman I'd met years ago at the Oasis of Peace. Her hair had turned silver, but her olive skin was still smooth. A Yemenite Jew, she conversed in Arabic with a woman in a long black embroidered dress whose hair was covered with a white *hijab*. Photographers swarmed around them as a symbol of friendship between Jews and Muslims.

Eliyahu and the Sheikh stretched the circle until it became a wavy line facing the Damascus Gate. A spirited *shalom/salaam* chant was followed by silence, broken by the ubiquitous sound of a Ram's horn, and then the singing of a Hebrew prayer, *ain k'elo-heinu*, and the Arabic call to prayer, *la ilaha illa Allah*—both of which pointed to one God above all.

To bestow a blessing on Jerusalem, we raised our palms towards the Old City and sang a rousing rendition of "Down by the Riverside." *I'm gonna lay down my sword and shield / down by the riverside / down by the riverside... Ain't gonna study war no more...* And we believed every word.

Almost 500 people gathered by the Jaffa Gate; about 50 held a drumming circle near the Lion's Gate; 100 stood by the Dung Gate near the Wailing Wall; and 30 walked the perimeter. There were not enough people to encircle the Old City, but no one had been shot or arrested, and there had been no violence.

Suddenly someone yelled, *"Moshiach! Moshiach!"* Like fulfillment of Biblical prophecy, everyone looked toward the imminent arrival of the anointed one. An old Arab man was leading a white donkey with a child riding on its back. Zechariah had foretold, "Your Messiah will come to you, triumphant and victorious, humble and riding an ass."

Highway One came to a temporary halt as we followed the white donkey across six lanes of endless traffic to celebrate our action in a nearby park. Someday this event might be hailed as another blast on the horn, weakening the walls of racism and fear. But the day after the Big Hug, nothing changed in the lives of Palestinians. Displacement, separation, and occupation continued.

Drunk on hope, it took me months to realize that Faisal's grandfather's house lay buried somewhere beneath that six-lane highway. After 1948, a Palestinian village languished in the desolation of No Man's Land. In 1967, it was rediscovered and destroyed. By 2007, the village had disappeared beneath black asphalt, its history erased.

Still hoping to find the former Mandelbaum Gate, I discovered the Museum on the Seam, located on the edge of the former border between east and west Jerusalem. IDF soldiers wandered through powerful art installations, dedicated to teaching Israelis about dialogue, coexistence, and social justice. Each soldier's face was a road map of their ethnic background—European, African, Arab and American. In the museum's gift shop, I found a historic photo of the sign that had once been posted on both sides of the divide known as No Man's Land. In Arabic, Hebrew, and English, it read, *Danger! Stop! Frontier Ahead!*

Shavuot, a Jewish holiday celebrating the harvest and the gift of the Torah, came on the heels of the Big Hug. In a custom dating back hundreds of years, people stayed up all night studying the holy texts at home or in synagogues. At dawn there were community gatherings to celebrate having received the Ten Commandments.

When Marc and I visited Susie in Jerusalem 1998, the middle aged matron who greeted us at the door of her modest apartment bore no resemblance to the construction-worker woman we'd known in Taos. She wore a wig, a long loose-fitting, ankle-length dress, and clunky shoes. Susie's dream of studying Jewish mysticism had taken her from the mountains of northern New Mexico to Jerusalem, where she'd become a Kabbalah teacher. After lighting the Friday night candles and serving us a sumptuous meal, Susie declared that Sabbath was a time to talk about anything and everything. I had just returned from traveling in Gaza and the West Bank and needed to express my horror about the occupation. I felt Israel was violating the heart of Judaism: treat your neighbor as you want to be treated. Susie countered by claiming the Torah required Jews to maintain a strong army. That she believed military might was the path to Jewish salvation shocked and disappointed me. We each remained unconvinced of the other's point of view.

Shavuot 2007: I hesitated to call Susie but very much wanted to be at a gathering where Jews were celebrating when the Law was given to humankind. Without referring to our contentious visit eight years before, Susie unhesitatingly invited me to her home. "Bring something sweet to share. There will be about twelve women." From the guest house on St. Mark's Road, I walked along Chabad Street to Susie's home in the Jewish Quarter near the Wailing Wall. She still lived in the same tiny third-floor apartment, which was decorated with leafy green plants and flowers in honor of the miraculous blooms that appeared on Mount Sinai in expectation of the Torah.

"Welcome, welcome Iris, *gut yontif*, happy holiday. I am now called Sarah Yehudi." She looked softer, almost priestess-like in a loose-fitting gown of greens, golds, and browns. A colorful *kippah* rested on her head, and a silver braid hung down her back. The table was set with bottles of wine, challah, pita bread, hummus, olives, a variety of salads, and cheesecakes. Roast chicken and a brisket simmered in the oven.

Before moving to Israel, the orthodox women gathered here had been secular Jewish Americans. They ranged in age from 20 to 60-something. I was treated like a sister who was still evolving. One woman took me by the hand and led me down the steep hill to join the community gathering at the Wailing Wall. She adroitly wove a path through the crowd until we were face-to-face with the Herodian stones. I was not carrying a *siddur* (prayer book) like most of the women, and the only prayer I had was a 40-year-old question: *When will Israelis and Palestinians be able to share this land as equals?*

Upon returning to the apartment, we recited the Hebrew blessing for washing hands. Sitting at the head of the table, Sarah Yehudi lit the holiday candles, blessed the wine and bread, and held up a cheesecake. "Studying Torah is sweet on your tongue, very sweet—like this cake." Everyone smiled.

The women around this table were curious to know about their teacher's past. "Tell us a secret about her. What was she like?" They could never have imagined Sarah Yehudi dressed in coveralls, a torn T-shirt, and a baseball cap worn backward while she filled old tires with dirt before stacking them to build the walls of an off-the-grid solar house. Sarah's hands were now soft. She had not done manual labor in years. The women enjoyed hearing bits and pieces of their teacher's life in Taos.

Sarah invited everyone to share a secret about themselves. One woman spoke of the humiliation she felt when falsely accused of stealing. My turn. I hesitated. What could I possibly share with these women? I shared what was on my mind.

"Yesterday I went to the Big Hug. People from all over the world surrounded Jerusalem with love. Israelis, Palestinians, and internationals held hands as equals. No one was held above the other. No one was singled out as 'The Chosen.' We sang and danced and celebrated as if peace had already descended. It was inspiring." Silence filled the room until one of the women finally spoke.

"You have just described what it will be like when the *Moshiach* comes."

"We are the Messiahs," I said daringly. "We are the ones we've been waiting for."

Sarah Yehudi spoke, shifting from Biblical jargon to psychological. "Those whom we perceive as the enemy reflect a part of ourselves not yet claimed." A few nodded, absorbing this profundity before moving to the next secret. I told the women I felt exhausted. They planned to study the holy texts all night and advised me to lie on the couch until the fatigue passed. Around midnight I said *layla tov* (goodnight) and walked alone through the deserted streets of the Old City. To my surprise and relief, I was not afraid.

At dawn I was awakened by Hebrew chants pouring through my window. The Jewish community was celebrating receiving the Law. At the same time church bells pealed, and the *muezzins'* call to prayer echoed through the streets. The cacophony mingled inside of me until they became joyously harmonic. I went to the rooftop of the guest house to watch the sky grow light and imagined the twelve women dancing by the Wailing Wall, ready to embrace their enemy as an unacknowledged part of themselves.

಄

After our witness tour ended, Rita and I went back to Ramallah. Khalil had invited us to visit his village in the Galilee. While getting ready to leave town, a seemingly mundane moment would come back to haunt us. Khalil and I were waiting impatiently in his car that was parked in front of a camera shop across the street from a plate-glass-fronted restaurant. I watched the people stream in and out of the restaurant, and was about to get a cup of coffee there when the sisters reappeared. They apologized for having taken so long, got in the car and we were on the road.

Traveling with Americans passports, in a car with yellow license plates, we anticipated no problems at checkpoints. In spite of this, to avoid the risk of being humiliated, Khalil drove on secondary roads. We were heading to Nazareth, where Israeli historian Ilan Pappé was being honored. There was no marker to indicate when we crossed an international border from the West Bank into Israel proper—no *Welcome to Israel* sign.

We got lost on the steep, narrow cobblestone streets of Nazareth, where mud and limestone houses clustered on terraced ridges. Huge satellite dishes and TV cameras announced the building where the event was happening. We arrived in time to hear Pappé being introduced in Arabic, listened to him speak in Hebrew, and stood with everyone for the final ovation. Rita and I were probably the only people in the crowd who didn't understand either language, but we had read his book, *The Ethnic Cleansing of Palestine.* Using declassified Israeli state archival sources, Pappé documented the expulsion of nearly one million people in 1948, when over 400 Palestinian villages were wiped off the map. Soon after being honored by Palestinian-Israelis, Pappé left his country, where he had been ostracized by Israeli academia, and moved to England.

The village of Rami hugged a rocky hillside in the Galilee. Khalil's extended family included a brother and sister-in-law, their children, grandchildren, and numerous cousins. His two-room efficiency apartment was attached to his brother's grander three-story home, but we were quite comfortable. Khalil's nephew invited us for dinner in his nearby restaurant that was quite famous in the Galilee. Platters of food kept appearing on a long banquet table in the main dining room reserved exclusively for the family. I ate my way through stuffed grape leaves, stuffed squash, roast lamb, tabouli, and endless salads. Khalil accompanied Rita and me on a much-needed walk through the village. We passed the cemetery where generations of his family lay buried. A dirt footpath skirted through olive groves framed by low stone walls that helped to conserve water and soil. We ignored the darkening clouds that had been building all morning until a sudden downpour cut our walk short. This Palestinian village inside Israel proper reminded me of Palestinian villages in the West Bank before the occupation. I better understood how Amty, Ibrahim, Yusra, Faisal, Samira, and Marwan felt after the 1967 War. Call it Israel or Palestine—they were home.

Three days later we returned to Ramallah. Dried blood stained the sidewalk in front of the restaurant with the plate-glass window where a makeshift memorial had been erected to honor a 22-year-old man who had been murdered here in broad daylight. He was eating in the restaurant when about 20 Israeli plainclothes military personnel jumped out of a minivan delivery truck with green license plates and forced him into the street where he was shot in the leg and neck. Some terrified bystanders retreated into the restaurant. Others began to throw stones. Several were injured in a spray of bullets. Gunning down a man in broad daylight was the action of the Mafia. Someone claimed he was a member of Mahmoud Abbas' Presidential Guard. Why didn't the Israelis arrest the suspect? Is international humanitarian law as dead as this young man?

ॐ

After heartfelt hugs and teary goodbyes, Rita and I left the comfort of Lois and Khalil's home in Ramallah. Before catching our plane, we had last-minute shopping and goodbyes. A human rights activist reverend had asked me to buy her a church cowl. I had no idea how to choose a religious garment for a Christian clergywoman, but the smiling white-haired gentleman who greeted me at the door of his shop with a measuring tape draped around his neck immediately put me at ease.

"Be welcomed. I am the Mukhtar of the Syriac Orthodox Community in Jerusalem—and the best tailor in the Christian Quarter." While helping myself to a piece of candy in a bowl on the countertop, I noticed a photograph hanging on the wall, signed and dated in the early 1970s. It was the tailor as a young man standing next to Teddy Kollek, then mayor of Jerusalem. Following my gaze, the tailor said, "This mayor believed in tolerance and acted fairly to all—Jews, Muslims, and Christians." Like my grandmother, the tailor judged leaders by how they treated their minority populations.

The *mukhtar*-tailor proudly showed me an array of handmade religious garments. "I sell these to people around the world. My father was a tailor and, *insha'Allah*, my son will take over this shop after me." Neighbors dropped in to visit while I browsed. This shop was the heart of a Christian community that could trace its roots back thousands of years—a community in danger of disappearing because of the oppressive, relentless occupation. Indigenous Christians now make up only two percent of the Holy Land's population.

I chose a cowl with red, black, and green hand-embroidered crosses running the length. The tailor looked at me with raised eyebrows. "Yes, I understand," I replied to his unasked question. Red, black, and green were the colors of the forbidden Palestinian flag. These perfectly stitched crosses sent a message to the world—Christian Palestinians still existed and still dreamed of their own country. Embroidery as a revolutionary act was inspiring. The tailor winked at me as I walked out the door and headed down the road.

"I never got to visit Samua," I complained to Khalid upon entering his shop. Pointing to several coarsely woven rugs, he told me they had been made in the village. "I have customers waiting for them, but I'll give you a killer deal because you are like family." I was tempted, not because of the exquisite magentas, umbers, and complex geometric design, but because they reminded me of the day I sat weaving in the sun with the women of the village. Owning this rug could be my consolation and proof that Samua still existed. Khalid sensed my hesitation (as I calculated cost plus shipping) and noticed my eyes shift to a gorgeous fabric of muted plum, purple, lavender, rose, mauve, and lime.

"This was made by the Druze. They are famous weavers from northern Israel." He led me to the middle of the pedestrian walkway, where we held the cloth open to the sunlight. On one side, the colors were soft and muted, but when we flipped the fabric over, they screamed with vibrancy and light. "This will be the perfect canopy for my daughter's wedding," I said, and of course Khalid gave his long-lost ex-sister-in-law a killer deal.

Farid entered Zalatimo's Sweet Shop like a Palestinian Santa Claus; a sack slung across his shoulder was full of gifts—two sets of Shabbat candlesticks, three *menorahs*, a *mezuzah*, a *jelabiya* for my husband, hand-embroidered purses for me, and a Hebrew Bible illustrated with black and white etchings.

"*Erees*, this Bible is to thank your mother for taking care of the Quran for so many years."

Farid's relaxed manner never hinted at his personal travails. The Israeli authorities had recently issued a warrant, ordering him to vacate the building that housed his precious library. The building was going to be demolished for the construction of a light rail system linking West Bank Jewish settlements, which the Israeli government considered permanent. No one seemed concerned that the street in question was on the Palestinian side of the Green Line.

In a land where homes were demolished, ancient fruit trees uprooted, arbitrary arrests commonplace, detentions indefinite, and checkpoints blocked freedom of movement, why should anyone be concerned with a collection of 30,000 books, periodicals, and newspapers issued in the Arab world since the 1930s? Because in a city filled with research centers and historical archives, there were no public libraries for Palestinians. The loss of this private library was a loss for the entire community. Volumes memorializing Palestinian history were every bit as precious as the keys to their lost homes.

"*Salaam aleikum.* Blessings on you and your family," Farid said before we parted.

"*Aleikum al salaam.* Blessings on you and your family." I was not sure if we would ever meet again. I always basked in his welcome and enjoyed the generosity of his family but could barely fathom the extent of his struggle and pain.

Rita and I spent our last two nights in Tel Aviv. Carrying over-stuffed suitcases and a backpack, I felt like a donkey trying to fit through a narrow turnstile at the entrance of the West Jerusalem bus depot where armed guards checked every piece of luggage. Rushing commuters threatened to step over and around me as if I were a boulder. On the bus to Tel Aviv, no one seemed worried about the possibility of a suicide bomber, and no one looked like an Arab, although I knew that identifying ethnicity or religious affiliations by skin tone, eye color, nose size, or clothing was sketchy at best. The bus descended the hills west of Jerusalem, past the minarets of Abu Ghosh, through miles of pine forests harboring the burnt carcasses of tanks from 1948, and into a broad irrigated valley. I always thought of the first time I crossed the narrow neck of Israel on a bus with Faisal.

Lois had warned us to get to our hotel before the onset of the Sabbath because most places closed early on Friday, even in cosmopolitan Tel Aviv. Tourist guides, history books, and Zionists claim that Israel's largest, most prominent city was built on 32 acres of barren sand dunes north of Jaffa on land bought in 1909 by the Jewish National Fund. Other historians acknowledge the fact that Tel Aviv was built on and around the existing Palestinian villages of Al-Sumayil, Salome, Sheikh Munis, Abu Kabir, and Al Manshiyeh.[29] *Tel* is a man-made mound consisting of layers of civilizations built on top of one another. *Aviv* is Hebrew for "spring," a word signifying renewal. It cannot be denied that Tel Aviv is a modern city built on the ruins of an indigenous people still struggling to survive.

Luxury hotels, apartment buildings, and glass skyscrapers blocked the sea breezes from entering our small hotel with few amenities. An uncomfortable bunk bed, glaring street lights, and never-ending traffic, in spite of the Sabbath, kept me awake. Toward dawn, I fell into a disturbed sleep and dreamed UFOs were targeting Earth with light beams that erased all memory. I woke tired and cranky.

We walked the few blocks to a gorgeous beach. Lulled by endless waves lapping the shore, we dug our toes in the sand while eating breakfast in a beach café. Bikini-clad women gabbed on cell phones. Families shared picnics. Music blasted from the latest technological gadgets. Kids played with Frisbees and made sand sculptures alongside the shore. After breakfast we headed south toward Jaffa, alternating between swimming in the turquoise waters and walking. We joined sun worshipers draped on black rocks and watched break dancers gyrate to the beat of live drummers. Were it not for the fact that everyone was speaking Hebrew, this could have been Miami Beach. How easy it was to

---

[29] Yonatan Mendel, "Fantasizing Israel," *London Review of Books,* January 25, 2009. www.lrb.co.uk/v31/n12/yonatan-mendel/fantasising-israel

forget about an occupation happening a few miles away—that is, until we met Maya. We'd been introduced to her through a mutual Israeli friend. "Meet me by the old clock tower in Jaffa," she'd said over the phone. "Everyone knows that landmark."

Only a small fraction of Palestinian-Israelis live in Tel Aviv, where the ethnically diverse Jewish community includes Jews from North and South America, Australia, South Africa, Southern Europe, North Africa, India and Central Asia. The bulk of the Muslim and Christian Arabs live in Jaffa, a few miles to the south. Until 1948, this ancient port city had been the most prosperous and cosmopolitan city in Palestine. Under intense shelling, more than 60,000 residents of Jaffa fled the city. Most went to Gaza.

Rita and I wandered through the alleyways of Old Jaffa, past upscale restaurants, galleries, souvenir shops, museums, a theatre, and buildings that might have been there since Biblical times. We noticed that the signs describing the local history were written in Hebrew, English, French, German and Spanish—but not in Arabic. Jaffa was believed to have been the first city built by one of Noah's sons after the Great Flood, Jonah's final port before being swallowed by a whale. Some claim the cedars of Lebanon passed through this port on the way to building Solomon's Temple in Jerusalem. According to archaeological evidence, Jaffa has been inhabited for over 7000 years.

We waited beneath the impressive clock tower built in 1906 by the Ottoman Turks until a stocky woman with black curly hair and olive skin unhesitatingly walked up to us and introduced herself with a welcoming *shalom*. Maya led us to the promenade overlooking a lighthouse that guarded the harbor. A vague scent of citrus mingled with the salty breeze. It was easy to understand why Palestinians forced out of Jaffa never forgot their homes. Over cold drinks in a seaside café, Maya told us about her family.

"Syria used to be home to a wealthy class of Jewish diamond merchants and jewelers. My grandparents lived a good life there. Jews were free to practice their religion and travel anywhere in the country, but were not allowed to return because they would be suspected of spying for Israel. Our Muslim and Christian neighbors envied us because Syrian Jews were not allowed to serve in the army." She laughed at this irony.

Maya complained that her son who lived in an illegal West Bank settlement had been forced to transfer his two daughters from the local settlement school to a separate school for *Mizrahi* Jews. "If my son could afford it, he would gladly leave the settlement," she said angrily. Having known life as second-class citizens in Syria, her family was disappointed to become second-class citizens in Israel. *Ashkenazi* Jews of European descent were the top economic tier in Israeli society. I was more saddened by this revelation than surprised.

Maya spoke about her work smuggling Palestinian children into Israel for medical care. Because Arabic was her mother tongue, she was able to reassure frightened children and their anxious families. As an Israeli civilian, she risked arrest every time she entered the Palestinian-administered areas of the West Bank.

One day while participating in an anti-occupation protest outside her son's settlement, Maya got an urgent cell phone call from her son. "Mom, I hope you're not out there. I hear shooting. I'm afraid the soldiers are being rough tonight." But his mother *was* there, being verbally bullied by a soldier after she told him the West Bank was a quagmire of violence, brutality, and contempt for Palestinian life. Maya may have looked like an Arab, but her sense of entitlement, casual dress, and fluent Hebrew convinced the soldier she was Jewish, and she was not arrested. When the protest was over and the crowd dispersed, Maya walked into the settlement to join her son and grandchildren for a Shabbat dinner.

Maya escorted us to our hotel. Along the way we passed a bizarre structure of steel and smoked glass rising out of an adobe ruin—a dissonant juxtaposition between a lost past and a modern present. The Etzel House was a museum dedicated to documenting the 1948 Jewish conquest of Jaffa. "The original part of the building was a Palestinian home destroyed during the war," Maya informed us. Near the museum stood an old mosque, another inconvenient reminder of a past most Israelis would just as soon ignore.

"When you get back to the States, tell your friends what you saw here. The critical mass to change Israeli society from within does not exist. We need a push from the outside world—especially America."

Maya's lament echoed statements we'd heard from other Israelis. She embodied a paradox in this society: an Arab-Jewish-Israeli peace activist whose family lived in an illegal settlement because of economic necessity. I was grateful to have met this woman with the courage of David and the wisdom of Solomon, and I definitely planned to tell friends about her.

When I got back to the States, I called Faisal, but he was not interested in hearing about the people I'd met, the Separation Wall, or anything to do with occupation. He only wanted to hear about my visit with Farid. The following year, Faisal's two sons traveled to the West Bank. He called to tell me about their trip.

"They wanted to see the places they'd heard about all their lives. They're Americans, born in New York, but Israeli soldiers at the Allenby Bridge crossing made them wait six hours before handing them a visa on a piece of paper. When my sons asked, 'Why don't you stamp our passports?' the soldiers said, 'This is what we're giving you. Don't lose it, or you'll be illegal and we can arrest you. Now get the hell out of here.' A short distance away, they came to another checkpoint where soldiers took their paper visa and questioned how they entered the country. Because of their Arab names, they were taken off the bus to Hebron, held for hours, and released when there were no more buses. They were forced to spend the night sitting outside the checkpoint, but they finally got to Samua and saw our land. We still own 85 *dunams,* about 16 acres. You remember how long it took us to ride donkeys out to the land? All that beautiful land is now crowded with roads and houses."

Faisal complained, "My sons didn't even bring home one jar of olive oil from our trees. Oh God, I was so relieved when they phoned from Amman to tell me they'd made it out of Israel without being arrested or killed. I will never return." He continued, "I'm 67 years old—too old to be insulted by young boys from Ethiopia, Russia, and Europe. Soldiers cannot tell me where to stand, where to go, or what to do on my own land. I was born there. I am part of the earth there."

He decried an international community that treated Palestinians with indifference at best, contempt at worst. Although Faisal spoke the words many Israelis longed to hear—"I will never return"—he had already passed the love of Palestine to the next generation. They hold the key, literally and symbolically.

Geologic time is measured by the creation and destruction of mountain ranges, canyons, rivers, and deserts. Human time is measured by generations. When Faisal and I met, our lives were all about the future. Now we are grandparents. My grandson's name, Aiden, means "paradise" in Hebrew and Arabic. Faisal's granddaughter Yusra, named to honor the memory of his mother, means "The easy path," as in, "May your life be smooth sailing." Joy about our grandchildren is dampened by the harsh realities in the West Bank, a place Faisal once considered home and I once considered the Promised Land.

A smile steals across my face when I think of happier times, immediately followed by thoughts of dissolution. There may be no happy ending in our lifetime. Technology has given us the image of a blue planet spinning through space at the outer edges of the Milky Way. Parents who fear their sons or daughters might fall in love with the sons or daughters of a tribe considered the enemy, know this: the Aidens and Yusras will surely find each other in this shrinking world. Love knows no boundaries. Love can penetrate apartheid walls, checkpoints, and international borders more effectively than military might.

In the twentieth year of my life, I learned that the enemy of my people were friends. In the sixtieth year of my life, I believe more than ever there is no reason to fear "the other." I came. I saw. I was welcomed.

"One can pay back the loan of gold,
but one dies forever in debt
to those who are kind."

— Ancient Mayan proverb

EPILOGUE

Myths grow into facts on the ground because emotions live in story. I grew up believing that tiny Israel, surrounded by dangerous enemies who hated us, was greening an empty wasteland in order to create a safe haven for world Jewry. I loved that story, but another truth was revealed to me when I became part of a Palestinian family. Middle East history is so laden with mythology it's often hard to tease them apart. Psychology understands that humans are not logical. Facts can be argued. Statistics can be used to prove anything. Religions use the Bible to justify the unjustifiable. History is filled with conflicting promises, disappointments, shifting alliances, betrayals and voices that were silenced. Truth is often a matter of perception; the power of beliefs cannot be denied.

I refuse to accept the decree that Muslims and Jews are natural-born enemies. Consider tenth and eleventh century Spain, known as *Sepharad* in Hebrew and *al-Andalus* in Arabic. As tolerant conquerors, Muslims allowed "the people of the book," a reference to Jews and Christians, to practice their religion and participate in mainstream cultural and civic life. For 800 years, in an era of coexistence known as *La Convivencia*, the Abrahamic faiths flourished under Moorish rule. When Queen Isabella of Spain proclaimed the Edict of Expulsion in 1492, Muslims and Jews who refused conversion to Christianity were banished. Jews who converted to Christianity, but secretly practiced their religion, risked being burnt alive. In 2000, I traveled to the Iberian Peninsula to see evidence of this history. I sat inside churches converted from mosques, round-domed structures ripped open, allowing the church spires to thrust heavenward. In Cordoba, I walked through the maze of streets and plazas in the *Judería*, the old Jewish quarter, visited one of the few surviving medieval synagogues, and sat beneath the statue of Moses Maimonides, the personal physician of Saladin, the Muslim warrior who vanquished the Crusaders. Maimonides's controversial text, *The Guide for the Perplexed*, was written around 1190 CE in Classical Arabic using Hebrew script. Intended to bridge the contradictions between philosophy and literal Torah, the book is cited and debated by people of all faiths.

Before the collapse of the Ottoman Empire in the 1920s, Muslims, Jews, and Christians of Jerusalem shared traditions and communal space. Everyone celebrated at local shrines, met at night in cafés during Ramadan to hear Arabic music, and loved the carnival atmosphere of Purim. Jews welcomed Muslim pilgrims returning from Mecca. Muslims and Jews vouched for each other at the bank and lived in the same neighborhoods in the Old City. The Jewish community in Jerusalem was proud to be part of the restoration of the Dome of the Rock mosque in 1898 on the occasion of a visit from Kaiser Wilhelm II and Augusta Viktoria. Rabbis, imams, and priests counseled anyone, regardless of religion.[30] That's the Jerusalem I yearn for.

Seiff, my mother's maiden name, means "sword" in Arabic. Perhaps our family lineage includes *Sephardic* or *Mizrahi* Jews, but the possibility of Middle Eastern heritage in our family is denied by my mother, who prefers to believe her maiden name means "soap" in German. That the

---

[30] Amy Dockser Marcus, *Jerusalem 1913: The Origins of the Arab-Israeli Conflict* (New York: Penguin, 2007), 45.

Nazis may have used Jewish cadavers to make soap does not affect her beliefs. She identifies as a Westerner. When I lived in Paris, I traveled to Alsace-Lorraine on the French-German border, but my imagination was filled with Holocaust novels, films and stories of Jews escaping the Nazis. Emotionally, I could not cross the border into Germany. Ironically, modern Berlin has become a world class artistic center, attracting thousands of American and Israeli Jews.

In her seventies, Mom had a bat mitzvah beside the Wailing Wall where she was given a Hebrew name. In her 99th year, Mom has moved beyond racial and religious stereotypes. "I wouldn't mind having Palestinians as neighbors," she recently declared. Her deeds preceded her words. "Mama Janet" had welcomed the Khatib family and was welcomed by them in turn during her visit to Jerusalem. "I don't understand why we can't share Israel. Enough killing."

"Mom, you've become a radical," I declared, but her suggestion, not nearly as audacious as claiming to be God's Chosen, has yet to become a fact on the ground.

When Faisal turned 75, I called to wish him a happy birthday. Israel's invasion of Gaza was raging, but we never spoke about the carnage and destruction happening there—or the ongoing land confiscation, settler expansion, illegal arrests, and continued occupation of the West Bank. We spoke of our children and grandkids and commiserated on the challenges of growing older. He attributed his painful arthritis to living in a cold and alien climate. After the death of Faisal's wife, his married daughter and her family moved in with him. One of his sons lived just over the border in Canada. His other son was engaged to a Jordanian woman and was considering a move to Amman. But for now, Faisal was enjoying the comfort of having his children and grandchildren nearby. He has sorrowfully accepted the fact that he will be buried in Buffalo beside his mother and will never return to Jerusalem—not even in death.

"*Erees*, did I tell you about a visit from the FBI? They came to my house after I mailed photos of myself to Jordan." Although a U.S. citizen for decades, Faisal was in the process of renewing his Jordanian passport, a passport he had once risked his life for. In an increasingly hostile environment for Muslim-Americans, this was *his* plan B—just like Israel is plan B for millions of Jewish-Americans.

In the words of Robert Frost—*Home is the place where, when you have to go there, They have to take you in.*

"I told the FBI agent I would gladly answer all his questions if he would agree to listen to me first." Faisal proceeded to give the agent a lesson on American history: the Native American genocide, the African slave trade, Chinese labor camps for the men who built the transcontinental railroad, Japanese internment camps during World War II, and State Department restrictions on Jewish refugees escaping the Third Reich.

"When I complained to FedEx, they told me everything mailed by an Arab to an Arab country is checked by Homeland Security."

"Faisal, how do you say 'justice' in Arabic? I want to make T-shirts and bumper stickers that say 'justice' in English, Arabic, and Hebrew."

"That reminds me of a story in the Quran," he said. "In order for there to be justice, you must have judges who cannot sleep at night because they are worrying about making the right decision." We both knew judges like that were hard to find.

Before saying goodbye, we agreed that if anything should happen to either of us, we wanted to be notified.

Faisal no longer believes a love story between a Muslim Palestinian man and a Jewish American woman matters. I disagree. Media commonly portrays Palestinians as less than human, as terrorists who hide behind their children. When reporting on events in the West Bank and Gaza, foreign and Palestinian journalists have been threatened by the Israeli military's use of rubber bullets, stun grenades, live munitions, beatings with batons, and more. Misleading headlines and articles, often written without context, cast Israel as a vulnerable country forced to defend itself against powerful enemies. That Israel has the strongest military in the Middle East—including nuclear capabilities—is rarely mentioned. The U.S. Congress has just passed a multi-billion-dollar deal increasing Israel's annual military aid from $3.1 billion to $3.8 billion dollars for the next ten years, more aid than any other country in the world receives. The money will be used to buy arms and security equipment from American defense companies—a Faustian deal for both countries.

So far, with the exception of Prime Minister Rabin, successive Israeli governments have condemned their country to live by the sword, but there is no "Iron Dome" (Israel's anti-missile defense system) that can keep them safe. The euphoria Israelis felt in 1967 after achieving the conquest of their dreams, especially the Old City of Jerusalem, has become a sobering reality as their civil society becomes more and more militarized. Neighbors who once were friends have become "the other." The enemy lives within. And the name of the enemy is racism and fear. If military might were the path to security, Israel would be the most secure nation on earth.

But social media has allowed us to see the connection between all oppression—whether it be the racial profiling of African-Americans, desperate refugees seeking sanctuary, climate change activists, or Native Americans protecting the water. The inspiring resistance movement against a 1,100-mile-long pipeline that was supposed to cross the Missouri River near the Standing Rock Sioux Reservation brought together over 300 indigenous groups and sympathetic internationals, including Palestinians. The human rights and environmental movements have met. The circle is widening.

In the late '60s, when Faisal and I helped organize a benefit in New York City for Palestinian refugees, most Americans were unaware of their plight. June 2017 marks the fiftieth year since the Six Day War, an event the Palestinians call *al-Naksa*, their second catastrophe, the first being the 1948 *al-Nakba*. It is also the 100-year anniversary of the Sykes–Picot Agreement, a secret accord between England, France and Russia that carved up the Middle East into the national entities we know today; and 100 years since Britain released the Balfour Declaration endorsing "the establishment of a national homeland for the Jewish people in Palestine, it being clearly understood that nothing shall be done which may prejudice the civil and religious rights of existing non-Jewish communities in Palestine…"

Faisal and I divorced decades ago, but we never argued about who had stronger rights to live in the Promised Land. With youthful innocence, I shared life with the Palestinians moments before the curtain of occupation fell. I am grateful to have seen the Wailing Wall when it was nestled in the heart of the ancient Moroccan Quarter, to have walked through the streets of Hebron with no soldiers in sight, and to have experienced village life before the onset of modernization, pollution, and occupation. I loved the pristine landscape between Jerusalem and Ramallah before it was riddled with settlements and checkpoints. It was a borderless, seamless world that welcomed me. Renowned Palestinian poet Mahmoud Darwish once wrote, *Unfortunately, it was Paradise.*

My heart breaks with shame about the inhumane treatment of Palestinians. I am not alone. For the first time in memory, an American rabbi committed to human rights live-streamed social justice-centered services between Rosh Hashanah and Yom Kippur, the Jewish days of awe. I ruminated. Did Jews move to the Middle East to become a military outpost for the Western world? Or, to create a sanctuary where Jewish culture and religion could flourish?

On December 23, 2016, two days after the Winter Solstice, the longest night of the year in the northern hemisphere, the UN Security

Council made a historic vote regarding the Israeli-Palestinian conflict. In an unusual synchronicity, Christmas Eve and the first night of Chanukah coincided. Christians were celebrating the birth of a Holy Baby who promised to bring love and redemption to a suffering humankind. Jews were remembering the Maccabees, a small but fierce band of warriors who defeated a powerful army allowing the Jewish community to reclaim and rededicate their holy temple in Jerusalem. Miracles are not everyday events, but when they happen, they must be acknowledged and celebrated.

In a break with our country's longstanding position to veto UN Security Council resolutions that "seek to impose solutions to final status issues," the United States abstained. Resolution 2334, that was passed 14 to 0. It was declared that Israel's Jewish-only settlements in the West Bank were "a violation of international law and had no legal validity." Furthermore, the settlements were "a major obstacle to the possibility of an Israeli and a Palestinian State living side-by-side in peace and security." Israel was advised to "stop all settlement building, including in East Jerusalem, and fulfill its obligation under the Fourth Geneva Convention as an occupying power." Israel and the United States, along with 194 other countries, are signatories to the Geneva Conventions, negotiated in the aftermath of World War II. Although a non-binding resolution is unenforceable, it is global affirmation of international law. The resolution was passed at a time when the Israeli Knesset was poised to retroactively legalize settler outposts and homes built on privately-owned Palestinian land. Many understand that if the internationally-recognized border were erased, the more than 4.5 million Palestinians living in the West Bank and Gaza would demand the rights of citizenship in Israel, as they are a people without an officially recognized country.

Since 1947 solutions have been put forth—two states, a confederation, internationalizing Jerusalem, people and land exchanges. We might even be witnessing the final phase of the conflict—Israel's painful transformation into a secular pluralistic democracy for all the people living between the Mediterranean Sea and the Jordan River—similar to the U.S. But solutions lie in a distant future paved with graves and broken families. Whatever compromises are reached, Israelis and Palestinians will remain entangled in each others' lives. We must learn to empathize with "the other." Change does not happen with arguable facts and conflicting narratives found in history books. Change starts with the human heart.

ARABIC, HEBREW, & YIDDISH GLOSSARY

Abu: (Arabic) Father of

Ahlan wa sahlan: (Arabic) Be welcome – a statement of hospitality to strangers

Alhamdulillah: (Arabic) All praise belongs to God

Amty: (Arabic) My paternal aunt. Also used as a term of endearment for an unrelated woman

Arak: A traditional anise-flavored liquor popular in the Middle East

Ashkenazim: (Hebrew) Jews from European and Russian descent whose main language was various dialects of Yiddish

Bar Mitzvah (Hebrew – male) / *Bat Mitzvah* (Hebrew – female) Literally means "son or daughter of the commandment." A coming of age ceremony in Judaism that happens at the age of 13, marking the beginning of religious responsibility

Baruch Hashem: (Hebrew) A traditional Hasidic greeting that means "Bless the Name," a reference to God. It is a way to avoid saying God's name in vain.

Bedouin: Arabs who traditionally maintain a nomadic way of life

Boker tov: (Hebrew) Good morning

Druze: Offshoot of eleventh-century Shiite Muslims with unique rituals and practices. They are found in Lebanon, Syria, Jordan, and northern Israel.

D'var Torah: (Hebrew) A talk or conversation based on the weekly Torah portion

Dunum(s): (Arabic) One dunum is about one quarter of an acre.

Eretz Yisrael: (Hebrew) The Land of Israel is one of several names for an indefinite geographical location in the Southern Levant. It is also known as the Land of Canaan, the Promised Land, the Holy Land, and Palestine. Biblical borders include Judea and Samaria, a reference to the West Bank.

Irgun (or ETZEL): A militant Zionist militia founded in Mandate Palestine; in 1946 they blew up the King David Hotel and committed other acts of terror against the British and Palestinian Arabs.

Fatah: (Arabic) An acronym that translates as the Palestine National Liberation Movement. This secular political party, founded in 1959, once was the cornerstone of the Palestinian cause.

Gut Yontif: (Yiddish) Happy holiday; a Yiddish expression that comes from the Hebrew words *yom tov*. Literally means "good day"

Habibi (male) / *Habibti* (female): (Arabic) My beloved

Haganah: (Hebrew, The Defense) A Zionist militia during Mandate Palestine that became the Israeli Defense Forces upon the founding of Israel in 1948

Hajji: (Arabic) A title of honor reserved for religious Muslims who have fulfilled a religious pilgrimage to Mecca, known as a Hajj

Halachic: (Hebrew) The collective body of Jewish religious laws derived from the written and oral Torah

Hamas: (Arabic) Acronym for the Islamic Resistance Movement that emerged throughout the West Bank and in Gaza at the start of the First Intifada in 1987. Running on a platform of reform and security, this political party was democratically elected in 2006 as the majority in the Palestinian Legislative Counsel. They worked to end the suicide bombings.

Hamsa: (Arabic and Hebrew) An ancient Middle Eastern amulet symbolizing the Hand of God. It is a universal sign of protection against the Evil Eye. It is also known as the Hand of Fatima or the Hand of Miriam.

Haraam: (Arabic) Shameful, forbidden

Haredim: (Hebrew) God-fearing. Orthodox Jews who follow a devout and fundamentalist lifestyle

Hatikvah: (Hebrew) Literal meaning: "the hope." The national anthem of Israel. The lyrics are adopted from a poem by Naftali Herz Imber, a Jewish poet from Ukraine.

Havdalah: (Hebrew) Separation. A Jewish ritual practiced at dusk on Saturday which separates sacred Sabbath time from the mundane. The ritual uses wine, spices, and a multi-wick candle.

Hijab: (Arabic) A head covering worn in public by some Muslim women beyond the age of puberty in the presence of adult males who are not part of the immediate family

Insha'Allah: (Arabic) God willing

Intifada: (Arabic) From a verb meaning "to shake off." It refers to the uprising of Palestinians against the Israeli occupation of the West Bank and Gaza.

Imam: (Arabic) The person who leads prayers in a mosque

Jelabiya: (Arabic) A long loose fitting robe, traditionally worn by Bedouins over clothing by males and females

Kabbalah: (Hebrew) Literally means "receiving." An esoteric discipline originating in Judaism that seeks to explain the nature of existence

Keef haalek: (Arabic) How are you?

Keffiyeh: (Arabic) A traditional headdress worn by Arab men, usually white with red or black checkered patterns

Khal: (Arabic) A maternal uncle

Khalti: (Arabic) A maternal aunt

Kibbeh: (Arabic) Ground lamb mixed with pine nuts, butter, onions and spices. Served with yogurt and rice.

Kibbutz: (Hebrew) A communal settlement in Israel where people live and work together, traditionally agriculturally based. Modern *kibbutz* are mainly corporations run by those who once were members of the *kibbutz*.

Kiddush: (Hebrew) Literally, "sanctification." The blessing recited over wine or grape juice at the onset of the sabbath and other Jewish holidays

Kippah: (Hebrew) Small round skullcap worn by religious Jews. Also known as a *yarmulke*

Knesset: (Hebrew and Arabic) Literal meaning: "the gathering" or "assembly." The name for Israel's parliament

Lahmeh: (Arabic) Beef

Lechem: (Hebrew) Bread

LEHI (aka the Stern Gang): Hebrew initials for "Fighters for the Freedom of Israel." This Zionist militia committed acts of terror during Mandate Palestine.

Mabrook: (Arabic) Congratulations

Machatunim: (Yiddish) The parents of our child's spouse

Mammeloshn: (Yiddish) The mother tongue

Mansaf: (Arabic) A lamb and rice dish served with a savory yogurt sauce

Matzah: (Hebrew) Cracker-like unleavened bread, traditionally eaten by Jews during Passover

Maqluba: (Arabic) Layered chicken or lamb, fried cauliflower and eggplant served on a bed of rice. Moments before serving, the pot is flipped over, which is why this popular dish is called "upside-down."

Mazel tov: (Hebrew) Congratulations; good luck

Mea She'arim: (Hebrew) The Orthodox Jewish Quarter in West Jerusalem.

Mechitza: (Hebrew) A curtain or wall used by Orthodox Jews to separate men and women during prayer

Menorah: (Hebrew) A nine-branched candelabrum lit during the eight-day holiday of Chanukah

Mezuzah: (Hebrew) A small decorative hollow case containing a parchment inscribed with a specific prayer from the Torah. It is usually fixed to the doorpost of a Jewish home.

Minyan: (Hebrew) A quorum of 10 men (or in some synagogues, men and women) over the age of 13 required for traditional Jewish worship

Mitzvah: (Hebrew) A good deed

Mizrahim: (Hebrew) East, or Oriental. The term refers to Jews who are from countries in North Africa and the Middle East. The reference includes Kurdish, Iraqi, Iranian, Yemenite, Moroccan, Lebanese, Afghani, Turkish, Indian, Pakistani, and Syrian Jews.

Moshiach: (Hebrew) The messiah. Literally means "the anointed one"

Moshav: (Hebrew) A cooperative community of separate farms. Pioneered by early Labor Zionists

Mossad: (Hebrew) Israeli Institute for Intelligence and Special Operations

Mukhtar: (Arabic) The head of a local government or town, usually chosen by consensus

Muezzin: (Arabic, Turkish, Persian) The crier who calls the faithful to prayer five times a day from the mosque's minaret

Nakba: (Arabic) Literal meaning is "the Catastrophe," referring to the ethnic cleansing of Palestine by Zionist forces beginning in 1947-48

Naksa Day: (Arabic) Literal meaning is "the setback" or "calamity." Commemorates the Arab defeat in the 1967 Six-Day War when Palestinians were displaced once again

Pushke: (Yiddish) Derived from a Polish word that means a little container kept in the home for the purpose of collecting charity

Quran: (Arabic) Literal meaning, "the recitation." Muslims believe these revelations were made to Muhammad by Allah through the angel Gabriel.

Sabah al khayr: (Arabic) Good morning

Salaam aleikum: (Arabic) Peace be with you

Sephardim: (Hebrew) Jews from the Iberian Peninsula who spoke Spanish and Ladino. They fled Spain (Sepharad) in 1492 during the Spanish Inquisition

Shavuot: (Hebrew) A Jewish holiday with double significance; it celebrates the grain harvest, and is the day the Torah was revealed to the Israelites gathered at Mt. Sinai

Sheikh: (Arabic) A title of honor that can denote royalty; a male member of a tribe who deserves respect; a person tasked with guiding a group of people; a respected scholar of Islam

Shvitz: (Yiddish) A traditional Jewish steam bath of Eastern European origin. Also refers to a Turkish bath house

Shtetle: (Yiddish) Small towns or villages in Central and Eastern Europe with large Jewish populations that existed before the Holocaust

Siddur: (Hebrew) A traditional Jewish prayer book that contains prayers for the Sabbath, the new month, holidays and for every day

Sidi: (Arabic) My grandfather; a masculine title of respect

Souq: (Arabic) A marketplace or bazaar

Sukkah: (Hebrew) A temporary dwelling built outside, covered with branches and used during the fall harvest celebration of Sukkoth

Sulha: (Arabic) A traditional Middle Eastern conflict resolution process

Taboun: (Arabic) An igloo-shaped outdoor clay oven used to bake bread

Tallit: (Hebrew) A fringed garment traditionally worn by religious Jews

Torah: (Hebrew) Literal meaning is "the law." Torah includes the first five books of the Old Testament which was given to Moses on Mount Sinai.

Tzaddik or Tzadik: (Hebrew) Righteous or good person; without sin; spiritual master. *Tzaddikim* (plural)

Umm: (Arabic) Mother of

Wadi: (Arabic) A valley, canyon, or seasonally dry riverbed

Yalla: (Arabic) Let's go

Yeshiva: (Hebrew) A Jewish institution that focuses on the study of religious texts, mainly the Talmud and the Torah, traditionally only open to men

Yom Kippur: (Hebrew) The Jewish Day of Atonement

Yom Yerushalayim: (Hebrew) Israel's "Jerusalem Day," a holiday celebrating the so-called "reunification" of East and West Jerusalem in 1967

Zikr: (Arabic) A ceremony in which supplicants repeatedly glorify the name of God

WORDS AND TERMS THAT MEAN THE SAME THING

Allenby Bridge (Israeli side) = **King Hussein Bridge** (Jordanian side)

Arab-Israelis = **Non-Jewish-Palestinians** who became citizens of Israel in 1948

Arabic coffee = **Turkish coffee**

Bethany = **Al-Azaria**

Damascus Gate = **Bab el-Amoud** (Arabic, meaning Gate of the Column)

Diaspora: Jewish Diaspora: a portion of the population of the Kingdom of Judah were sent to Babylon in 586 BCE; the dispersion of Jews after the Romans destroyed Jerusalem, including the Second Temple in 70 CE. **Palestinian Diaspora:** the expulsion of hundreds of thousands of Palestinian Muslims and Christians from their homes and villages by militant Zionists in what became Israel in 1947-1948.

Har Homa (Jewish settlement built on Palestinian land overlooking East Jerusalem) = **Jabal Abu Ghneim** (Palestinian name for their hillside)

Hebron = **Al-Khalil**

Historic Palestine = **Israel + West Bank + Gaza**

Ibrahimi Mosque = **Cave of Machpelah** = **Tomb of the Patriarchs**

Israel (modern) = **Palestine** (historic) = **Canaan** (Biblical) = **Judea** (Biblical)

Israeli War of Independence (1947-48) = **First Arab/Israeli War** = **Palestinian Nakba**

Jaffa Gate = **Bab al-Khalil**

Jerusalem = **Yerushalayim** (Hebrew: the City of Peace) = **Al-Quds** (Arabic: the Sacred City)

Lake Tiberias = Kinneret = Sea of Galilee (New Testament name)

Mizrahi Jews = Arab Jews = Jews from North Africa and the Middle East

Moroccan Quarter = Mughrabi Quarter = current site of **open-air synagogue by the Wailing Wall**

Nablus = Shechem (Hebrew)

Occupied Territories = Disputed Territories = West Bank + Gaza + Golan Heights

Old City = Ancient walled city of **Jerusalem**

Separation Wall = Security Wall = Apartheid Wall

Six-Day War = 1967 Arab-Israeli War = Al Naksa

Temple Mount = Haram al-Sharif (Arabic) = **Har HaBayit** (Hebrew) = **Mount Moriah** (biblical name)

The Promised Land (Jewish reference) = **The Holy Land** (Christian reference)

Wailing Wall = Kotel = Western Wall

West Bank = Judea and Samaria

Yom Kippur War = Ramadan War (1973)

HISTORIC TIMELINE

1516–1918: Ottoman rule over Palestine

1880–1890: A million-plus Eastern European Jews flee to the United States

1881–1903: 10,000 European Jews immigrate to Palestine

1894: The Dreyfus Affair: the trial of a Jewish captain in the French army becomes the symbol of European anti-Semitism

1896: Father of Zionism, Theodor Herzl, publishes *The Jewish State*, a political manifesto

1897: World Zionist Organization is established with the objective to create a Jewish homeland in Palestine. About 50,000 Jews already lived there.

1898: Theodore Herzl makes his only trip to Jerusalem to meet Kaiser Wilhelm II and plead the case for a Jewish state in Palestine. The Prussian King and his wife, Augusta Viktoria, a German monarch, were welcomed by thousands of people as they entered Jerusalem.

1901: Establishment of Jewish National Fund (JNF): land bought by JNF became Jewish national property that was protected from private property speculation

1904: Second wave (40,000) of European Jewish immigrants arrive in Palestine

1908: The Young Turk Revolt creates a constitution that allows criticism of the Ottoman government, inspiring Arab and Jewish nationalism.

1909: Establishment of Tel Aviv and the first *kibbutz*, both on the outskirts of Jaffa

1914: World War I begins. Ottoman Empire enters the war on the side of Germany

1916: Sykes-Picot, a secret agreement, is signed between England, France, and Russia, carving up the Middle East into spheres of influence.

1916: The McMahon-Hussein Correspondence was an exchange of letters during World War I between the Sharif of Mecca and the British High Commissioner in Egypt. The correspondence supported an independent Arab state in exchange for Arab help in defeating the Ottoman Empire.

1917: The Balfour Declaration: Britain endorses the establishment of a national homeland for the Jewish people in Palestine, as long as it does not violate the civil and religious rights of existing non-Jewish communities. Borders were not defined.

1919–1923: Third wave (35,000) of Russian and Eastern European Jews arrive in Palestine

1919-1928: Seven Palestinian Arab Congresses. Organized by Muslim-Christian Associations in British Mandate Palestine, they rejected Zionist immigration but welcomed Jews who had been living in Palestine before World War I, known as *Yahud awlad Arab* (Jewish sons of Arabs).

1920: *Haganah*, a paramilitary militia, is founded by Zionists in British Mandate Palestine. In 1948, the militia became the Israel Defense Force.

1922: British Mandate Palestine ratified by the League of Nations at the end of World War I

1924–1928: Fourth wave: 78,000 Jews arrive in Palestine, fleeing poor economic conditions and anti-Semitism in Poland

1925: Hebrew University opens on Mount Scopus

1929: Riots break out at the Wailing Wall; Jews and Arabs are killed in Jerusalem, Safed, and Hebron

1933–1936: Fifth wave (165,000) enters Palestine. This includes educated German Jews.

1933–1935: Hitler is elected and assumes power in Germany; Nuremberg Laws are passed against Jews living in Germany

1938: *Kristallnacht*: Nazi gangs destroy Jewish property and synagogues throughout Germany

1939: World War II begins

1939–1947: Britain restricts Jewish immigration to Palestine

1946: The Irgun, a Zionist militant militia led by Menachem Begin, bombs British headquarters in the King David Hotel in Jerusalem, killing 91 people of various nationalities.

1947: Palestinians reject the UN Partition of Mandate Palestine into Jewish and Arab areas. Partition allocates 55 percent of Palestine to Jews who only own seven percent of the land. Most are recent immigrants from Europe.

1947–1948: First Arab-Israeli War begins, also called the Israeli War for Independence. Jewish militias attack Deir Yassin, a Palestinian village 18 miles outside of Israel's boundaries as outlined in UN partition. Two-thirds of the villagers are murdered.

1948: Plan Dalet: Zionist leaders' plan for the expulsion of the non-Jewish majority of Palestinians by large-scale intimidation.

May 14, 1948: David Ben-Gurion declares the establishment of the State of Israel. Their Declaration of Independence says: "The state will insure for the complete equality of social and political rights to all its inhabitants, irrespective of religion, race, or sex; the state will guarantee freedom of religion, conscience, language, education, and culture."

1949: Armistice agreement between Israel, Egypt, Jordan, Syria, and Lebanon establishes the Green Line. The *de facto* borders give Israel 78 percent of Mandatory Palestine, including West Jerusalem, parts of the Galilee, and the Negev Desert. Jordan annexes the West Bank, including East Jerusalem. Gaza comes under Egyptian control.

1953: Hussein becomes King of Jordan at the age of 18 after the assassination of his grandfather, King Abdullah

1954: American Israel Public Affairs Committee (AIPAC) becomes a registered lobby in Washington, D.C. It has become one of the most influential lobbies in the U.S. Congress.

1956: Egyptian President Gamal Abdel Nasser nationalizes the Suez Canal. Soon after, Israel invades the Sinai and the Suez Canal and takes control of the Straits of Tiran.

1957: U.S. pressures Israel to withdraw from the Gaza Strip and Sinai in return for safe passage through the Straits of Tiran. UN forces monitor the Suez Canal.

1966: Clashes arise between Israel and Syria over water issues. Syria attempts to divert the headwaters of the Jordan River in an effort to stop Israel from pumping water from the Sea of Galilee, but attacks by the Israeli military make this hazardous.

1966: Israel raids Palestinian villages in the West Bank, including Samua, outside of Hebron.

1967: Israel becomes capable of assembling its first nuclear bomb.

1967: May 14: Egyptian combat units cross the Suez into the Sinai; Egypt demands the withdrawal of UN troops in Gaza and the United Arab Republic; Egyptian troops take over UN positions in Suez. **May 22:** Egypt closes the Gulf of Aqaba to Israeli shipping. **May 30:** Egypt and Jordan sign a mutual defense pact. **June 5:** Israeli planes destroy the Egyptian Air Force. **June 8:** Israel attacks the *USS Liberty*, an intelligence-gathering ship off the Egyptian coast—34 sailors killed, 164 wounded. **June 10:** Cease-fire, Israel is left in possession of West Bank, Gaza, Sinai Desert, and the Golan Heights.

1967: UN Resolution 242 passes in Security Council. It calls for the "inadmissibility of the acquisition of territory by force and the need for a just and lasting peace in which every state can live in security." Israel is a signatory to this resolution.

1967: Israel demolishes about 2,000 Palestinian homes, including four villages in the Latrun area and the Mughrabi Quarter in the Old City of Jerusalem

1969: Palestine National Council (PNC) elects Yasser Arafat as Chairman of the Palestine Liberation Organization (PLO)

1970: U.S. asks Israel to withdraw from the Occupied Territories in return for official recognition. Rogers Plan was the first land-for-peace deal.

1971: As General Officer of the Southern Command, Ariel Sharon orders the razing of 2,000 houses in Gaza refugee camps.

1973: Yom Kippur War, also known as Ramadan War. Egypt and Syria attack Israeli positions in the occupied Sinai and the Golan Heights. Israel forces them back with U.S. support.

1973: UN Resolution 338: All concerned parties are asked to terminate all military activity and implement UN Resolution 242.

1974: The PLO is recognized as a legitimate representative of Palestinians; Arafat speaks at the UN appealing for the establishment of an independent Palestinian state alongside Israel. Israel and Syria also sign disengagement accord.

1974: Israel and Egypt sign the first disengagement accord; the U.S. and Egypt resume full diplomatic relations. Israeli-Syrian disengagement accord.

1974: *Gush Emunim* (Bloc of the Faithful) is founded on the belief that Israel should settle the West Bank on religious grounds.

1975: The Suez Canal is opened after an eight-year closure. UN General Assembly passes a resolution equating Zionism with racism.

1977: Eighty-five settlements are established in Gaza, the Jordan Valley, and the Golan Heights. Anwar Sadat addresses the Israeli Knesset on the importance of establishing a permanent peace based on justice.

1978: Camp David Accords brokered by U.S. President Jimmy Carter normalize relations between Israel and Egypt in exchange for Israeli withdrawal from the Sinai. Israel also agrees to full autonomy for Palestinians within five years, but this is never implemented.

1979: Egypt and Israel sign peace treaty; Israel agrees to withdraw from the Sinai Peninsula; first Israeli freighter since Israeli independence passes through the Suez Canal

1980: The Israeli Knesset officially annexes East Jerusalem; the international community does not recognize this annexation to date

1981: Israel bombs Iraqi nuclear reactor; Egyptian President Anwar Sadat assassinated; Hosni Mubarak becomes president of Egypt; Israel illegally annexes Golan Heights

1982: Israel invades Lebanon. Israel responsible for massacres in Sabra and Shatila, two Palestinian refugee camps in West Beirut. Israel returns last portion of Sinai to Egypt.

1982: Fez Peace Plan: In exchange for Israeli withdrawal from occupied Palestinian territories, Arab leaders offer recognition of Israel's right to exist in peace.

1986: Israeli whistleblower and peace activist Mordechai Vanunu reveals to the world his knowledge of Israel's secret nuclear program

1987: First Intifada: spontaneous, mainly nonviolent uprising to protest growing Jewish settlements on Palestinian land

1988: King Hussein renounces Jordan's claim to the West Bank; The PLO recognizes Israel, gives up claim to 78 percent of historic Palestine, condemns all forms of terrorism, including state terrorism, and proclaims a Palestinian state in the West Bank and Gaza. Launching of *Hamas* (Arabic acronym for Islamic Resistance Movement)

1990: Iraq invades and annexes Kuwait; UN sets deadline for withdrawal

1991–92: The Madrid Conference: bilateral talks between Israel and Syria, Israel and Lebanon, and Israel and a Jordanian-Palestinian delegation.

UN Resolution 242 is the foundation of talks

1992: Israeli Prime Minister Rabin supports land for peace deal; about 100,000 demonstrators oppose withdrawal from the Golan Heights

1993: Oslo Accords: Israel and the PLO sign Interim Self-government Arrangements. Arafat and Rabin agree to mutual recognition

1994: American-born Jewish settler in Hebron kills 29 Muslim Palestinians worshipping in the Ibrahimi Mosque; Palestinian Authority (PA) takes control over Jericho and the Gaza Strip; Prime Minister Rabin and King Hussein declare the end of war between Israel and Jordan; Rabin and Arafat receive the Nobel Peace Prize

1995: Israel withdraws from major Arab population centers in the West Bank—except Hebron

1995: Taba Agreement (Oslo II) divides the West Bank into areas of control: **Area A**—direct Palestinian civil and internal security control; **Area B**—Palestinians have civil and police authority, but Israel retains security responsibility; **Area C**—exclusive Israeli control in most of the West Bank

1995: Israeli Prime Minister Rabin is assassinated by a Jewish-Israeli religious extremist

1995: Sharm el-Sheikh Memorandum: an interim agreement between Israel and the PLO that provided a timetable for final status on Jerusalem, borders between Israel and Palestine, return of refugees, settlements, prisoner release, safe passage between West Bank and Gaza, and a seaport in Gaza. Permanent agreement was scheduled to be reached by 2000.

1996: Palestine National Council (PNC) cancels the clauses in the Palestinian National Charter calling for the destruction of Israel; Israeli Prime Minister Netanyahu and Arafat meet at the Erez checkpoint. Palestinians protest an Israeli archaeological project that opens a tunnel beneath the Temple Mount

1997: Division of Hebron. **H1**—160,000 Palestinians (80 percent of the city) to be administered by Palestinian Authority. **H2**—800 settlers are guarded by 2,000 Israeli soldiers. The Palestinian population is around 30,000. Israel maintains full military control in the Old City of Hebron, including the Ibrahimi Mosque.

1997: Netanyahu announces plans to build 6,500 housing units for Jews only on Har Homa, a hill overlooking East Jerusalem, known to Palestinians as Jabal Abu Ghneim

1997: Sheikh Yassin, spiritual leader of Hamas, is released from house arrest in Israel

1999: King Hussein dies and is succeeded by son Abdullah; the PLO postpones declaration of statehood

2000: Camp David Summit fails to achieve final status agreement between Israel and the PLO

2000: West Bank villages of Abu Dis, Al-Azaria, and Suwahra are returned to Palestinian control

2000: The Second Intifada is triggered when Ariel Sharon visits the Temple Mount/Haram al-Sharif with a massive police force

2001: Ariel Sharon is elected Israeli Prime Minister

2001: Terrorists destroy the World Trade Center in New York City

2001: President George W. Bush endorses a Palestinian state in the West Bank and Gaza

2001: Women In Black is nominated for the Nobel Peace Prize

2002: Israel launches "Operation Defensive Shield," the largest military operation in the West Bank since the 1967 Six-Day War

2002: Arab Peace Initiative: Twenty-two Arab countries offer to integrate Israel into the region in exchange for an end to the occupation, a "just solution" to the refugee problem, and security guarantees for all states. Israel rejects the offer and begins building the Separation Wall/Security Fence

2002: Bulldozers demolish over 300 homes in the Jenin refugee camp

2003: The United States invades Iraq and topples Saddam Hussein; Israel expands the Security Fence/Separation Wall

2003–2004: The Road Map to Peace is developed by the United States, the European Union, Russia, and the UN. The initiative is supported by Palestinians but rejected by Israel.

2004: The International Court of Justice finds the Separation Wall in violation of international humanitarian law and calls for its immediate dismantling and for Israel to make reparations

2005: Mahmoud Abbas is elected President of the Palestinian National Authority

2005: Sharm el Sheikh Conference is held between Israelis, Palestinians, Egyptians, and Jordanians. Israel releases 900 Palestinian prisoners and withdraws from Jericho; the Second Intifada ends

2005: Israel evacuates 8,000 Jewish settlers from Gaza but retains control of border crossings, airspace, and coastline. Israel constructs 13,000 new housing units for Jews in the West Bank

2005: Palestinian civil society initiates a global campaign for Boycott, Divestment, and Sanctions (BDS) against Israel until it complies with human rights and international law

2006: In a democratic election, Hamas wins more seats in the Palestinian Legislative Council than Fatah. The United States and European Union declare an embargo on the new Palestinian government. The loss of aid undermines Palestinian civil society.

2006: Hezbollah abducts three Israeli soldiers and murders two, triggering the Second Lebanon War. A million civilians are displaced and more than 1,000 people, mostly civilians, are killed, including hundreds of children.

2006: Operation Summer Rains: Israel attacks Gaza to recover kidnapped

Israeli soldier, Gilad Shalit. Several hundred Palestinians are killed

2007: Fatah and Hamas agree to share power, but violence continues

2007: The 40th year of the military occupation of the West Bank including East Jerusalem, Gaza, and Golan Heights

2008–2009: Operation Cast Lead. Israel invades Gaza blaming Hamas for rocket attacks; Goldstone Report, commissioned by the UN, claims Israel was responsible for "deliberate attacks designed to punish, humiliate, and terrorize a civilian population." More than 1,400 Palestinians are killed, including 300 children. Thirteen Israelis are killed.

2008: Free Gaza Movement: International human rights activists attempt to break the blockade of Gaza by sea

2009: President Barack Obama speaks in Cairo, calling for an end to new Israeli settlement construction in the Occupied Territories. He also calls for Arab recognition of Israel.

2009: Gaza Freedom March: Another nonviolent attempt to end the blockade of Gaza, this time by land. More than 1,300 people from 42 countries try to enter Gaza through the Egyptian border, but authorities do not allow the march to take place as planned.

2010: Gaza Freedom Flotilla. Several ships, including the Turkish ship, *Mavi Marmara*, with a capacity of over 1,000 passengers, attempt to bring humanitarian aid to Gaza. All ships are forcefully boarded by Israeli commandos in international waters. Nine passengers are killed.

2011: Gilad Shalit, an Israeli soldier, is exchanged for more than 1,000 Palestinian prisoners

2011: Palestine bids for statehood at the United Nations General Assembly

2017: June 5 marks the 50th year of the military occupation of the West Bank, including East Jerusalem, Gaza, and Golan Heights.

Sources for Timeline:

Baltzer, Anna. *Witness in Palestine: A Jewish American Woman in the Occupied Territories* (Boulder, CO: Paradigm Publishers, 2007).

Bickerton, Ian J., and Carla L. Klausner. *A Concise History of the Arab-Israeli Conflict* (Englewood Cliffs, NJ: Prentice Hall, 2004).

Forced Migration Review, no. 26 (August 2006). (Published by the Refugee Studies Centre in association with the Norwegian Refugee Council.) Oxford, United Kingdom.

Hass, Amira. *Reporting from Ramallah: An Israeli Journalist in an Occupied Land* (New York and Los Angeles: Semiotext(e), 2003).

Jewish Virtual Library. An online encyclopedia of Jewish history and culture. www.jewishvirtuallibrary.org

McCarthy, Justin. *The Population of Palestine* (New York: Columbia University Press, 1990)

WEBSITES FOR MORE INFORMATION

Adalah: The Legal Center for Arab Minority Rights in Israel. **www.adalah.org**

Al-Haq: Palestinian legal and human rights organization. **www.alhaq.org**

Amnesty International: www.amnesty.org

BADIL Resource Center for Palestinian Residency and Refugee Rights: **www.badil.org**

Breaking the Silence: Israeli soldiers speaking out about the occupation. **www.breakingthesilence.org.il**

B'Tselem: Israeli Information Center for Human Rights in the Occupied Territories. **www.btselem.org**

Center for Jewish Nonviolence: https://centerforjewishnonviolence.org/

Christian Peacemaker Teams: www.cpt.org

Coalition of Women for Peace (Machsom Watch, Women in Black, New Profile): **www.coalitionofwomen.org**

Counterpunch: Fearless journalistic muckraking since 1993. **www.counterpunch.org**

Electronic Intifada: A major media online outlet that promotes the Palestinian perspective with news article and commentary. **https://electronicintifada.net**

Friends of Sabeel—North America (FOSNA): An international peace movement initiated by Palestinian Christians who seek a just peace as defined by international law and existing United Nations Resolutions. **http://www.fosna.org/about/sabeel**

Grassroots Jerusalem: This is an online platform resulting from a partnership from 80 grassroots community organizations in 40 Palestinian communities of Jerusalem. **http://www.grassrootsalquds.net**

Gush-Shalom: Israeli Peace Bloc: **http://gush-shalom.org**

Haaretz (Israeli center-left newspaper): **www.haaretz.com**

Israeli Committee Against House Demolitions (ICAHD): www.icahd.org

J Street: Political home for pro-Israel, pro-peace Americans who want Israel to be secure, democratic and the national home of the Jewish people. **www.jstreet.org**

Jerusalem Center for Social & Economic Rights (JCSER): www.jcser.org/eng

Jewish Voice for Peace: A diverse community of activists inspired by Jewish tradition to achieve peace for Palestinians and Jewish Israelis based on equality. They focus on the critical role of the United States in the conflict. **www.jewishvoiceforpeace.org**

MachsomWatch: Israeli women observing at checkpoints. **www.en.machsomwatch.org**

Mondoweiss: An independent website devoted to informing readers about developments in Israel/Palestine and related US foreign policy. **http://mondoweiss.net**

Open Hillel: Promotes pluralism and open discourse in Jewish campus communities. **www.openhillel.org**

PalMap: Palestine Mapping Center. **www.palmap.org**

PASSIA (Palestinian Academic Society for the Study of International Affairs). **www.passia.org**

Rabbis for Human Rights: www.rhr.israel.net

Roots: Non-violent grassroots movement for understanding among Israelis and Palestinians. **www.friendsofroots.net, info@friendsofroots.net**

T'ruah: The rabbinic call for human rights. **www.truah.org**

United Nations Office for the Coordination of Humanitarian Affairs OCHA): **www.ochaopt.org**

U.S. Campaign for Palestinian Rights (USCPR): Formerly known as the U.S. Campaign to End the Israeli Occupation. They're a national coalition of groups working to advocate for Palestinian rights and a shift in U.S. policy. **http://uscpr.org/about-us**

+972 Magazine: Independent blog-based web magazine owned by a group of journalists, bloggers, and photographers whose goal is to provide eyewitness reporting and analysis of events in Israel and Palestine. **www.972mag.com**

WEST BANK SEPARATION BORDER
APRIL, 2007

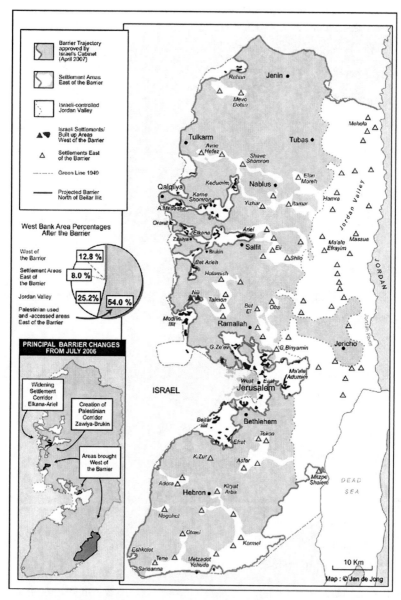

Map of West Bank Separation Wall: Reprinted with permission from Foundation for
Middle East Peace / Jan de Jong. http://fmep.org

PALESTINIAN LOSS OF LAND
1947 TO PRESENT

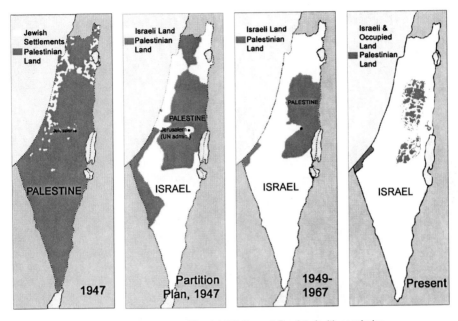

Maps of Palestinian Loss of Land, 1946-Present: Reprinted with permission
from Anne Remley, *If Americans Knew.* www.ifamericansknew.org

ACKNOWLEDGMENTS

The writing of this book has followed me through the seasons of my life—from innocent young traveler to hippie, teacher, mother, grandmother, and human rights activist. The learning curve has been long and steep. Like a historical detective, I found myself asking *why, what if,* and *why not*, more times than I can remember. Along the way, I was encouraged and helped by many people. I wish to thank Kyra Ryan, my first editor; Bill Whaley, for his insightful comments and encouragement; Ibrahim Kazerooni, Pamela Olson, Pat Risso, for historical input and editing. To Pam Parker and Barbara Paul for bringing some of these stories to the stage. Thank you to my friends and fellow writers for their encouragement, especially Elaine Sutton, Rose Gordon, Phaedra Greenwood, Lynn Hamrick, Stan Hordes, Ariana Kramer, Sarah Wilkinson, and Amanda Sutton. Thanks to my editor, Susan Schuurman and to my book designer, Barbara Davis.

Thank you to my children, Minka and Eli, and to my grandchildren, Aiden, Maya, Treska and Ellatova, who turned this task into a labor of love. These stories are for you to take forward. And thanks to my husband Marc, who traveled with me to Jerusalem and met the stranger with a handshake and a smile.

ABOUT THE AUTHOR

PHOTO: MARLEY MUSELLA

Iris Keltz was born and raised in New York City with a family that ˅ stressed the Jewish narrative of suffering in a 2000-year Diaspora culminating in the Holocaust. She grew up believing that tiny Israel surrounded by dangerous enemies was greening an empty wasteland in order to create a safe haven for world Jewry. But another truth was revealed when she married into a Palestinian family and found sanctuary with them during the 1967 War. Keltz has returned several times to the West Bank, Gaza, and Israel to bear witness to the repercussions of that war.

Her first book, *Scrapbook of a Taos Hippie: Tribal Tales from the Heart of a Cultural Revolution* (Cinco Puntos Press, 2000) is an award-winning historical memoir that documents the counterculture in northern New Mexico through vignettes, oral histories, photographs, newspaper articles, and other memorabilia. It was named one of the top ten reads of the century in *New Mexico Magazine's* Centennial Issue.

As a freelance journalist, Keltz's articles, op-eds, and essays have appeared in print and electronic media, locally, nationally and internationally, including *The Taos News*, *The Albuquerque Journal*, *New Mexico Magazine*, *Counterpunch*, *Mondoweiss*, and *Haaretz Newspaper*. She was interviewed on a live radio broadcast in Jerusalem (2010), and she is a guest lecturer at universities, high schools, synagogues, churches and civic centers. Keltz represented her congressional district as part of a national lobby with the Tikkun Community. She is a founding member of several social justice groups in New Mexico.

Keltz holds a Masters Degree in Education from the University of New Mexico. Recently retired from a 40-year teaching career that began as a storyteller in Harlem, New York and ended as a reading teacher in Albuquerque, New Mexico, she is now free to write, travel, and visit her grandchildren, who live on opposite coasts.